INHERITING A CANOE PADDLE

The Canoe in Discourses of English-Canadian Nationalism

If the canoe is a symbol of Canada, what kind of Canada does it symbolize? *Inheriting a Canoe Paddle* looks at how the canoe has come to symbolize a love of Canada for non-aboriginal Canadians and provides a critique of this identification's unintended consequences for First Nations. Written in an engaging style, it is a scholarly examination and a personal reflection, delving into representations of canoes and canoeing in museum displays, historical re-enactments, travel narratives, the history of wilderness expeditions, artwork, film, and popular literature.

Misao Dean opens the book with the story of inheriting her father's canoe paddle and goes on to explore the paddle as a national symbol – integral to historical tales of exploration and trade, central to Pierre Trudeau's patriotism, and unique to Canadians wanting to distance themselves from British and American national myths. Throughout, *Inheriting a Canoe Paddle* emphasizes the importance of self-consciously evaluating the meaning we give to canoes as objects and to canoeing as an activity.

(Cultural Spaces)

MISAO DEAN is a professor in the Department of English at the University of Victoria.

Inheriting a Canoe Paddle

The Canoe in Discourses of
English-Canadian Nationalism

MISAO DEAN

UNIVERSITY OF TORONTO PRESS
Toronto Buffalo London

ISBN 978-1-4426-4480-9 (cloth)
ISBN 978-1-4426-1287-7 (paper)

Library and Archives Canada Cataloguing in Publication

Dean, Misao
Inheriting a canoe paddle : the canoe in discourses of English-Canadian
nationalism / Misao Dean.

(Cultural spaces)
Includes bibliographical references and index.
ISBN 978-1-4426-4480-9 (bound)   ISBN 978-1-4426-1287-7 (pbk.)

1. Canoes and canoeing – Social aspects – Canada – History.   2. Popular
culture – Canada.   3. Nationalism – Canada.   4. National characteristics,
Canadian.   I. Title.   II. Series: Cultural spaces

GV776.15.A2D42 2013   797.1220971   C2012-907605-8

University of Toronto Press acknowledges the financial assistance to its publishing
program of the Canada Council for the Arts and the Ontario Arts Council.

ONTARIO ARTS COUNCIL
CONSEIL DES ARTS DE L'ONTARIO
50 YEARS OF ONTARIO GOVERNMENT SUPPORT OF THE ARTS
50 ANS DE SOUTIEN DU GOUVERNEMENT DE L'ONTARIO AUX ARTS

Canada Council   Conseil des Arts
for the Arts   du Canada

This book has been published with the help of a grant from the Canadian
Federation for the Humanities and Social Sciences, through the Awards to Scholarly
Publications Program, using funds provided by the Social Sciences and Humanities
Research Council of Canada.

University of Toronto Press acknowledges the financial support of the Government of
Canada through the Canada Book Fund for its publishing activities.

*How do you get to be the sort of victor who can claim
to be the vanquished also?*
Jamaica Kincaid

Shame, as Marx said, is a revolutionary sentiment.
J.P. Sartre

Contents

Acknowledgments

I've spent a long time writing this book; it's been delayed over and over again due to both unavoidable illness and avoidable bone-headedness. I want to thank everyone who has encouraged me, supported me, and talked to me about it over the years, especially Jamie Dopp and my colleagues in the English department at the University of Victoria, both current and retired; Tina Loo and Eric Sager; Bruce Hodgins, Dale Standen, John Jennings, and Jeremy Ward in Peterborough; Norm Crerar, Gib Perrault, and Jim Rheaume; Jamie Benidickson; and Ted Chamberlin, Cecily Devereux, and Cynthia Sugars. I received financial support from the University of Victoria and the SSHRC; I also spent a very productive six weeks at the Gibraltar Point Centre for the Arts working on a final draft. An earlier version of the introduction was published in *Home-Work: Postcolonialism, Pedagogy, and Canadian Literature,* edited by Cynthia Sugars (Ottawa: University of Ottawa Press, 2004); chapter four appeared in *Journal of Canadian Studies* 40, no. 3 (2006): 43–67. My personal thanks go to Nancy Nigro and Michael Rensing for being there when I needed them, and to my daughters for taking care of me.

INHERITING A CANOE PADDLE

The Canoe in Discourses of English-Canadian Nationalism

Inheriting a Canoe Paddle

My father died in 2000, after a year-long illness with colon cancer. The doctors performed some palliative surgery at the time of his diagnosis, but as the cancer grew he could digest less and less of what he ate. So the year was spent, essentially, waiting for him to starve to death. It was a long time to wait. His illness affected all his children profoundly, and made me, like him, demanding and reflective and distraught in turns. But it also caused me to rethink who I am as an academic, as well as a daughter, a mother, and a person. I certainly feel, profoundly, that I am his daughter; my drive to achieve and my intellectual curiosity are a product of his influence, no less than my awkward social sense, my blasted sense of humour, and my crooked baby fingers. Like Margaret Laurence's heroine in *The Diviners*, Morag Gunn, I often hear my father's words emerge from my mouth, and I hear them in the mouths of my daughters. I rarely thought of these things extending back more than one generation, but now I know they must; I feel an incredible sense of loss that I do not know more about my own family history, and I want to use my skills as an academic to think about that. In a way, I now realize, I have always been exploring that heritage in my academic work: my work on Brantford-born novelist Sara Jeannette Duncan was partly an exploration of the ideas and sly ironies I recognized as typical of my mother's family, who are descended from pioneer farmers in Flesherton, Ontario; I associate my interest in the left-nationalist politics of the 1970s with the historical marker for Montgomery's Tavern, which my Dad introduced me to on a shopping trip when I was about eight. White, anglophone academics, especially those of us who are committed to a progressive politics, do not often celebrate familial and cultural continuity; instead we emphasize diversity, mobility, hybridity, the breaking down of the systems of power

that continue to sustain violence and inequality both in our own country and in the world, the family among them. But at some moments, it
becomes not only appropriate but necessary to think about what we have
inherited from previous generations, and how that inheritance both enables and limits who we can be.

Most of my inheritance is intangible; my memories, my mannerisms,
my interests, my vocabulary are all part of it. It might be misleading to
attribute those to my parents; maybe they came from their parents, or
even further back – maybe there is no source but only a retreating path
through genealogy, an unsatisfactory path of repeated bereavement. But
after my father's death, when I resumed my life in Victoria, a life that has
no connection to my childhood family, I realized how much inheritance
has come to mean tangible things: the rugs and bookshelves I inherited
when my mom moved into an apartment, my dad's canoe paddle that
hangs on the wall in my office, and his old fleece jacket that I wear curl-
ing. These things survive through time, and their materiality comes to
compensate for the way that people disappear, leaving no trace.

Inherited objects are a visible sign of loss; as Ethel Wilson wrote in
Swamp Angel, the symbol comes to substitute for the reality. The material objects I have inherited have become signifiers of my father, and
their histories of manufacture, exchange, and use allow them to serve as
reminders of the meanings and histories lost with his death. Their function as mnemonics is a stark illustration of the relationship between signs
and their referents: the sign is a substitute for the referent, an admission
of its absence, an attempt to recall to presence that which we can never
recover. Even an accumulation of objects owned by my father can never
be more than a Derridian supplement, a fruitless attempt to fill in the
gap between their materiality and his. Their very constitution as signifiers of my father is an admission of his material absence: as Peter Schwenger has written, 'The death of the thing, then, is the price we pay for
the word.'[1] The objects themselves, constituted as signs of a reality that
can never be recovered, are what remains to be interrogated.

The inherited object with most meaning for me is my father's canoe
paddle. It's not an old paddle – he received it as a retirement gift from
a colleague when he left his law firm, about ten years before his death.
This paddle is made from a single piece of hardwood – cherry – not
laminated: this makes it more flexible and responsive to the pressure of
water. Some people don't like paddles made this way because the slight
give in the blade leads to a loss of power in the stroke. But I am not much
of a power paddler – I don't have the upper body strength, for one thing

– and I would rather go someplace at a leisurely pace than wear myself out half a mile from home. I like it, and my Dad liked it, because it's a beautiful piece of wood, an example of craftsmanship, and its possession marks us as particular kinds of people, who can afford to own and appreciate beautiful things, and particular kinds of paddlers, who stick to the flat water and think of ourselves as sensitive to the natural world. Though it's a little too big for me, I like to use it when I take my kids canoeing.

The last time I saw my Dad use this paddle, I was six months pregnant with my second daughter, and we were going to canoe around the lake a bit, as we often did on vacation. I was not much help getting the canoe into the water, but I could paddle, and the landscape always made much more sense from the water. This paddle also reminds me of the cottage we had in Haliburton when we were children and of the time we spent there. The first canoe I remember was a fifteen-foot canvas and cedar canoe, which we discarded after my brother and my Dad tried chopping down a few trees to improve the view from the deck. They assured my mother that they knew how to make the tree fall where they wanted; luckily, only the ribs of the canoe were broken. In that canoe, I learned that I was strong enough to propel myself where I wanted to go; I learned to be still, and to watch for the blue heron that sometimes came to our lake. So, besides the memories of my father and my family, this paddle reminds me of important things about myself.

One of the places we used to go in Muskoka was a cottage near Kilworthy, a place where members of my Dad's family had a hunting camp in the first decades of the twentieth century. I never knew any of these people: I struggle to make a connection with the picture of my grandfather as a young man with a thin moustache, holding up a lake trout by the gills, and with his mother in a white middy blouse in the background of a photograph featuring rifles and a dead deer. My father's interest in canoeing must derive from this history, and so my paddle is inextricably related to these images. This paddle means that members of my family have been vacationing in Muskoka for a hundred years and reminds me that my grandmother and great-grandmother probably had their own paddles.

Thus far, this paddle appears to have meaning transparently and naturally: it is associated with my childhood, my love of canoeing, my father, and his family. But I know that these meanings are an illusion, a product of a process that resulted in what Marx called the fetishism of commodities. Marx argued that the social relations that produce value in objects

Grandma Cadman and unidentified members of the author's family on vacation
in Muskoka. Date unknown.

are obscured in the process of exchange, and the illusion is created that
value inheres objectively in the objects themselves, rather than in the
social relations that produced them. Thus 'productions of the human
brain appear as independent beings endowed with life, and entering
into relation both with one another and the human race.'[2] My paddle
seems to brim with meaning, connecting me to my father, my mother
and siblings, and my father's family, but I know that this life, this meaning, is socially constituted. Things can only be constituted as objects in
the social process of identity formation, for when a thing is named 'it
is also changed. It is assimilated into the terms of the human subject
at the same time that it is opposed to it as object, an opposition that is
indeed necessary for the subject's separation and definition.'[3] Thus, 'all
of our knowledge of the object is only knowledge of its modes of representation – or rather of *our* modes of representation, the ways in which
we set forth the object to the understanding.'[4] While objects come into
being through social processes, and their meanings are culturally created, this process is obscured as the meanings projected onto the object

are attributed to the object itself. The paddle does not really have any of these meanings in and of itself; it has these meanings because I have externalized the aspects of my identity that I associate with my father and his family, and certain memories of my childhood, and projected them onto the paddle. According to Daniel Miller, in *Material Culture and Mass Consumption*, my coming to own the paddle is part of a process whereby I will recognize that these meanings are self-created and re-incorporate them into my own identity.

An analysis of this kind affords different sorts of satisfaction. By thinking about my father's paddle, I express my longing for his presence; I also construct characteristics of my own identity – my self-reliance, my love of the natural world, my occasional stillness – by attributing those associations to the paddle. The paddle acts as a souvenir, literally, reminding me of who I am as a daughter, a scholar, a person. I have a whole collection of these souvenirs of myself: the brooch my mother gave me when I graduated from high school, the desk I bought when I moved to Victoria, first editions of Sara Jeannette Duncan's novels, a copy of George Whalley's *Legend of John Hornby*. Each one is a 'souvenir' of some aspect of myself, a reminder of episodes in my personal history. But these personal histories are not the only meanings I associate with my father's canoe paddle. Even as a child, I knew that the canoe was the means whereby Canada 'became a nation': it facilitated exploration and the fur trade, those two east-west movements that eventually united the nation 'a mari usque ad mare.' The canoe occupies a unique place in the nationalist discourse I study: Pierre Trudeau wrote in his famous essay, 'Exhaustion and Fulfillment,' that it was the means whereby a Canadian could learn a patriotism that was 'felt in his bones.'[5] The canoe is still an important means by which urban Canadians like myself claim a first-hand experience of the landscape and a sense of themselves in relation to it. My canoe paddle is also the means by which I identify myself with the larger political community and with the aims of the Canadian state, an identification that seems fully compatible with my family, who as third-generation Ontarians have always been disparaging of anything 'American,' and suspicious of anything British. Because my paddle is a material object that I have used and inherited, that identification seems 'natural.'

In his book *National Dreams*, Daniel Francis has written the best account of the way that the canoe functions as a symbol of Canada. While the book is intended for a general audience, in a straightforward and uncomplicated way Francis makes it clear that he is familiar with most of the recent academic theorizing about the nation. Beginning with an epigraph from Edward Said, 'nations are narrations,' Francis explains that he intends to 'locate and describe some of the most persistent images and stories that seem to express the fundamental beliefs that Canadians hold about themselves.'⁶ According to Francis, 'The Ideology of the Canoe' is one of these stories, which through repetition has become part of the 'master narrative which explains the culture to itself' (10). For Francis, the motif of the canoe journey into the wilderness and back is a defining one for Canadian culture, summoning up the history of indigenous peoples, the history of the fur trade and exploration, and the reaction against urbanization in the early twentieth century that led to summer camps and cottages. However, despite the easy and accessible way Francis tells the story of the canoe as myth, the canoe does not merely 'emerge' as a symbol of nationality as a natural result of its ubiquity in Canadian history. The canoe becomes mythic because this shift is in the interests of the 'elites' who 'use [myths] to reinforce the status quo and further their claims to privilege' (12). This single narrative of the omnipresence of the canoe is the result of a particular historiography, which is both incomplete and gendered. 'This does not mean that the myths are false,' Francis avers, 'only that they are partial' (12). Neither does it mean that they are timeless, or natural. In the case of the 'ideology of the canoe,' this 'tradition' was invented, popularized, promulgated, and underwritten by specific individuals in a specific time period, from the mid-1950s and into the nationalist 1960s and 70s. Certainly Canadians canoed before this; but in travelling from one place to another by canoe, or racing canoes in First Nations or northern communities, they were not self-consciously participating in an activity that promised an imaginative encounter with the history of the nation *qua* nation and the creation of an experiential patriotic identity. If the nation is, as Francis asserts, 'a group of people who share the same illusions about themselves' (10), one of the illusions that unites us as Canadians is a belief that the canoe is 'the symbol of our oneness with a rugged northern landscape, the vessel in which we are re-created as Canadians' (129). It is one of the 'core myths' (10) of Canada.

Roland Barthes gives an account of the way that material objects can operate as 'myth,' making historically contingent concepts like nationality seem to have the validity of objective science. In Barthes's account, myths offer an artificial resolution for cultural contradictions by referencing two levels of signification that he calls first and second orders.⁷ Similarly, Susan Pearce, in *Museums, Objects and Collections*, suggests that objects function like myth to naturalize cultural hegemony by resolving metonymic and symbolic values.[8] Both theorists suggest that the materiality of objects allows them to function as evidence or 'proof' of the cultural values they seem to symbolize. Taking my canoe paddle as an example: I invest the paddle as signifier with the signifieds of my family history of paddling, and thereby objectify the paddle as a signifier of me-in-relation-to-my-family. The relationship between the paddle and its signification is not arbitrary – because it was my father's and now is mine, because both he and I have used it to paddle, it is metonymically a *part* of the family activity of paddling, and to that extent it seems to be a *natural* or intrinsic sign of this activity; in addition, because the paddle endures in time, and has indeed outlived my father, it carries into the present the memories associated with him in a material form. But the paddle-as-sign of me-in-relation-to-my-family also operates as signifier in a secondary system in which it mythically or symbolically represents a second signified – the metanarrative of Canadian nationality constructed around exploration, the fur trade, and, more recently, wilderness camping and environmental protection. In this system, the paddle is emptied of its metonymic significance – that is, its status as a real part of my family history – and is available to be filled up with symbolic meaning as a signifier of a particular version of the history of Canada. Because the paddle can function alternately as sign (paddle as natural sign of me) and as signifier (paddle as historically constructed symbol of the nation), it works to insert me into the narrative of nationality.

The materiality of the paddle is an important aspect of the way it functions in this system. Material objects are perceived first through what theorists of material culture call their presentational qualities; that is, their weight, solidity, colour, texture, dimensions, and aesthetic and sensual appeal. My paddle is demonstrably 'real'; it is also beautiful and valuable, and for that reason I will keep it, allowing it to carry forward its history of manufacture, use, and exchange. Because the paddle has weight and solidity, it can serve as material evidence to prove the validity of the narratives within which it is an important signifier. Beyond this, the paddle is materially in my possession: because it is materially a part of my relationship to my father and my canoeing memories, and because it is old enough to have survived my father, it can serve as 'proof' of my narrative of self, and of the interrelationship between my personal narrative and the larger cultural narrative, as 'proof' of my Canadianness. As Daniel Miller writes, 'The artefact ... tends to imply a certain innocence of facticity; it seems to offer the clarity of realism, an assertion of certainty against the buffeting of debate, an end or resting point which resolves the disorder of uncertain perspectives.'[9] Its materiality is instrumental to the stability of the larger cultural myth it comes to represent.

That cultural myth of Canadian nationality became the subject of much of my work as a scholar. I was trained at graduate school in the seventies, when the focus of Canadian literary studies was the definition and elaboration of the nation in literary works. I never doubted that a 'Canadian identity' existed, as the question was posed in those days: I knew what it was, and it was mine. I knew what it was because I had a personal, and multi-generational, attachment to a particular place that was in Canada; I knew it because I connected my personal history and my family history to the history of Canada that extended beyond my lifetime; I knew it because I had paddled. The 'ideology of the canoe,' as Daniel Francis calls it, allows Canadians like me to construct an identity in which subjectivity and nationality form a seamless whole, and each seems to both confirm and contribute a satisfying depth to the other.

But because my paddle is material, and because material objects can 'bear perpetual symbolic reinterpretation,'[10] it can also represent radically different and even contradictory identities and values. The interpretation of my paddle-as-sign-of-me elides many alternative inter- pretations that challenge the stable, integrated Canadian identity I have constructed for myself, and of which I have become increasingly aware, especially since I moved to the other end of the country. At least one of these must be the paddle as an 'intrinsic' or natural sign of the tech- nologies and material possessions our culture appropriated from First Nations. Birch-bark canoes are unique to northern North America; while other cultures built frames and covered them with skins or bark, Cree people and Mi'kmaq and Anishnabe built frames inside pieces of birch-bark and propelled them with paddles carved by hand out of single pieces of wood, rather like my paddle. Europeans adopted this technol- ogy, 'improved' it with the techniques of mass production, and used it to try to make money out of the land inhabited by the canoe-makers. Here in British Columbia, this happened without even the treaties that exist in some other parts of the country. My paddle has come to be a reminder that my 'Canadianness' also implicates me in the theft of the land that constitutes Canada. In this system of signification, the paddle-as-sign-of- me, and of my most intimate memories of a happy and materially com- fortable childhood, is tied directly to my status as a beneficiary of white privilege and to the complicity of my forebears in cultural genocide and theft.

From this point of view, my paddle no longer resolves the issues raised by my longing for my father; instead, the personal identity objectified in my paddle, which I experienced as a vital, natural, and self-defining connection between the geographical spaces of Canada and my personal history, is undermined and destabilized. Instead, it seems more like a cue for evoking the feeling of 'imperialist nostalgia' defined by Renato Rosaldo in his book *Culture and Truth*: 'a particular kind of nostalgia, often found under imperialism, where people mourn the passing of what they themselves have transformed.'[11] Indeed, any reading of my paddle must acknowledge that it signifies at least two incompatible systems of meanings, meanings that work to contradict each other and that cannot be reconciled into a single system. The feeling of 'being at home,' of 'topophilia' (as Yi-Fu Tuan calls it)[12] or love of place that is the effect of its physicality, and of the link that I construct between it and my family, is contaminated. Minnie Bruce Pratt, a lesbian poet from a southern US white family, recounts a similar recognition in her essay 'Identity: Skin Blood Heart,' when she concludes that her childhood home was built on 'the grave of the people [her] kin had killed, and [her] foundation, [her] birth culture, was mortared with blood.'[13] Pratt's nostalgia for her childhood home is undone by her recognition of the racism that underpins it, her understanding that 'home was an illusion of coherence and safety based on the exclusion of specific histories of oppression and resistance, the repression of differences even in oneself.'[14] Rather than resolving differences like these into a comfortable sentimentalism, my paddle becomes their repository and the means of constructing a link between my personal identity and the history of colonialism that shapes it. And so it becomes a sign of more than one kind of loss: loss, not only of my childhood home, but of the narrative of nationality that secured it.

George Grant's great work about loss, *Lament for a Nation*, was formative of the consciousness of a whole generation of Canadians, many of whom were my professors and are my colleagues. Grant lamented the loss of an autonomous nationality that he felt had resulted from the triumph of the liberal will to technique that characterized modern Canada. The sense that Canada would provide an alternative to the social (dis)organization of the United States, that Canada could be an alternative way to think about human political relationships even while located on the North American continent, was defeated, he thought, with the defeat of the Diefenbaker government: the Chief's obstreperous and clumsy attempt to keep US nuclear warheads off Canadian soil had been opposed by Lester Pearson, who was reasonably and moderately prepared to cooperate in the US Cold War. But Grant lamented more than

the loss of sovereignty: he lamented the loss of a sense of citizenship that
he thought was necessary to full humanity. And that loss, he thought, was
partly the result of the very idea of North America.

The nation is a very recent idea in the history of human societies. It
was born in the Romantic era (late eighteenth–mid-nineteenth centuries) and became the rationale for a reorganization of European states
on the principle of the self-determination of peoples, a reorganization
that persisted through the peace negotiations after the First World War
and continues today. In Europe, the theory of the nation emphasized the
unity of the land and the people through the supposed traditional peasant culture and its links to ancient agricultural practices. The concept of
the 'folk,' a people unified by shared language, history, and religious/
cultural practices and linked to the land through agriculture, became
central to the idea of nationality. Their lives spent working the land,
responding to its seasonal rhythms and knowing its fertile potentialities,
were held to create in the peasant classes a unique character literally
dictated by the land itself; attempts were made to revive agriculturalist
pagan traditions and to resituate the values of the peasant small land-
holder at the centre of the culture in contrast to the educated urban
elite.[15] Margery Fee notes that: 'The intimate relationship of a people
with the soil – a relationship seen as quasi-biological – was used to support the argument that their rulers should come from a local elite rather
than a foreign aristocracy. The peasants, because closest to the soil and
the most uncorrupted by foreign influences, were felt to be the most
representative of their "race" and nation.'[16] In this theory of nationalism,
the underlying unity of the people and the soil formed a natural check
on the resource extraction and technological manipulation that came
along with industrialization.

In contrast, George Grant argues, the idea of North America was conceived in a historical period that was dominated by a rationalism that
created an absolute split between man and nature. North America was
'discovered,' explored, invaded, settled, and made into a state by a culture that saw the landscape it encountered as nothing more than an
object, composed of resources, potentials, riches, obstacles, and means
– in short, what Don McKay would call *materiel*, available for manipulation, development, and sale. For this reason, Grant argues that the unity
of people and land that the nation represents is closed to us, for the idea
of participation in a civic order presupposes the communal unity that
the image of 'roots in the soil' represents. Because North Americans
'discovered' the land within recent historical memory, and because our

motivation in migrating here was merely our confidence in the power of technology to create prosperity from material resources, what Grant calls the 'will to technique,' for us the land can never be the sacred place of our ancestors and the repository of a mystical unity that creates the nation. For First Nations, the very dust under their feet is composed of the remains of their ancestors, whereas, Grant argues, 'there can be nothing immemorial for us except the environment as object.' 'That conquering relation to place has left its mark within us,' Grant writes, and we are perpetually aware of ourselves as alien:

> When we go into the Rockies we may have the sense that gods are there. But if so, they cannot manifest themselves to us as ours. They are the gods of another race, and we cannot know them because of what we are, and what we did.[17]

What we are, and what we did – these words resonate for me, and they form the underlying rhythm of my personal quest for a sense of connection to place. For me, as for Grant, the originary violence that established title to North America can never be forgotten; it persists as a contradiction within the idea that Canada is and can be identical to the geographical space it occupies.

This contradiction, which splits off the geography of the nation from its culture (settler-invader culture) is central in most theories of what makes Canada unique as a nation. Many locate this split in the psychology of individuals rather than, as Grant does, in history. Northrop Frye detects 'a tone of deep terror with regard to nature' that is both literal, 'in a country where the winters are so cold, and where conditions of life have so often been bleak and comfortless, where even the mosquitoes have been described as "mementoes of the fall,"' and psychological, 'a terror of the soul at something these things manifest.'[18] For Margaret Atwood, in her influential study of Canadian literature, *Survival*, the actual land that makes up Canada is 'often dead or unanswering or actively hostile to man;' the landscape betrays the trust of the Canadian, and so becomes an obstacle to 'conquer and enslave' rather than a nurturing or generous ally.[19] Dennis Lee's poem *Civil Elegies*, strongly influenced by both Grant's and Atwood's ideas, complains that Canadians are a people who 'take that land in greedy/ innocence but will not live it,'[20] in the sense of adapting to it, understanding it, and internalizing it as home. Robin Mathews's thesis that Canadians prioritize community good over individual liberty is also founded in the premise that cooperation and community solidarity are/were necessary to ensure survival in a landscape that is both harsh and harshly capitalist.[21] The land only becomes part of these Canadas by force. This is a nation turned against itself, one which defines itself not just by distance from, but by opposition to, the geography it encompasses.

There are alternative characterizations of the relationship between Canada and the land. Some Canadian authors have attempted to create an idea of nation based on an agricultural relationship with the land: Frederick Philip Grove's *Fruits of the Earth* comes to mind, with its central character, Abe Spaulding, eventually learning how to 'read' the flat prairie for its values as landscape. Robin Mathews developed this idea in relation to French- and Anglo-Canadian nationalism in his work on the *roman de la terre* in Canada. John Ralston Saul has recently argued that Canada is 'a métis nation' based on the pre-Confederation mixed-race culture that existed before Canada came into being. Carl Berger, in a well-known essay 'The True North Strong and Free,' has recounted the way that many nineteenth-century Canadian nationalists based their sense of nationality on the interaction of the climate and the people, arguing that the challenges of living in a northern climate would inevitably mould a unique 'race' of active, healthy, and democratic people adapted to the climate. But many have seen only the absence of connection to the land and the lack of a European folk culture. C.P. Traill famously lamented the way that the Canadian woods seemed bereft of the fairies and druids of England, and poet Earle Birney complained that 'it's only by our lack of ghosts we're haunted.'[22] As Margery Fee points out, some have seen Canada's First Nations, rather than its agricultural communities, as the 'folk' who have an authentic connection to the land. Fee comments in her essay on 'Romantic Nationalism and the Image of Native People in Contemporary English-Canadian Literature' on the way that contemporary Canadian writers create narratives that resolve their insecurity about 'belonging' by referring to First Nations cultures. However, she suggests, this strategy is flawed because 'those closest to the soil are not blood ancestors, their cultural traditions are alien, and [for Canadians] to become their mouthpieces in any valid sense is to betray both one's culture and its claim to the land' (17). This fundamental break between the 'folk' and the people of Canada, between the land and the story that is supposed to explain why we are here, is the source of the 'bad fit between Old World Romantic theory and the New World situation' (17), according to Fee. While Canadian writers frequently refer to Native mythologies as sources for poetry, and

First Nations peoples as the unique and distinctive element of Canadian culture, few non-indigenous writers manage to successfully incorporate them: Northrop Frye comments in his 'Conclusion to the *Literary History of Canada*' that while 'the Indians began with a mythology which included all the main elements of our own. It was, of course, impossible for [non-indigenous] Canadians to establish any real continuity with it' (233). The result is the continuing awareness of a slippage between the nation as concept and the geographical space that purports to embody it, between the idea and the thing, between the people and the place, and a continuing sense of loss and displacement.

Terry Goldie, in his book *Fear and Temptation*, puts the paradox plainly: 'The white Canadian looks at the Indian. The Indian is Other and therefore alien. But the Indian is indigenous and therefore cannot be alien. So the Canadian must be alien. But how can the Canadian be alien within Canada?'[23] Goldie describes the fundamental ways that European-derived cultures try to 'erase this separation of belonging' (12). He coins the term *indigenization* for the process whereby non-indigenous Canadians try to make themselves either literally Native, or merely native to place. Goldie identifies two images that represent the encounter between non-indigenous peoples and the landscape and peoples of the settler colony: penetration and appropriation (15). For Goldie, penetration is the image that dominates explorer narratives: this is the attitude that sees 'Indians,' like the landscape, as Other, something to be subdued, changed, civilized, or removed. Appropriation characterizes more complex literary works, says Goldie, and operates through either impersonation or incorporation: impersonation is the attempt to assume the subjectivity of the indigene, either by writing in the first person as a First Nations person (like Anne Cameron or Rudy Wiebe), or by literal impersonation (like Grey Owl or the 'tribe of the Wannabees' identified by Deborah Root[24]); incorporation subsumes First Nations cultures, technologies, and lands under the rubric of 'Canada.'

The nationalist narrative that sees the canoe as a symbol of the nation incorporates First Nations cultures as the proof of Canada's link to the land. In her article 'Becoming Indigenous: Land, Belonging and the Appropriation of Aboriginality in Canadian Nationalist Narratives,' Eva Mackey shows how in such nationalist discourse First Nations cultures are transformed into the 'heritage' of all Canadians, which 'enables the culture of the colonized to be appropriated by the colonisers and put to service in building national and international identity.'[25] The narrative of incorporation elides the long history of colonization and produces what Mackey calls 'settler innocence': 'The celebration of Canadian national "heritage," made possible by appropriating Aboriginal culture, entails no less than the erasure of a history of *conquest*. Aboriginal people become the ancestors of a nation who pass on an inheritance, not the survivors of conquest and colonization' (161). By taking my canoe paddle as the symbol of my interpellation as Canadian, I participate in that erasure, even as I am haunted by 'what we are, and what we did.'

More recently, environmentalists have tried to remake a physical and emotional connection to the land through a rejection of the ethics of consumer culture and corresponding political action to preserve wilderness areas from development. Wilderness areas, defined as natural spaces untouched by humans and home to the biologically diverse ecosystems that supposedly pre-existed human interference with the natural world, are valued in environmentalist discourse as havens of beauty and spiritual renewal, as well as repositories of valuable undiscovered species and 'carbon sinks' in the fight against global warming. However, as William Cronon has argued, wilderness as a concept can never erase the history of exploitation that created it; it is a space created by the removal of indigenous peoples from their traditional territories and 'a product of the very history it seeks to deny' – the history of the conquest and theft of North America. The spiritual sustenance that Canadians derive from their appreciation of the aesthetic and tactile joys of the 'wilderness experience' and their sense that knowledge of (love of) wilderness creates or augments their sense of nationality is derived at the expense of the 'thoroughgoing erasure of the history from which it sprang.'[26]

This book is about loss: loss of many different kinds. It is the loss that my paddle represents to me, a loss of childhood, family, stability, but also a loss of fixed political identity that I think is common to many other Canadians of my generation. For if my paddle represents to me the attempt to bridge the gap between myself as Canadian and the landscape of Canada, then this book is about the absolute incommensurability of these two and the way that the desire for a nation that is material and experiential, felt in the bones (as Pierre Trudeau put it),[27] will always be frustrated. If my paddle represents to me the way that the ideal canoe trip is supposed to create an identity encompassing the human world and the wilderness, my paddle represents the truth that the ideal world of glaciated lakes and loons remains, and will remain, beyond my reach in a conceptual and spiritual way. And if my paddle represents my desire, as a non-indigenous Canadian, to be vitally and historically and spiritually connected to place, indigenous to Canada, then this book represents both the loss of that dream for me and my attempt to disrupt, trouble, and denaturalize that dream for other non-indigenous Canadians. It represents my recognition of the cultural imperative to tease apart the easy way that the contradictions of 'settler culture,' the culture of the Euro-Canadian majority, are resolved by the 'myth of the canoe,' and my belief that to live those contradictions, actively and self-consciously, is the only justifiable way to call oneself Canadian in the twenty-first century.

This book demonstrates the way that canoeing, as it is represented in Canadian literature, non-fiction, and popular culture, and as it is prac- tised by non-indigenous recreational canoeists, is a strategy of appropria- tion whereby non-indigenous Canadians hope to indigenize themselves to 'erase the separation of belonging' that characterizes white settlement in the northern part of North America. Growing out of the groundbreak- ing and important work by Terry Goldie and Margery Fee, it applies their concepts of indigenization and appropriation to suggest that the canoe was and is appropriated from First Nations cultures by middle-class white Canadians in order to re-signify themselves in an unbroken line of descent from First Nations peoples, and so create themselves as 'natural' inheritors of the land. It argues that while canoes and canoeing were adopted by non-indigenous traders and settlers as practical and neces- sary tools for the exploitation of First Nations lands and peoples, since the advent of the engine canoeing has become a fetishized activity in Marx's sense, an activity that no longer has use value and instead appears to have, in itself, the power to heal the split between Canada, as an idea and an ideological construct, and the real, physical land it occupies.

However, the narrative that appropriates the canoe as 'heritage' and First Nations peoples as the ancestors of Canada is only apparently seamless. This book also suggests that this narrative embodies the con- tradictions it seems to deny by continually calling to remembrance the existence of Canada's First Nations peoples and the originary violence that deprived them of their traditional territories. Ernst Renan suggests that the narrative of nation can only be unified if some things are forgot- ten: historical events, facts, responsibilities, obligations. But many Cana- dians still remember what we are, and what we did: canoeists in Canadian culture are metaphorically (and sometimes literally) haunted by the nar- rative that is elided in the dominance of the ideology of the canoe, the narrative of the way that First Nations were invaded, colonized, and sub- sumed by non-indigenous culture in Canada. For paddlers who can hear that narrative, and who accept the contradictions it poses, the canoe has become a way to become more aware of issues of social justice for First Nations. And, as my last chapter will show, the canoe has also become a means for healing, community-building, and political awareness among First Nations peoples in Canada.

This book begins with a chapter that describes the way the canoe evokes the uncanny in many Canadian literary texts. Drawing on David Bentley's concept of 'uncannyda,' chapter one analyses the way the canoe provides a link to the landscape that signifies connection to and love of place, but also evokes 'the other,' resulting in the kinds of illusion or vertigo suggested by Bentley as indications of 'uncannyda.' Chapter two critiques the historiographic tradition that argues for the importance of the canoe in the founding of Canada and represents the voyageurs as its founders. It argues that despite the way that this tradition figures First Nations as ancestors or partners, it cannot escape the contradiction that the beginning of the Canadian state is the end of indigenous sovereignty. Chapter three introduces Eric Morse, a central figure in the popularizing of recreational wilderness canoeing. Morse was inspired by the work of Harold Innis and other historians to 're-trace the routes of the voyageurs' throughout the 1950s and 1960s. Morse conflated the geography of Canada with the nation as an ideological construct and suggested that both were available through the experience of canoeing; he introduced influential men in Ottawa to the idea that by canoeing, they could become more Canadian. The published accounts of his trips inspired many Canadians to follow in his wake. Chapter four describes the Centennial Voyageur Canoe Pageant, a cross-Canada canoe race that took place in 1967. The race was imagined as a historical re-enactment by its government sponsors (and by Morse, who advised race organizers); the way that the race figured First Nations and women embodied the contradictions of the historiography that justified it. Chapter five links the contemporary tradition of retracing the routes of historical canoeists to the concept of 'uncannyda' by considering multiple popular and literary texts based on the life and death of John Hornby. Each version of the events that led to his death situates them in a different moral landscape, and while each follows the same route, it leads to several different meanings. Chapter six focuses on the films and books of Bill Mason, Canada's 'canoeing guru.' Mason's work argued that canoeists could remake a harmonious relationship with nature through revaluing wilderness spaces uncontaminated by human interference, and through them gain access to a benevolent Creator. His view of the wilderness, however, is structured by a desire to elide the consequences of history; his use of

First Nations spirituality obscures rather than reveals the way that wilderness was constructed by the removal of First Nations peoples. Chapter seven revisits many of these themes in a history of the Canadian Canoe Museum collection and a reading of its permanent displays.

The final chapter in this book describes a way that canoeing can be part of a process of decolonization by considering the revival of canoe journeys among west coast First Nations. Rather than seeing the canoe as a way to become Canadian, First Nations from the Puget Sound area and up the coast to Alaska see canoe journeys as a way to assert their presence and their sovereignty and to promote health and traditional values in their communities. These journeys are not re-enactments, nor are they costumed performances for an audience; instead, they are cultural practices that have remade diplomatic and informal ties between nations, necessitated the recovery of traditional skills and protocols, and challenged the imposition of borders and reserves. They are a reminder that the only way that settler society can ever have a relationship with the land is by first ensuring justice for First Nations.

This book will inevitably leave out many representations of canoeing. Jamie Benidickson offers an encyclopaedic listing of instances of the canoe in popular culture, including advertising, Hollywood movies, newspaper cartoons, women's magazines, and summer camping handbooks, and I am greatly indebted to his book *Idleness, Water, and a Canoe*, which offers a comprehensive history of canoeing in Canada. Readers interested in such a history can hardly do better. However, my purpose in writing this book is not to write about the canoe, *per se*, but about what it has been made to represent in a certain strain of Canadian cultural thought. Rather than justifying the view that the canoe is a symbol of the nation, I want to show the way that the signifier 'nation' is itself ambiguous and unstable, and available to be filled up with meanings associated with the canoe. Calling the canoe a symbol of the nation does not tell us anything about the canoe *qua* canoe; instead, it allows historians or canoeists or cultural analysts to say what the nation is: indigenous, natural, democratic, multicultural, tippy, or whatever else. The designation of the canoe as a symbol of the nation is a metaphoric statement designed to give the nation the qualities attributed to the canoe, both historical and material. And so I am only interested in the history of the canoe insofar as that history is mobilized to attribute characteristics to the nation it is supposed to symbolize.

This book also argues that instead of accepting the non-indigenous characterization of the canoe as a symbol of Canada, First Nations com-

munities have reappropriated it in order to represent their own journeys towards both healing and justice. In events like the journey of Bill
Reid's LooTaas to Vancouver, and the Qatuwas Festival and the tradition
of tribal journeys that it inaugurated, First Nations are re-signifying the
canoe as integral to their own culture, with historical, practical, and symbolic value. Some commentators suggest that community ownership of
canoes and the continuing participation of paddlers in traditional ceremonies enlarges the symbolic significance of the canoe to include First
Nations as part of Canada and to express the non-indigenous values of
multiculturalism and racial equality. I will argue that instead it represents an assertion of indigenous sovereignty and a rejection of incorporation into mainstream Canadian culture under the current regime of
land and resource ownership.

In arguing that both the practice of (recreational) canoeing and its
representation in historical and literary texts in Canada is an attempt
to indigenize the non-indigenous population and to elide the history
of First Nations peoples, to substitute a conflict-free history of inclusion
for the reality of genocide and theft, this book does not attempt to lay
blame on individuals or to promote feelings of guilt in white Canadians,
least of all in canoeists. The idea of guilt, it seems to me, is a red herring
– a diversion from the real issues. Because I was born a non-indigenous
Canadian I have already benefitted from that genocide and theft – that is
a reality I cannot evade. The real question is, what do I do now? Instead
of attempting the futile practice of laying blame for past events, or evoking the paralysis of guilt, I have been inspired by the spirit of an essay by
Jurgen Habermas, 'On the Public Uses of History,' which advocates the
re-examination of the relationships between the historical traditions that
form our self-understanding and present knowledge of the way those
traditions led to injustices. 'We have to stand by our traditions, then, if
we do not want to disavow ourselves … What follows from this existential
connection between traditions and forms of life that have been poisoned
by unspeakable crimes? … Later generations … cannot be blamed for
their parents' and grandparents' failure to act. Is there still a problem of
joint liability for them?' he asks, and answers in the affirmative.[28]

The recognition that my love of canoeing hides my implication in genocide may seem like a naive one. Yet it's possible to know these things
without assimilating them into one's personal universe; without understanding how they can modify, or undermine, the reality of one's identity, the way they inflect one's pleasures, one's desires, one's material
sense of being in the world. It is a naive recognition, but one that I am

not afraid to own; I think it's quite possible that in the sense I mean it, most Canadians are naive. I think it's clear that most non-indigenous Canadians are unaware when they walk on 'Indian land,' and perhaps are only now becoming aware of the frustration and powerlessness that unresolved land claims can provoke. These things just aren't uppermost in our minds, even when they should be. When I visited Alert Bay, I was surprised when I was told that I could not enter the graveyard to read the tombstones: 'We're kind of sensitive about graves.' I should have thought of that: in my British Columbia literature class, I teach M. Wylie Blanchet's popular autobiography, *The Curve of Time*, in which she writes unblushingly about her children amusing themselves by robbing isolated grave sites on the BC coast. Asking the question about the graveyard reiterated for me what I already knew, what I needed to remain aware of. This book reiterates what we already know, what we need to remain aware of, what we are haunted by, all unknowing, when we canoe. If the way that canoeing is signified in Canada hides my implication in geno- cide, it may also reveal it.

Deborah Root has written that white North American culture often 'seems so bankrupt and uninteresting' as to be 'emptied of meaning,' composed of nothing but strip malls and sitcom television. She argues that the inability of white anglophone Canadians to rethink our own tra- dition, to oppose the 'destructive soulless ethos' of capitalism, prevents us from being able to act in solidarity with First Nations or truly under- stand what a racially diverse and equal society would be like. 'Rather than seeking authenticity elsewhere, we need to transform how we look at our histories and traditions and find ways to unravel these from all the racist versions to which we have been subjected.'[29] Thinking about my canoe paddle may be a good way to rediscover the continuity between the per- sonal and the cultural, and to tease out my personal investments in the cultural discourses of colonialism. But it might also be a way to oppose the paralysis that a burgeoning postcolonial awareness can provoke and to investigate what might have been inherited from within Western cul- ture that can help to address the inequities that have resulted from those discourses. In this way, my canoe paddle can still represent the familial and cultural continuity I want to preserve. I can use my inheritance of self-reliance and stillness, good memories, and commitment to place to change the way I think of Canada and my place in it.

Chapter One

Inheriting a Literary Tradition:
Paddling the Uncanny Canoe

Duncan Campbell Scott's 'Night Hymns on Lake Nipigon'[1] is one of my favourite poems. It evokes everything about canoeing that I love: the silence of the empty lake, the muted knock of the paddle on the gunwales, the whisper of the bow cutting through the water, the silvery whirlpool off the end of the paddle. The poem represents a group of canoes gliding through the darkness under a starry sky, racing an oncoming storm, the paddlers singing old familiar hymns back against the sound of distant thunder. The swinging rhythm of the poem evokes the rhythm of paddling: the lines are irregularly dactylic with five main stresses, each line concluding with Scott's trademark trochee. The final line of each stanza, five syllables arranged in his recognizable dum-da-da dum-da rhythm (the rhythm comes from the Sapphic stanza Scott was imitating[2]), always seems unfinished, ready to swing into the next stanza or stroke, until the storm breaks in at the end, 'Ringing like cymbals.' I love the sound of the words, too: 'the wild pellucid Nipigon reaches,' and the description of the hymns, 'the sonorous vowels in the noble Latin / ... married with the long-drawn Ojibwa / Uncouth and mournful.' I always teach this poem when I am teaching Scott, just because of the physical pleasure it evokes in me: the *chora* of the sounds, rhythms, and images play out directly on the senses and recall pleasant memories.[3]

But 'Night Hymns on Lake Nipigon' is a melancholy poem; it evokes that feeling of eerie isolation in darkness that suggests the uncanny. Like many of Scott's poems, it represents the encounter of two cultures, one which we might call 'Western' or European, the other, Ojibwa. The paddlers are singing 'Adeste Fideles' ('Oh Come, All Ye Faithful'), a melody developed for words in ancient Latin, rewritten in English, and now in an Ojibwa translation: 'Tones that were fashioned when the faith brooded in darkness' are especially suited to voices raised on the other side of the world, where, Scott says, 'Hunted the savage.' 'Now have the ages met in the Northern midnight,' says Scott, as the ancient melody rises 'on the lonely loon-haunted Nipigon reaches.' But despite the cultural similarity, for Scott, of the ancient peoples chanting 'in old-world nooks of the desert' and the Ojibwa peoples who now sing 'Adeste Fideles' in their own language, the natural world expresses the violence of the encounter between these two cultures with its own clash of forces: like Scott's other poems of cultural encounter, the poem ends with a violent storm that obscures the phrases of the song. The storm 'whelms them,' 'wraps them in rain'; 'back they falter' as their outlines fade in the driving rain.

The shadowy sounds fade away in the storm, but nothing is resolved.[4] Scott sets out his central problematic, which is the simultaneous strangeness and appropriateness of hearing the sounds of 'Adeste Fideles' in this setting, in this language; and then he drowns it. The issues of contact, opposition, and overlap of the two cultures are also drowned by the pleasure of rhythm, sound, and image. But they are still there, unresolved, contradictory. Does Scott think it's a good thing that the Ojibwa sing Christian hymns? He says that the hymn expresses 'a bygone age whose soul is eternal,' and the phrases fly into the air in a movement that mimics the movement of the paddles, 'Falling in rhythm, timed with the liquid, plangent / Sounds from the blades where the whirlpools break and are carried / Down into darkness.' But the eternal and presumably universal human sentiments expressed by the song are overwhelmed by thunder and 'falter / Back into quiet.' It's not clear.

'Night Hymns on Lake Nipigon,' of all Canadian poems, is the one that most represents for me the idea that David Bentley calls 'uncannyda,' the uncanny-ness of Canada. Following Freud, Bentley describes the uncanny as 'a process of repression [whereby] something that was once homely – cosy, familiar, and comforting – becomes the opposite – strange, mysterious, and disconcerting.'[5] Bentley suggests that the concept of the uncanny is particularly useful 'as a means of illuminating certain passages of early writing about Canada which emphasize the country's strangeness and unfamiliarity.'[6] In the examples Bentley cites, the uncanny is evoked by new experiences, confusions of perception, unnerving and mysterious phenomena that Europeans could not understand or only partially understood, experiences and objects that seemed to be like their European counterparts, but were different. 'Night Hymns on Lake Nipigon' evokes that eerie feeling. But for Scott, seated on the bottom of his canoe on Lake Nipigon, what was familiar, and what strange? The tune was familiar, though not the Ojibwa words; the land-scape was familiar, but not in the company of those sounds. Scott was Canadian, so the landscape was his 'native' land; the tune was Latin, and Christian, and so also his by right of ancestry, yet it seemed incongruous in the setting; the Ojibwa language belonged to the land, but not to him. Scott found the two aspects of his familiar nationality in stark opposi-tion and wrote a poem that represents the paradox that Terry Goldie identifies in *Fear and Temptation*: 'how can the Canadian be alien within Canada?'[7]

Duncan Campbell Scott is the perfect poet to begin a discussion of the contradictions inherent in the literary tradition of the canoe in Canada because it is impossible to discuss his work without discussing him, and he embodied those contradictions. A humane and educated man who practised classical piano on a silent keyboard in his Ottawa office and wrote poems and stories that ironized federal policies of assimilation for Native people, he was also the civil servant who authored and adminis-tered those policies. He conceived and enforced the residential schools policy that forced children into the care of people who beat them and sexually abused them; he was the face of the Indian Affairs department that confiscated the regalia of the Cranmer family at the famous pot-latch in 1921 in Alert Bay and sent twenty-six people to jail for refusing to abide by the law that forbade feasts, religious ceremonies, and give-aways. A well-known historian told me he had no hesitation in using the word 'evil' to describe Scott[8] because, he said, even if you think of Scott as a mere bureaucrat enacting the will of the (racist) government, he should have known better; he should have been paying more attention. Yet Scott is also the poet who spent his weekends paddling the Lièvres, the Gatineau, and the Rideau near Ottawa with fellow poet Archibald Lampman and wrote beautifully about canoeing on the Mattagami and portaging over the height of land.

The contradictions Scott embodies are like two sides of a piece of paper; you really can't separate them. His longing descriptions of the Canadian landscape, his accurate representation of the pleasures of the canoe trip, and his nationalist fervour for creating art from uniquely Canadian 'materials' are of a piece with his administrative attempts to extinguish Aboriginal title and to assimilate First Nations. His appropria-tion of the canoe as a symbol of his own indigeneity, and his construc-tion of the land as Canada and of himself as native to it, as Canadian, is premised on the extinguishment of any other way of seeing the land, and any other way to be native to it. Indeed, by seeing Canada as a politi-

cal colony in relation to Britain, and by being largely unable to see to
First Nations as colonized *by* Canada, Scott and his fellow 'Confederation Poets,' Charles G.D. Roberts, Lampman, and Bliss Carman, create
themselves as the colonials struggling for national self-definition and
independence and thereby substitute themselves for the real indigenes.
It seems to me that he perfectly represents the contradictions inherent
in English Canadian nationalism, the contradictions inherent in me and
in the intellectual tradition I represent. DCS 'R' Us, as it were.

This is not to say that the Confederation Poets were in any way distinctive in their form of settler nationalism; indeed, these contradictions
are inherent in the concept of the nation itself. Homi Bhabha suggests
that they derive from the instability of the concept of nation itself, from
its 'conceptual indeterminacy, its wavering between vocabularies'[9] and
from the 'impossible unity of the nation as a symbolic force' (1). This
indeterminacy is expressed by Bhabha in the form of pairs of opposi-
tions that are masked by the fiction of the unified nation, including 'the
heimlich pleasures of the hearth, the *unheimlich* terror of the space or
race of the Other' (2), the opposition that signifies the uncanny. The
uncanny expresses the impossible coexistence of both Canadian sovereignty and Aboriginal title, European descent and Canadian aboriginality, come from away and come from here, justice for indigenous and
non-indigenous Canadians alike. As Bhabha notes, 'this is not to deny
the attempt by nationalist discourses persistently to produce the idea of
the nation as a continuous narrative of social progress, the narcissism of
self-generation, the primeval present of the *Volk*' (1), but it is to question
the adequacy of those narratives of unity and draw attention to the way
they evoke the uncanny even as they try to resolve its contradictions. As
a mnemonic symbol of those narratives, the motif of the canoe in Canadian literature signifies doubly, in the sense that its very presence signals
an attempt by a literary text to claim a place in a unified discourse of
'nativeness,' to situate itself as Canadian, yet it also evokes that 'terror of
the space or race of the Other' (2).

The uncanny appears in the literature of the canoe as a singular motif,
that of a motionless canoe seemingly suspended in a bubble, surrounded
by an indeterminate element composed of reflection, illusion, light, and
depth. The persistence of this image through over a hundred years of
literature suggests the way it represents a moment of panic that is com-
pulsively revisited in generation after generation of Canadians.[10] Bentley
proposes that 'What makes Canada uncanny at certain times and places
is the transgression or dissolution of (European) spatial categories: small

seems large, far appears near, outside comes inside, above resembles below.'[11] The poetry of the 'northern romantics' uses the image of the canoe suspended between two reflective surfaces, the water and the sky – an image of isolation, illusion, and mirage – to turn the perception of nature, familiar from the Romantic tradition as an opportunity for emotional renewal, suddenly strange and threatening.

One of the best-known canoeing poems of the Confederation period is Archibald Lampman's 'Morning on the Lièvres.'[12] Like much of the poetry written by the generation of writers who grew up after Confederation, 'Morning on the Lièvres' seeks to indigenize the white Canadian by representing him in connection with a natural world described in terms recognizably and uniquely Canadian. The poem describes the familiar elements of a Romantic landscape – mists, effects of light and shadow, stillness and reflection, the mystery of landscape, and its ability to evoke and reflect emotional states. But the reader is clearly not with Wordsworth in his rowboat, for the birds, animals, and landscape features are specific to the Canadian Shield: jays, muskrats, the drowned trees at the edge of a reed bed, a rocky spur that juts into the river. This landscape portrait actually depends on the canoe; its ability to navigate shallow water provides access to locations inaccessible otherwise, and the speaker's point of view from low on the surface of the water effectively creates his link with the landscape. But the sense of 'uncannyda' intrudes here to undermine the idea of a seamless fit between culture and nature. 'Softly as a cloud we go / Sky above and sky below' are the often-quoted lines that open the second stanza of 'Morning on the Lièvres,' and they indicate the way that the reflective surface of the water makes the canoe seem suspended in the air rather than placed on the water. The bottom similarly drops out from under the speaker in one of the lyrics in Isabella Valancy Crawford's 'Malcolm's Katie': 'O light canoe, where dost thou glide?'[13] The speaker of the poem declares that 'Below ... gleams no silver'd tide' but instead a 'concave Heaven' containing the evening star and 'round worlds.' Indeed, there is 'no earth, no wave' either above or below the canoe; instead, it is surrounded by 'jewell'd skies' (part I, 136–45).[14] 'The canoe sits in the centre of a globe,' comments Robin Mathews, that implies perfection in the love of the two main characters in the poem, Max and Katie.[15] This image is foreign to Crawford's source, the lyric 'O légère hirondelle' from Gounod's opera *Mirielle*, but Robert Alan Burns notes that in this verse the canoe moves through an 'ambiguous' and 'illusory' medium to become 'a vehicle of communion, an image of containment whose destination is uncertain.'[16]

David Bentley cites an earlier example of the suspended canoe image in his article, 'Uncannyda.' He quotes from Thomas Moore's poem, 'To the Lady Charlotte Rawdon from the Banks of the St. Lawrence' (1806), which includes both a verse and a lengthy explanatory footnote containing this image. The footnote, drawn from the *Travels* (1778) of US explorer Jonathan Carver, reads: 'When it was calm, and the sun shone bright, I could sit in my canoe, where the depth was upward of six fathoms, and plainly see huge piles of stone at the bottom, of different shapes, some of which appeared as if they had been hewn; the water at this time was as pure and transparent as air, and my canoe seemed as if it hung suspended in that element. It was impossible to look attentively through this limpid medium, at the rocks below, without finding, before many minutes were elapsed, your head swim and your eyes no longer able to behold the dazzling scene.'[17] This footnote provides the basis for the canoe imagery in a verse of Moore's poem, also cited by Bentley:

> Over Huron's lucid lake,
> Where the wave, as clear as dew,
> Sleeps beneath the light canoe,
> Which, reflected, floating there,
> Looks as if it hung in air.[18]

The confusion of perception that creates both the illusion of a canoe floating in the air and vertigo in the speaker, the uncanny canoe, exemplifies Bentley's idea of uncannyda.

The image of the suspended canoe as a union of lovers is used in another poem by Isabella Valancy Crawford, 'The Lily Bed,' described by Ian Lancashire as 'among the most reticently erotic poems in English.'[19] In this poem the masculine canoe lays upon the breast of the maiden wave, the two joined as 'His cedar paddle, scented, red / He thrust down through the lily bed.' The 'He' of the poem is identified as 'the wood' who speaks with a tongue 'of loud, strong pines' and kisses with lips made of blossoms; the reflection of the wood in the water represents 'His image painted in her breast,' while the bark canoe upon the water represents 'one isle' that ''tween blue [sky] and blue [water] did melt.' They remain 'All lily-locked, all lily-locked' as 'His light bark in the blossoms rocked,' the rhythmic structure of the couplet stanzas underlining the metaphorical significance of the action. In Crawford's poem, the canoe represents the joining of opposites in such a way as to blur their separate being. In contrast, Pauline Johnson uses the suspended canoe

Pauline Johnson in her canoe, Wildcat. Image number BHS 563g. Courtesy of
the Brant Historical Society and Chiefswood Historic Site.

to explore a more conventional feminine sexuality in 'The Idlers.'[20] The
couple lounges in a 'lotus-land' created by their drifting canoe under a
hot July sun. The speaker's characterization of the sun, 'Full prodigal
of heat/ Full lavish of its lustre unrepressed,' placing his 'kisses' on the
water foretells the physicality of her description of her canoeing partner,
whose 'indolently crude' pose against the thwart of the canoe suggests
his 'might / Of muscle, half suspected, half defined' and his 'splendid
sunburnt throat that pulses unconfined.' While the drifting canoe is
merely the venue for the consummation of their relationship, the confusion of perception suggested by the suspended canoe image is evoked by
the melting and blurring of vision as the speaker turns to meet the gaze
of her lover, and the motif of reflection is recalled in his 'cloud-grey eyes,
wherein cloud shadows burn.'[21]
    Pauline Johnson's 'Shadow River: Muskoka' uses the image of the sus-

pended canoe to create a metaphor of the relationship between life and art, and of the poet as a manipulator of 'shadows' rather than reality.[22] The canoe is suspended as 'A bubble in the pearly air … Midway twixt earth and heaven' that seems to 'float upon the sapphire floor' with drifting clouds both above and below. The objects above the water are doubled by their reflections so that 'The border line' between the real and its shadow is indistinguishable: 'The keenest vision can't define / So perfect is the blending.' The poet claims a power over the reflection that she could never have in reality:

> The beauty, strength and power of the land
> Will never stir or bend at my command
> But all the shade
> Is marred or made,
> If I but dip my paddle blade;
> And it is mine alone.

The final stanza defines the 'the shadows and the dreaming' as the realm of the poet, because they are the home of the 'deep ideal' that the poet seeks to represent. In an extended analysis of this poem, Glenn Will-mott perceptively notes the way the poem both reproduces and rewrites English Aestheticism by politicizing the act of claiming allegiance to the aesthetic realm in preference to the 'world.' He attributes the poet's uncanny suspension in her canoe to her position as a First Nations writer, cut off from her Mohawk language by English education and deprived of power over the traditional lands of her people. In his reading, the paddle performs as pen, creating and destroying the shadow world, 'her *signifying* world.'[23]

'The Third Generation,' a short story by turn-of-the-century novel-ist and poet Marjorie Pickthall (1883–1922), evokes the uncanny to simultaneously assert and undercut the narrative of claiming land for the nation.[24] The two main characters are explorers on a canoe trip, retracing the path laid down through a 'vast wilderness' claimed by Bob Lemaire's grandfather fifty years earlier. In this narrative of white self-definition, a solitary Montagnais[25] man haunts the explorers, 'a living shadow' (127) on the edge of their evening campfire. This ghostly figure claims to know Bob, and he may indeed recognize him; the Montagnais man turns out to be the sole survivor of a smallpox epidemic introduced to the area by Bob's grandfather, an epidemic that wiped out the very people to whom the paddlers hope to turn for assistance when they run out of food. 'The Third Generation' challenges the way that the narrative of nationality incorporates First Nations as 'our ancestors' and their cultures as 'our heritage' by metaphorically depicting the way this narrative is haunted by cultural and actual genocide.

Bob's claim to the valley of the P'tite Babiche River is based on his grandfather's journals and his map, 'drawn on parchment in faded ink' (125). This textual evidence of both the enterprise and the achievement of Bob's grandfather, 'the only ... white man before themselves [who] had ever tried the journey from the Gran' Babiche due west to the P'tite Babiche' (126), legitimates Bob's status as the inheritor of the land, but this is only the beginning of Bob's indigenization. Although he was raised in the city by a father who 'worked in an office all his life' (125), Bob experiences a feeling of being at home, of 'stillness and a strange content' (125), when he first surveys his isolated domain. His inexperience in the ways of wilderness travel disappears when he enters the land claimed for him by his grandfather: 'when I saw it, it just seemed to – come natural' (126), he explains. When the expedition extends past September and risks the winter cold, Bob's 'instincts, inherited from generations' (133), allow him to understand more accurately the dangers confronting him and Barrett. And when the pair face the challenge of running a violent rapid in a snowstorm, Bob's 'instincts' again come to the fore, 'the sleeping instincts of a brain inherited from far generations of wanderers and voyageurs' (134). Inherited property is a privileged signifier of the inner self in turn-of-the-century fiction, in which newly purchased consumer goods can signal artificiality, pretentiousness, and falsity. Bob's instinctive knowledge of the landscape he moves through privileges this particular inheritance as representing his inner self, creating him as indigenous to this place.

But the mysterious presence of the Montagnais man undercuts Bob's claim to indigeneity. The Montagnais is characterized as both repulsive and ghostly, 'about the oldest old Indian' (127) they have ever seen: poverty-stricken, dependent, and less than human. Even though he soon drops several days behind, the man follows in their tracks like a stray dog, a 'ragged, dirty, old imbecile, forever following them' (129). Bob's partner, Barrett, finds his presence deeply disturbing: he 'was increasingly conscious that the old man was close upon their trail ... creeping, creeping, creeping, under the great gaunt stars, creeping, creeping, creeping, under the flying dawns, the stormy moons' (129). Similarly, the indigence and illness of the Montagnais reminds Bob that his grandfather was responsible for knowingly introducing smallpox to the indigenous community, and he describes the ghastly results to Barrett over the campfire: 'only one family, they say, escaped. All the others died; they died as if the Angel of Destruction had come among them with his sword – they died like flies, they died in heaps. And over the bones of the dead the tepees stood for years, ragged, blowing in the winds. And then the skins rotted, and the bare poles stood, gleaming white, over the rotting bones that covered an acre of ground, they say' (129). The evocation of death, physical and final, and the mysterious and disturbing survivor, perhaps driven mad by age and loneliness, evokes the uncanny in the familiar ghostly forms of turn-of-the-century fiction.

Bob feels that '[his] family – anyone of [his] name' (129) owes a debt to the indigenous people of the area, and he gives food and other supplies to the Montagnais man, as he would to a beggar. But Barrett disputes Bob's feeling of responsibility: he is not the conqueror of the land, but merely its inheritor. Indeed the story emphasizes his status as inheritor with its title, 'The Third Generation,' which alludes to the statement in the Bible that the 'iniquity of the fathers' will be visited 'upon the children unto the third and fourth generation.'[26] Bob's status as the blameless inheritor of the land is called into question by this title, which suggests that he inherits the sins of his forefathers, as well as their possessions. Bob explains that: 'Men had no souls in those days … the tremendous loneliness – the newness – the lack of responsibility – something killed their souls' (127). However, he leaves the obvious unspoken – something also killed the Montagnais. While the narrative of pioneer exploration and suffering legitimates white possession, and the trope of inheritance personalizes the right of possession, Bob's position in relation to this landscape remains unstable, not just because the indigene haunts the borders of these claims, but also because by Christian standards Bob bears the responsibility for his grandfather's actions.

But Bob's signification as the legitimate heir to the land is radically contradicted by the ending of the story. As the winter landscape becomes more and more threatening, Bob loses his sense of connection to and mastery over it. The canoe is destroyed by rocks and the two white men turn to their Montagnais companion for help. He promises to deliver them in short order to his village, 'a very strong tribe, and kind to the white men' (137). And with the logic of closure, he leads Bob to the very village depopulated by the smallpox his grandfather had introduced fifty years ago, still deserted, a landscape of rotting homes and unburied corpses. As Bob steps out of the canoe, the story declares 'the whole world was waiting for him' (136). But he steps into a landscape of death that signifies the way in which he is barred from confidently assuming the position of subject in the national narrative. As he moves through the deserted village, his feet of necessity '[crush] the bones of the dead' (136), symbolically implicating Bob in the deaths of these 'Indians.' Bob's claim to be at home in this landscape is based upon his inheritance; but in taking up that inheritance, Bob will die, and die without issue, unlike his grandfather, leaving no heirs to materialize his possession of the land in the founding of the nation. Bob's claim to be the new indigene is radically contradicted by the material evidence of violence that impedes his very steps. The actions that legitimated Bob's sense of himself as native to the place, the actions of his grandfather in claiming the land and so bequeathing it to his male heirs also bar those heirs from its possession.

'The Third Generation' dramatizes both the necessity and the impossibility of becoming indigenous, as Terry Goldie puts it,[27] and demonstrates the way that the attempt to construct Canada as a unitary nation is fundamentally contradictory. The infection and extermination of the Montagnais band is the founding violence that allows Bob's narrative of patriarchal succession to begin, the unchallengeable proof of his claim to ownership of the valley. Bob's knowledge of this violence determines his initial attitude towards the Montagnais man: an attitude of liberal condescension, which laments the losses of the past while in no way intending to remediate them. However, this attitude is made untenable by the final image of 'The Third Generation,' in which the white men recognize their own destruction in the destruction of the Montagnais. By ending with Bob's realization of his own death, 'The Third Generation' resists the desire for closure that would resolve the competing claims of settler and indigenous culture; the story is paralysed by its recognition of white responsibility and by its inability to remake an autochthonous unitary nation on the romantic model within a nation-space inscribed by multiple claims. Pickthall's critique of white Canadian imperialism reifies an alternative tradition of nation-building, one which evokes the uncanny in its inability to resolve its own contradictions.

A contemporary example of the uncanny canoe appears in Margaret Atwood's second novel, *Surfacing* (1972). Atwood's suspended canoe represents the narrator's detachment from her surroundings and her fellow canoeists: 'Around us the illusion of infinite space or of no space, ourselves and the obscure shore which it seems we could touch, the water between an absence. The canoe's reflection floats with us, the paddles twin in the lake. It's like moving on air, nothing beneath us holding us up; suspended, we drift home.'[28] This image is drawn from the beginning of the book, when the narrator finds herself unable to feel emotion and unable to trust her own memory: she has endured an abusive relationship and an abortion, both of which she has blocked from her memory and replaced with a fantasy of a marriage, birth, and divorce. The suspended canoe suggests the illusions that sustain her identity, as well as her sense of isolation from her friends. In addition, it represents the difficulties of perception she encounters as she revisits the 'near wilderness' landscape of her childhood, where she has come to investigate her father's disappearance. She is on her 'home ground,' which is also 'foreign territory,' uncannyda.[29]

Atwood is the author many Canadians think of when they think of the canoe in literature. Her representations of canoeing in *Surfacing* have a realistic precision that evokes a shock of recognition from a recreational paddler, even as we remark how strange it seems (as participants in a culture traditionally marginalized in English literature) to see references to our own experiences in a popular novel. The narrator evokes the familiar gender politics of canoeing when she describes struggling in the bow to correct the steering of her male lover, who will not give up the authoritative position in the stern despite his incompetence. She relates the challenges of instructing passengers how and where to sit, and of managing a canoe over-laden with inexperienced paddlers. She uses specialist vocabulary such as the verb ship (meaning to bring her paddle into the boat) and the nouns thwart and portage. She also describes diving off the stern gunwales of the wood canoe, a dangerous trick that many Canadians master as children (along with 'gunwale bobbing,' a method of propelling the canoe by standing on the gunwales in the stern and pushing down with your feet). The popularity of *Surfacing* with readers like me is explained not only by its feminist plot and its historical resonances with our own lives, but also by its realist representations of interactions with a landscape we recognize, an eerily familiar landscape not just of trees and lakes, but also of attitudes, practices, and ideologies that rarely appear in the books we read because they are mostly from the literatures of other English-speaking countries.

But Atwood's realist canoes are also canoes that represent alienation from the landscape and recall their origins among First Nations now displaced and usurped. Atwood's story 'Death by Landscape' uses the details of a recreational canoe trip to create what David Bentley calls her 'most eerie treatment of the Canadian environment as uncanny.'[30] The main character in the story, Lois, lives among a collection of landscape paintings by the Group of Seven and David Milne, paintings that 'fill her with a wordless unease' despite the fact that she personally selected them. Her feeling of simultaneous attraction and repulsion for the paintings is explained by an account of a canoe trip she took as a child. Partway through the trip her best friend, Lucy, disappears; the story offers clues that suggest Lucy may have committed suicide, run away, or perhaps simply gotten lost, but the disappearance is never explained. Lois feels blamed for the disappearance, and indeed she is blamed: as she acknowledges, people want 'a real story with a reason in it; anything but the senseless vacancy Lucy had left.'[31] Lucy's disappearance has left Lois feeling haunted by the life she might have had if Lucy had lived: 'she felt as if she were living not one life but two: her own, and another shadowy life that hovered around her and would not let itself be realized' (120).

The canoe trip that Lois and Lucy take is accompanied by ceremonies that give it the aspect of a ritual coming of age. Before they leave, the summer-camp leaders dress up as 'Indians' and hold a campfire send-off, painting each camper's face with a streak of red paint and enjoining them to 'go where no man has ever trod.' Lois knows that this ritual is fake: 'She knows too much about Indians ... she knows they have enough worries without other people taking their names and dressing up as them. It has all been a form of stealing' (110). When the camp staff enjoin the campers to 'follow in the paths of their ancestors,' she imagines daguerreotypes of her real ancestors, black-coated gentlemen and ladies in corsets, who 'would never have considered heading off onto an open lake, in a canoe, just for fun' (109). But despite this conscious knowledge, she yearns for the feelings of naturalness, freedom, and being at home in the landscape that the 'Indian' represents: 'She wanted to be an Indian. She wanted to be adventurous and pure, and aboriginal' (110), and she imagines the canoe trip will fulfil this desire. Accordingly, when the campers set out the next morning, 'Lois feels as if an invisible rope has broken' (112). She experiences this freedom as the vertigo suggested by the suspended canoe image: 'They're floating free, on their own, cut loose. Beneath the canoe the lake goes down, deeper and colder than it was a minute ago' (112). The deepness and coldness of the water imply danger as well as freedom, and Lucy's disappearance from the top of the lookout at lunchtime on the second day confirms the danger inherent in the fantasy of aboriginality.

Lois never returns to the northern landscape of her summer camp, but instead keeps it contained in the paintings on her wall. She imagines that Lucy has turned into a tree, like the suicides in Dante's *Inferno*, or is hidden in the paintings 'behind the pink stone island, or the one behind that' (121). As David Bentley comments, the paintings are both doors and windows, which, like the literary texts in the tradition of 'uncannyda,' 'simultaneously subject the disconcerting aspects of the environment to rational control and open the reader to unnerving puzzles and mysteries.'[32]

Another common motif in canoeing literature is that of the canoe trip as a quest for knowledge, an opportunity for reflection and self-understanding. This derives from the ideology of the 'New Romantics'[33] in late-nineteenth-century North America, who reacted against the increasing urbanization (and feminization) of space by characterizing 'wilderness' spaces as places that provided a respite from the supposed stresses of urban life. Canoe trips in these spaces represented an escape from time and progress into a life defined by the fulfilment of material needs and emptied of the supposed excesses of commercial culture. In the early twentieth century, these spaces were also defined as masculine places where men's greater physical strength would reinstate traditional gender relations in contradistinction to the feminine space of the city, where social rules supposedly determined by women reigned. William Closson James, in his article 'The Quest Pattern and the Canoe Trip,' argues that the contemporary canoe trip includes all of the elements of the romantic quest: 'departure from the known, the voyage into the unknown, and the return to civilization; the obstacles of high winds, rough waters, brutal portages, dissension, and long dreary rainy days; the unexpected pleasures of new vistas, of wildlife seen, of achievements and minor triumphs, and the joy of one's companions; the sense of participation in a primitive reality, or the re-enactment of an archetypal event, the sloughing off the inessential, and the experience of renewal.'[34]

James stresses the way that in modern literature the canoe journey is internalized, 'the exploration of the wilderness becoming a journey into the interior of the self'[35] in search of revelation, spiritual transformation, and renewal. For James, the transformation is explicitly one that indigenizes the paddler and makes him or her native to place: 'In enabling us to encounter our geographical uniqueness, in making possible a completion of that circuit of separation, initiation and return, and bequeathed to us by those peoples who were here before we were, the canoe may well be an effective vehicle, not only for the exploration of the wilderness of the Shield, but also for exploring that inner frontier, perhaps for effecting an appropriate transformation of attitudes through a kind of indigenization.'[36] Central to James's argument is the prospect of return, the 'crossing of the threshold' back into prosaic, everyday life,

carrying the knowledge acquired through struggle and hardship, 'the
circular quest in which the quester returns to his starting point inwardly
changed.'[37]

While it's easy to find examples of a quest narrative in Canadian canoeing literature, it's more difficult to identify the nature of the revelation
that the canoeist receives. Perhaps this is the result of the failure of the
'Victorian consensus' in the modern period; in the absence of any stable,
communally defined truth, knowledge granted by revelation or even by
self-analysis is bound to be contingent, partial, evocative. D.C. Scott's
poem 'The Height of Land'[38] ends with a series of questions that remain
unanswered, 'inappellable' in the language of the poem, their meanings
both unnameable and unable to be called forth. The canoe defines the
'prospect' in this prospect poem; only canoeists would know this spot,
and only for canoeists would it become symbolic of the divide between
the urban lowlands of Ontario and the (in 1916) relatively sparsely populated north-west of Canada. The height of land separating the watersheds of the Great Lakes and Hudson Bay serves as a place to weigh
the relationship between the solitary contemplative life of the wilderness
and the social responsibility of the Victorian urban environment. The
figure of the canoeist, sitting by the dying embers of his fire, reaching
out (to what?) for answers that do not come underlines the spiritual
disconnect between white settler society and the land and evokes the
incongruity of the uncanny.

Modernist poet and avid canoeist Douglas LePan included three poems
that use canoe imagery in his 1948 collection, *The Wounded Prince, and
Other Poems*, that might be read in the context of James's argument about
the canoe trip as quest.[39] Indeed James cites them as examples of canoe-
trip narratives in which the encounter with the wilderness is a healing
journey.[40] But LePan's canoeing poems are susceptible to at least two
other readings: one, an allegorical reading of the relationship between
the canoeist and the landscape as a metaphor for the psychological division between Canadians and their wilderness surroundings; the other, a
reading of the canoe trip as an extended metaphor for a voyage into a
threatening but compelling landscape of desire. LePan's two poems 'A
Country without a Mythology' and 'Canoe-trip' have often been read the
first way, as contributions to a well-known Canadian theme: how does a
poet make poetry out of a landscape that seems to be both unsignified
(by literary antecedents) and unsignifiable (because of its vastness, emptiness, and violent sublimity). Margaret Atwood reads them this way in
Survival: in her analysis of 'A Country without a Mythology,' she writes,
'someone called "the stranger" is travelling toward no discernable goal

through a land without "monuments or landmarks." ... What is missing
for him in this alien land are the emblems of tradition-saturated European civilization.'[41] The 'stranger' longs for a landscape that is gentle
and embracing, one in which 'The hills will fall in folds, the wilderness
/ Will be a garment innocent and lustrous / To wear upon a birthday,
under a light / That curls and smiles,' but instead he sees 'not a sign, no
emblem in the sky / Or boughs to friend him as he goes.' His progress is
flanked by a 'lust red manitou' that he ignores. For Atwood, this traveller
is emblematic of the Anglo-Canadian, struggling through a harsh and
inhospitable landscape unable to enjoy or even clearly see his surroundings and hopelessly 'retain[ing] his desire for a Wordsworthian experience of Nature as divine and kindly.'[42] The trip is unsatisfying, and the
knowledge gained is of alienation and loss.

An alternative reading of LePan's canoe-scapes is made possible by his
coming out as a gay man in his 1990 collection, *Far Voyages*. Read from
this perspective, the poem can easily be seen as an allegory of the clos-
eted gay man, travelling through the harsh landscape of repression and
social condemnation, guided by 'no monuments or landmarks,' surviving in what ways he can. In this reading, the violent weather that marks
the landscape both expresses his passion and marks him as the passionate man compelled to travel here:

> The land is open to all violent weathers ...
> Passion is not more quick. Lightnings in August
> Stagger, rocks split, tongues in the forest hiss,
> As fire drinks up the lovely sea-dream coolness.
> This is the land the passionate man must travel.

The 'lust red manitou' is the emblem of forbidden desire, an emblem
that the traveller fears and yet acknowledges as a sign of his 'native'
country. This canoe trip, which on one level represents a healing trip to
the centre of the self, also represents the burning experience of desire
in the threatening context of disciplinary power. Similarly, LePan's
poem from the same collection, 'Canoe-trip,' is open to both an allegorical nationalist reading and decoding as a representation of forbidden
desire. The 'fabulous country' through which the speaker has travelled is
'enamelled' with blueberries and contains 'pinelands whose limits seem
distant as Thule'; from the reservoir of wilderness the speaker and his
companions 'dipped and pulled out lakes and rivers,' which they 'strung
... together' to create a circuit, the circular canoe trip of quest and revelation that William James describes. The land they discover is 'good,' a

place that has the potential for holding 'a gold mine of a hydro-plant' 'here and there,' but this 'curious country' is mainly characterized by its wildness:

> Night falls, the gulls scream sharp defiance;
> Let whoever comes to tame this land, beware!
> Can you put a bit to the lunging wind?
> Can you hold wild horses by the hair?
> Then have no hope to harness the energy here,
> It gallops along the wind away.

These lines are recognizable as a contribution to the myth of the North as untamed, wild, in the European sense, as opposed to the urban landscape to which the speaker returns in the final lines of the poem, with his nerves soothed and his mental state restored. This reading of the poem as an account of a retreat to a natural world that is both challenging and restorative makes 'Canoe-trip' a favourite source of quotations for canoeing writers who interpret their recreational pastime as a retreat from the city to the wilderness. However, this poem is also an allegory of a journey into a necessarily hidden inner state; the untameable wilderness is an emblem of desire, and its wildness signifies a place that can never be tamed by the prosaic considerations of ownership and money-making – a place of passion only, without reference to the limitations of heterosexual love. 'Nerves are mended' and broken bones made straight, but the return to civilization is only illusory; the speaker has healed himself by his journey into his own desire and its expression, but that place persists as contradictory other to the urban landscape of conformity.

'But what of a different kind of canoe trip – one which is linear, rather than circular?'[43] James imagines such a trip as supported by 'the internal combustion engine,' and so potentially 'more likely to become an aggressive assault upon the wilderness' rather than a 'natural, adaptive and harmonious'[44] exploration of self. But another kind of one-way canoe trip, the trip that ends in death, is a persistent image in Canadian modernism, where it self-consciously represents how the violence and instability of modernism undercuts any naive attempt to 'go native.' The mysterious and dangerous landscape can swallow up travellers, as Atwood's 'Death by Landscape' indicates: Lucy remains in the forest, hidden behind or in the trees, and even though Lois returns to the city, a vital part of her is still in the woods, trying to find Lucy. In modernist texts the one-way canoe trip wends its way through a landscape for which the paddler is ill-equipped; a landscape of uncanny mysteries, of compelling and hypnotic obsession, or of actively hostile natural or social forces.

In Hugh MacLennan's novel, *The Watch that Ends the Night* (1954) the lone paddler in a canoe becomes a symbol of the isolated individual trying to navigate the currents of history without being overwhelmed. In the middle of the novel, one of the characters, Jerome, who represents a kind of 'everyman' figure in the novel, recounts an episode from his childhood, in which he escapes from his mother's murderer by paddling a child-size, birch-bark canoe down a New Brunswick river and into the ocean. The image of Jerome alone in his canoe in the chaos of the Gulf of St. Lawrence is repeatedly cited by the narrator as representative of the individual paddling furiously through the nightmare of history and of the ego struggling against the dark drives of the id. The narrator comments: 'The canoe in which [Jerome] had issued from the forest had now taken him out into the ocean. A canoe in the ocean, at night, with a hurricane rising. Jerome. Myself. Everyone.'[45] Jerome's persistence and his struggle become an intrinsic symbol of the isolation of the individual and of the existential importance of persistence. Although in the novel Jerome does land his canoe and begin a new life with an adoptive family, his journey figuratively remains at sea, a metaphor for the reality of 'living under the bomb' in the mid-twentieth century.

Canadian literature provides multiple illustrations of the way that Canadians still remember what we are, and what we did. These literary texts are metaphorically (and sometimes literally) haunted by the narrative that is elided in the dominance of the ideology of the canoe, the narrative of the way that First Nations were invaded, colonized, and subsumed by non-indigenous culture in Canada. The uncanniness of the canoe in Canadian literature embodies the way that the desire for a nation that is material and experiential will always be frustrated. And if the canoe is an emblem of the desire of non-indigenous Canadians to create a fully 'Canadian' literature, literally grounded, vitally and historically and spiritually connected to place, indigenous to Canada, then this chapter represents an analysis of the way that imagery of the canoe also disrupts, troubles, and denaturalizes that desire. It represents my recognition of the cultural imperative to tease apart the easy way that the contradictions of 'settler culture,' the culture of the Euro-Canadian majority, are resolved by the 'myth of the canoe.'

Chapter Two

Inheriting a Historiographic Tradition: Canada Is a Canoe Route

The 'Prologue' to Grey Owl's popular book of stories, *The Men of the Last Frontier* (1931), consists of a two-page description of an encounter with history. It begins on the quiet bank of a 'deep, slow-flowing river' in a shadowy, mysterious forest. An eagle soars overhead, and an otter snoozes nearby. 'Far-off in midstream appears a tiny dot' that, coming closer, becomes a bark canoe paddled by 'six brown, high featured savages. Eagle feathers bob in unison, copper-hued backs bend and sway, driving forward the fragile craft, high of prow and stern, with a leaping undulation that is the poetry of motion.' The canoe is dominated by a single white man who stands in the centre. '[H]is burning gaze is fixed ahead: Westward, Westward, from whence the river flows.' The canoe passes swiftly by, 'diminishes again to a speck and disappears into the unknown … the tiny waves of its passing find their way to shore, and so die. The two wild creatures stare in idle curiosity, and return each to his occupation … and little know that, for a moment, they have gazed on History.'[1]

In this vignette, History, with a capital H, is the visual pageant of the canoe and its central position at a nexus of the encounter of active 'man' with the passive, unchanging 'face of Nature as it was since the Beginning.'[2] The bark canoe and the 'savages' bedecked with eagle feathers supply the clues that this scene is set in the northern part of North America; the white man and his driving obsession with westward travel is a familiar figure from imperialist mythology, representing the restless quest of the 'white race' for commercial opportunity, land, and freedom. Yet this pageant is removed from both space and time; it happens in no specific place and in no specific year, as though it happens over and over again, in many different places and at many different times. The white man has no context and no motivation: the remnants of his clothes suggest 'the courts of Europe,' but his gaunt cheeks and burning gaze signify only endurance and compulsion. He operates in obscurity, 'all unknown to the teeming millions of the Eastern Hemisphere,' to open 'the long closed portals of the Western world.'[3] History is his conquest of North America, and the canoe is at its centre.

The quotation, 'Canada is a canoe route,' attributed to historian A.R.M. Lower on the website maintained by the Canadian Museum of Civilization, sums up the historiographic tradition that grounds the fetishization of the canoe as a symbol of the nation. According to this tradition, the fur trade of the eighteenth and early nineteenth centuries determined the economic and political shape of Canada, and the canoe was the necessary technology that allowed the exploration and economic development of the nascent nation. This narrative of the founding of Canada also holds that the canoe was instrumental in the formation of a unique national character: as a direct response to the unique geography of the nation, the canoe required adaptation of European commercial and cultural modes to local requirements. In addition, the sophistication of the canoe as a technology prompted respect for First Nations, which was reinforced by the importance of their role in the fur trade. This historiographic tradition connects the foundations of the state and of Canada's unique and independent nationality to the land through the canoe, and it incorporates First Nations as 'partners' in the founding of Canada or 'ancestors' who have 'bequeathed' the nation to us.

But 'history,' as Hayden White among others has pointed out, is not a neutral record of the material reality of the past, but a narrative that merely claims a kind of objectivity in order to allow it to function as 'arbitrator of the realism of contending political programs'[4] in the present. The historiographic tradition that posits that 'Canada is a canoe route' is similarly not an objective narrative of the facts of the past, but an argument for nationalism in the present that sets out to prove Canada's economic and political independence, especially from the United States, and also Canada's cultural uniqueness, again as distinguished from the US. It aims to construct a relationship between Euro-Canadian culture and the traditions of North American indigenous peoples that would justify seeing the Canadian state as a 'natural' or inevitable successor to indigenous sovereignties, and to argue that Euro-Canadians have a natural, emotional, and ancestral tie to the land. Finally, it positions the canoe as the means to the realization (and defence) of Canadian nationality, through preserving and regulating recreational canoeing rivers, practices, artefacts, and documents.

Like all historical narratives of nationality, the idea that 'Canada is a canoe route' functions to disguise and naturalize contradictions and to subsume difference under the banner of the same. While depending upon the premise that the nation was constructed by historical, political, and economic forces, it also holds that the shape and character of the nation are the natural and inevitable result of its physical geography. While admitting that the majority of the founders of the nation were not indigenous, it also holds that they were indigenized by their experiences in canoes. And while suggesting that the fur trade inevitably and naturally led to respect for, and partnership with, First Nations, it also holds that the fur trade led to the founding of the Canadian state, whose central purpose was the extinguishment of indigenous sovereignty in favour of Canadian. As Stuart Hall has written, such 'narratives of nationhood are discursive devices that represent difference as unity, and which try to "stitch up" differences into one identity, an identity that represents everyone as belonging to the "same great national family."'[5] The continuing paradox identified by Terry Goldie, of the Canadians who are also alien in Canada, has to be taken into account. The trope of the canoe as a symbol of Canada confronts this contradiction by figuring First Nations as 'partners' in a common enterprise that is of benefit to both and by indulging in imperialist nostalgia for a past time in which Euro-Canadians and First Nations shared a common economic enterprise, without acknowledging that the narrative that sees the fur trade as the initial step towards the political constitution of the Canadian state must take its place in the history of the attempted destruction of First Nations peoples by that same state.

Current academic historians embrace diverse methodologies, antecedents, and approaches; but only one of these traditions provides the basis for the nationalist argument that the canoe belongs at the centre of Canadian history. Works by historians such as Harold Innis, Donald Creighton, and A.R.M. Lower locate the beginning of the nation in the fur trade of the eighteenth and nineteenth centuries, a trade that was made possible by the east-west canoe routes that facilitated penetration into the centre of the continent. For these historians, the adoption of the canoe to transport trade goods on a commercial scale was integral to the spread of European and eventually Canadian sovereignty across the continent. In addition, A.R.M. Lower argued that the Canadian character continued to be formed by canoeing into the mid-twentieth century, as not only working-class but middle-class young men spent their summers working as surveyors, fire wardens, and guides in remote wilderness locations accessible only by canoe. In more recent times, John Jennings has argued that the canoe is as important a symbol for Canadians as the covered wagon for the US, and Bruce Hodgins has used his interest in canoeing as an entrée into research and writing in environmental and indigenous histories. For these historians, and many others, the medium that made Canadian economic sovereignty possible was the canoe.

This tradition of academic historiography begins with the work of Harold Innis, who, in his influential study *The Fur Trade in Canada*, argued that Canada's east-west political orientation was determined specifically by the east-west movement of goods along the canoe routes established by fur traders, especially the 'peddlers from Montreal,' the XY and North West Companies, who developed a well-travelled route from Lachine, up the Ottawa river and across the Mattawa to the French River and Georgian Bay; through the Great Lakes to the Grand Portage just south of Fort William; along the Pigeon and Rainy Rivers to Lake of the Woods, then down the Winnipeg River to Lake Winnipeg; west into the prairies and to Edmonton via the Saskatchewan; and/or north-west to Fort Chipewyan by way of Methye portage and the Athabasca River. Innis further argued that this route, and the fur trade posts developed to support it, became the basic line of communication and determined the initial form of settlement of Canada's north-west.

The Fur Trade in Canada was published in a revised edition prepared after Innis's death by his wife, Mary Quayle Innis, incorporating all of his revisions, corrections, marginal notations, and suggestions for reorganization. This republication in 1956 provided a basis for the nationalist histories that were written and taught throughout the 1960s and 1970s in Canada, inaugurating a tradition of nationalist historiography that countered the arguments of historians who suggested that the Canada-US border was arbitrary and an impediment to what they considered the more 'natural' north-south trade. This interpretation of Innis's work is reiterated in Robin Winks's introduction to the 1956 revised edition: 'the chief significance of this book is not that it is a nearly definitive history of the economics of the fur trade. It is more than that; it is the beginning of an entire re-orientation of Canadian (and therefore North American) history. Contrary to those historians who insist that Canada is a nation despite her geography, Innis asserted that Canada is a nation because of it. Rather than a series of regions each of which has more natural affinity with a like region in the United States than with other Canadian regions, she is a single, coherent unit created on the east-west line of imperial communications, a line based on the St. Lawrence River, the Great Lakes, and the western waterways and trails, penetrating via the natural extension of the Atlantic Ocean into the capitals of Europe.'[6] Winks goes on to summarize Innis's argument that the centralized communications and transportation system that had its roots in the fur trade canoe routes of the North West Company became the basis for transportation and communications in industrialized Canada, and the forts and trading posts along its length the basis for present-day Canadian towns and cities.

A similar argument appears in Donald Creighton's *Commercial Empire of the St. Lawrence* (1937). Creighton states that 'The St. Lawrence river inspired and supported a trading system which was both transatlantic and transcontinental in extent' and determined 'the political development of Canada.'[7] For Creighton, the geography of the St. Lawrence River had a spiritual as well as a commercial effect on European settlers: they 'read the meaning of the region, they evoked its spirit, and they first dreamed the dream which the river inspired in the minds of all who came to live upon its banks' (20). 'Geography directed the activities of men' (11), Creighton wrote, and his 'Laurentian thesis' of Canadian history, 'the dominant interpretation of Canadian history until the 1960s,'[8] is a story of cultural and commercial adaptation, inspired by geography and initiated by the fur trade.

For both Creighton and Innis, the political and economic development of Canada created an opposition between the fur trade and settlement. Unlike the US, which developed westward by exterminating and dispossessing First Nations in favour of Anglo-European agricultural settlement, Canada extended its sovereignty and commercial activity in the west through the fur trade, which initially required First Nations to remain on the land. The commercial interests of Montreal (and the political interests of Canada, which were funded through an excise tax on exported furs) required that the land west of the Ottawa remain populated by animals and that First Nations living on the land fulfil the role of primary harvesters of fur. As Creighton points out, the protection afforded to Aboriginal title in the Proclamation of 1763 was partly designed to protect fur-producing lands in the western part of North America, and only partly to protect First Nations from white incursions: 'the primitive culture of the hunting Indians was essential to the fur-trading state, and the fur-trading state would alone preserve the Indians from extinction' (16). Creighton attributes Canada's relatively liberal policy towards First Nations (in comparison, for example, to US and Australian policies of extermination and forced relocation) to their initial importance to Canada's economic development through the fur trade. John Jennings brings this argument into the present with his concept of a 'canoe frontier,'[9] a frontier populated by fur traders who moved over the land without claiming it.

Historian Arthur Lower was interested in the canoe and canoeing from another perspective. Lower's early work as an economic historian had been strongly influenced by Innis's interpretation of the fur trade as a model for a staples-based economy. In *Canadians in the Making* (1958), Lower calls Montreal the jumping-off point for 'the canoe route that built Canada,'[10] suggesting that he accepted Innis's argument that the fur trade was the single most important element in determining the political shape of the nation. But in his later career he became much more interested in the formative effect of wilderness on Canadian institutions and identity. In his memoir, *Unconventional Voyages* (1953), he recounts his own experiences as a canoeist. Like many young middle-class men of his generation, Lower had worked in the bush to earn his university tuition, and he argued that such experiences, whether of tree-planting, working on a survey or fire-fighting crew, guiding, or summer camp leadership, were something that Canadians held in common. He speculated that the qualities that such an experience developed must necessarily have their effects on Canadian institutions: 'To go into the bush in the spring, soft from a city winter … and come out as hard as nails in the fall, rejoicing in your ability to carry a canoe over a two-mile portage without setting it down, or to paddle at racing speed up the length of a twenty-mile lake … to learn tolerance of others with whom you must live at very close range, to acquire the adaptableness and self-reliance which only the woods and their counterpart, the sea, impart: these are matters which must leave their mark [on countless Canadians].'[11] Historian Bruce Hodgins, who studied with Lower in the fifties, recalled that Lower 'emphasized the importance of the "permanent" northern bush to the Canadian experience of nation building, and believed it important that the Canadian historian and engaged citizen combine on the one hand the sophisticated and rational, and on the other, experience of bush lore, the canoe and the North.'[12]

The assertion that Canadian geography and history were intertwined in the narrative of Canada's canoe routes was given popular form in Hugh MacLennan's beautiful book, *Seven Rivers of Canada* (1961). Originally conceived as a series of articles in the popular general circulation magazine, *Maclean's*, *Seven Rivers of Canada* opened with the chapter, 'The Rivers that Made a Nation,' which argued for the centrality of rivers and canoe transportation in the development of Canada by focusing on the history of the fur trade. MacLennan declared that 'in the early days the Canadian experience was epic'[13] and that the canoe voyageur was a 'superman' (21) who 'staked out Canadian – or at that time British – claims to the whole northwestern hinterland from the head of the Lakes to the Pacific' (28). MacLennan's series of personal essays, intended to 'give a sense of the mystery, the beauty and variety of our rivers, to indicate in passing how they link us to the past' (viii), declared its debt to the work of historians 'Harold Innis, Bartlet Brebner, Donald Creighton, Arthur S. Morton and others' (viii).

Historians today would accept none of these assertions. W.J. Eccles wrote the definitive challenge to Innis's work as early as 1979; in his article, 'A Belated Review of Harold Adams Innis, *The Fur Trade in Canada*,' Eccles asserts that neither Innis's 'premises, both stated and unstated, his use of historical evidence, nor the conclusions drawn will stand up to close scrutiny and all too many erroneous interpretations of North American history have been made in consequence.'[14] Eccles points out specific omissions in Innis's evidence and errors in his interpretation of his primary sources; he challenges Innis's general economic determinism, pointing out that both the French and British imperial governments pursued the fur trade even when it was unprofitable in order to cement military alliances with First Nations, and he counters Innis's assertions that the British had an advantage in trade over the French and that the fur trade and settlement were incompatible. Indeed, he points out how early profits from the fur trade supported settlement in French Canada (420) and later trading posts subsidized occupation of territory 'for purely political and military reasons' (440). Bruce Hodgins specifically points out in 'Canoe Irony' that 'Despite the canoe's mythological purity as a symbol, it was, in fact part of the "idea of progress" which led to the continuing destruction of wilderness'[15] and the extinguishment of Native sovereignty. But popular historians of the canoe continue to treat the arguments of Innis and Creighton as 'proof' of the importance of the canoe in the development of the nation; citations from their works dominate the literature of canoes and canoeing that has appeared in the last forty years and provide a basis for the idea that the canoe is both a symbol of the nation and a means whereby one can access it.

The main arguments that canoeing enthusiasts take from the academic tradition are that the fur trade determined the economic and political shape of Canada: the shape of the fur trade was a direct response to the geography of the nation and required adaptation of European commercial and cultural modes to something Canadian; the fur trade required a liberal state policy towards First Nations, which laid the basis for Canada's current 'liberal' policies; and the common experience of life in the bush and its requirements moulded Canadians as individuals and as a nation. From these premises, canoeing writers argue that the canoe is a means to becoming identified both with the landscape and with the nation, based on three interrelated arguments: the canoe was the only way for Europeans to get around in the northern part of North America, and thus the landscape required them to change their cultural assumptions; the canoe provides access to indigenous cultures and world-views because it is an indigenous form of transportation, created by indigenous peoples from local materials and uniquely adapted to the particular geography that became Canada; and canoeists (in the form of explorers, voyageurs, and traders) who experienced the landscape by canoe were the founders of Canada.

The effect of these histories is to fetishize the canoe as a direct means of patriotic national transformation. The canoe becomes, as Daniel Francis puts it, the 'vessel in which we are recreated as Canadians,'[16] a vessel endowed with power to change mind-sets from non-Canadian to Canadian. For recreational canoeists, the histories of canoes and canoeing detach the canoe from its metonymic significance as a literal necessity for some kinds of travel for some people at some historical periods, from its undoubted 'use-value' in Marx's sense, and attach to it the metaphorical value of a nationality drawn from the land and determined by it. These histories substitute the canoeist, whether indigenous, French Canadian, or Anglo-European, for the 'folk' in European theories of nationality, and argue that the canoeist – forced to adapt to requirements of the landscape and to engage with its geographical conformation, varying levels of fertility, and seasonal change in a physical way – are the 'closest to the land' and therefore the most 'Canadian.' This fetishization of the canoe as the means to nationality works to heal the split between landscape and people because it purports to demonstrate how canoeists, by virtue of their canoeing, are not European anymore, but something new, Canadian.

The narrative that creates the canoe as a fetish of nationality directly addresses the role of First Nations in the modern nation by exempting the fur trade from any hint of its effects on indigenous peoples, including exploitation, disease, and diversion of economic activity into trade with Europeans. It asserts the innocence of Anglo-Canadian society by suggesting that since the fur trade depended on keeping First Nations on the land and preserving their traditional hunting way of life, the fur trade could not be the first step towards depriving them of their lands without adequate compensation or the seed of government policies of assimilation that attempted to destroy their cultures. And since the nation was founded on the fur trade, any policies inimical to First Nations must also be alien to the nation. Further, it argues that by adopting the canoe, Anglo-Canadians adopt the point of view of First Nations and can themselves achieve that connection to the land that is traditionally the attribute of the 'folk' in nationalist thought. Indigenous peoples are not excluded from these nationalist histories: indeed they are everywhere present, but the problem is, as Bruce Willems-Braun puts it, 'how they are made present.'[17] In the narrative that sees the canoe as a symbol of the nation, the cultural heritage of First Nations is appropriated as 'our' heritage, the heritage of non-indigenous Canadians, in order to 'bolster settler nationalist mythology.'[18]

The premise that the canoe is an indigenous form of transportation would seem to need no demonstration. The canoe was constructed and used by the First Nations peoples of North America long before contact with Europeans, and 'Indians' are often appealed to in early canoeing literature as experts. In 'The Canoe: Half Stolen,' an article published in *Outing* magazine in 1913, the author proclaims that only 'the Indian's wisdom' provides the authority on how to paddle, because the canoe is 'his' craft.[19] Canoeing manuals had to battle the preconception that paddling techniques were 'naturally' part of 'the Indian's' skill set, a 'forest virtue unattainable by a man with a white skin.'[20] As C.E.S. Franks puts it, nineteenth-century 'Europeans did not treat Indian skills in white water as techniques that could be broken down into their components and studied and learned, but rather as an art which was part of the birthright of the wilderness native.'[21]

The association of the canoe with First Nations peoples also provides an argument for its identification with the natural world. The idea of the 'Indian' as a 'natural man,' identified with the landscape and its wild inhabitants and unformed (or uncontaminated) by urban society, arose as an ideal in Romantic ideology and was often marshalled by authors who wished to critique the limitations of European life. Terry Goldie suggests that early Europeans in Canada 'seldom present the slightest doubt that the indigene is part of nature'[22] and recounts the way that explorers like Columbus treat the inhabitants of North America as identical to the landscape. More recently, Goldie suggests, the identification of indigenous peoples and nature is performed by 'texts which present the indigene as an emissary of untouched nature and fear the ecological dangers of white technology.'[23] Eva Mackey makes the same point: 'Aboriginal peoples and nature have long been equated in colonial, nationalist, and tourist discourses.'[24]

The 'natural' derivation of the canoe from the Indian/landscape is further reinforced in popular histories of canoeing by the argument that the canoe is metonymically part of the landscape. Kirk Wipper points out that canoes were made from indigenous woods, barks, pitches, and roots, which themselves derive from the landscape.[25] Moreover, as James Raffan argues, these materials determine the shape and limitations of canoe design: 'Workable canoes never contravene the properties and capabilities of the natural materials from which they were made,'[26] he writes, and canoe-makers 'work with the bends the natural material allows.'[27] The huge *canot de maître* used in the fur trade 'likely developed from the finely crafted bark canoes created by the eastern Algonkians,' writes Peter Labor in 'The Canot du Maître,' and was 'developed by Aboriginal builders to meet the needs of geography ... [−] a shell of bark, roots, sinew and wood' that nonetheless 'danc[ed] and fl[ew] like a living creature.'[28] The resulting canoe is identical to the land: 'an island – a part of the changing landscape.'[29] Bill Mason writes in *Canoescapes* that the canoe 'is as much a part of our land as the rocks, trees, lakes and rivers.'[30]

The landscape that canoe historians associate with the canoe is the landscape of the Canadian Shield: dense boreal forests underlain with glaciated rock and drained by a network of lakes and rivers broken by swamps and rapids. Such a landscape is almost impossible to travel through in the summer except by water, and early European travellers, who were focused on returning to seaports in time for the yearly crossing of the Atlantic, wanted to travel in the summertime. The canoe, with its shallow draft, manoeuvrability, and light weight, seemed perfectly adapted to this purpose. John Murray Gibbon, in *The Romance of the Canadian Canoe* (1951), cites Samuel de Champlain in 1603: 'He who would pass [the Lachine Rapids] must provide himself with the canoes of the savages, which a man can easily carry; for to transport a boat is a thing that cannot be done in the short time necessary to enable one to return to France to winter ... But with the canoes of the savages one may travel freely and quickly throughout the country, as well up the little rivers as the large ones. So that by directing one's course with the help of the savages and their canoes, a man may see all that is to be seen, good and bad, within the space of a year or two.'[31] Early observers of

First Nations peoples tended to attribute the remarkable suitability of the canoe to summer travel in the Canadian Shield to the cleverness and experience of indigenous craftsmen; however, more recent writers have tended to mystify this relationship. Bill Mason famously commented that 'God created the canoe, and then set about making a country in which it could flourish,' but he was not alone in attributing the adaptation of the canoe to the landscape to forces beyond logical representation. James Raffan includes the canoe-builder in his representation of the relationship between canoe and landscape as a dance: 'Tight curves beget smooth pirouettes on the surface of time, sweeping curves add purpose and elegance in the dance from here to there, the builder and the boat, the tree and the river together in form and function limited only by a maker's imagination.'[32] John Wadland uses the metaphor of a birth to express the relationship between the canoe, 'an indigenous craft, [and] the landscape.'[33]

However, despite the way that these arguments all seem to rely on the metonymic identity of the birch-bark or wood canoe with the landscape itself, many of these same commentators suggest that an identical spiritual or nationalizing experience can be attained in any well-designed canoe, no matter what materials are used. Peter Labor states that 'fibreglass and wood reconstructions allow an authentic experience in Montreal canoe culture.'[34] Most of the wilderness canoe-trip advocates recommend fibreglass, aluminium, or Kevlar canoes for lighter weight and greater durability, and only Bill Mason suggests that the aesthetic of the canvas-covered wood canoe, despite its tendency to gain weight over a long trip, is still preferable (though the company that made his preferred wood canoe, the Chestnut Prospector, went out of business in 1979). Eric Morse advocated using Grumann aluminium canoes and wrote that 'A Chestnut is 19th century ... romantic, but for the birds.'[35] As James N. Gladden remarks in his book, *The Boundary Waters Canoe Area*, canoeists who want the 'experience of direct contact with nature' do not seem to be averse to using whatever new technologies can facilitate their goal.[36] The canoe, originally metonymically 'part of the landscape' itself because of the materials it was made of, has become a fetish of that landscape by being detached from the very evidence that underwrites its symbolic meaning.

Canoe commentators have made much of the assertion by historians like Donald Creighton that Canadian geography forced early European immigrants to adapt both materially and spiritually to the landscape. This argument, along with comments by Cartier and Champlain endorsing the canoe as a means of travel that allowed a return to the ship before freeze-up, became generalized to suggest that the canoe, because it was identified with the landscape itself, was the only possible means of travel inland. For example, James Raffan comments: 'To go inland into Canada, Cartier realised he needed the boat derived of the landscape realities of the New World. Cartier realized he needed a canoe.'[37] Similarly, on the Alexander MacKenzie Voyageur Route website, Peter Labor states: 'One account of Jacques Cartier describes his first experience with the canoe at the Lachine Rapids, a point at which he could sail no further up the St. Lawrence, and even his best men in row boats could make little headway. Cartier, then, was resigned to "swallow [his] pride and imitate 'les sauvages' in adapting to the demands of geography." His adaptation was the acceptance of the canoe as the best "technology" for travelling the Canadian waterways.'[38] The comments of other European visitors, such as Anna Jameson, Frances Simpson, and Susanna Moodie, on the novelty of the canoe and their enjoyment of canoe travel are also frequently cited as evidence of the way that Europeans were 'recreated as Canadians' in the canoe. Susanna Moodie recounts in *Roughing It in the Bush* how she learned to manage a canoe by herself, and travelled and fished on the Otonabee River and nearby lakes in the early 1830s: 'The pure beauty of the Canadian water, the sombre but august grandeur of the vast forest that hemmed us in on every side and shut us out from the rest of the world, soon cast a magic spell upon our spirits, and we began to feel charmed with the freedom and solitude around us. Every object was new to us. We felt as if we were the discoverers of every beautiful flower and stately tree that attracted our attention, and we gave names to fantastic rocks and fairy isles, and raised imaginary houses and bridges on every picturesque spot which we floated past during our aquatic excursions. I learned the use of the paddle, and became quite proficient in the gentle craft.'[39] Anna Jameson travelled by canoe to Sault Ste. Marie and persuaded her Anishinabe guides to run the rapids for her enjoyment, an experience she described in *Winter Studies and Summer Rambles in Canada*: 'in a minute we were within the verge of the rapids, and down we went with a whirl and a splash! – the white surge leaping around me – over me. The Indian with astonishing dexterity kept the head of the canoe to the breakers, and somehow or other we danced through them ... I had not even a momentary sensation of fear, but rather of giddy, breathless, delicious excitement.'[40]

Frances Simpson travelled to the Red River settlement with her husband, Hudson's Bay Company governor George Simpson, and while she wrote in her journal that 'a canoe journey is not one which an English Lady would take for pleasure,' she seems to have found sufficient pleasure in the landscape and the company to mitigate the discomfort she experienced. She describes the head of the Mattawa River where it connects to the Ottawa as: 'the most wild & romantic place I ever beheld: it reminded me of the description I have read (in some of Sir Walter Scott's beautiful tales) of Scottish scenery. The approach to this Portage is truly picturesque: the river from being a considerable width, here branches into a variety of channels, one of which we entered, so narrow as scarcely to leave a passage for the Canoe – on either side are stupendous rocks of the most fantastic forms: some bear the appearance of Gothic Castles, others exhibit rows of the most regular, and beautifully carved Corinthian Pillars: deep caverns are formed in some, while others present a smooth level surface, crowned with tufts of Pines, and Cedars.'[41]

However, Beverly Haun-Moss has pointed out the many ways that the written record demonstrates that the adoption of the canoe, rather than forcing Europeans to change their preconceptions about the natural world (and the Canadian landscape in particular), instead offered an opportunity to discursively construct that landscape according to European ideological paradigms. Susanna Moodie and Frances Simpson order their landscape descriptions according to the eighteenth-century conventions of the picturesque and the sublime; Jameson's account of her trip down the Ste. Marie Rapids is a textbook example of the way that Romantic ideology valued the landscape for its ability to evoke strong emotional experience.[42] As Haun-Moss argues in her article, 'Layered Hegemonies: The Production and Regulation of Canoeing Desire in the Province of Ontario,' canoeists both historical and contemporary have been motivated by contradictory desires that nonetheless derived from European ideologies. On the one hand, the canoe allowed access to the land, and therefore 'colonizers used the canoe to explore and map the land, ultimately overlaying it with a gridwork "of square mile sections and concession line roads." Parsing down the land to manageable subsections was part of the effort to know it, name it, and lay their claim upon it' (40). But in contrast: 'The pathways of the canoe, the lakes and rivers of the province, refused to comply with the imperial regulating project, instead cutting and meandering through the landscape, offering the colonizers a way to subvert their own desire to claim, document, and contain' (40). Haun-Moss argues that the 'subversion' of the European project of knowing, naming, and claiming, rather than deriving directly from the land, took the forms of Romantic and Victorian cultural ideologies: her three examples of paradigmatic canoeing attitudes, Moodie, Jameson, and John 'Rob Roy' McGregor, are governed by ideologies common to their historical period in Europe. Haun-Moss presents Moodie as an Enlightenment observer of nature, Jameson as the Romantic individualist in a quest for intense emotional interaction with nature, and MacGregor, the inventor and popularizer of the 'Rob Roy' canoe in Europe, as a Victorian using his canoe full of Protestant tracts and New Testaments to make the world a better place. These three figures are paradigmatic, for Haun-Moss, of the three kinds of canoeing desire that persist in the non-Native community in Canada: recreational canoeing that offers 'leisurely interaction with nature' (44), competitive and 'recreational whitewater canoeing' (45), and the tradition of 'the restorative canoe trip' (47) that offers a respite from stressful urban life. Haun-Moss offers an argument that substantiates the idea that in adopting the canoe, Europeans and their descendants did not need to/could not/did not change anything but their mode of transportation.

A more specific attempt to create a historiographic connection to the land is the practice of appropriating First Nations beliefs about the land as part of canoeing history. John Murray Gibbon devotes an entire chapter of *The Romance of the Canadian Canoe* to First Nations ancestral stories that involve canoeing. Similarly, James Raffan reproduces a version of the story of Glooscap and stories drawn from Huron and Ottawa traditions, as well as French-Canadian folk tales about the canoe. Dennis Coolican, in his 'Canoe Trip Diary' of a trip he took with Eric Morse in 1955, reports that the group adopted the practice of leaving an offering before a rapid for the Annishnabe spirits known as mannegishi, the 'little men without noses who live in the rocks of the rapids'[43] and might upset canoes. Grey Owl (Archie Belaney) not only adopted a First Nations identity, but also included Cree stories in his history of the 'lost' canoe brigade: he refers to local geographical features by their Native names, and points out places where spirits and supernatural creatures may be found (he also refers to the little men, whom he calls May-May-Gwense). These examples of appropriation reinforce the way that the narrative of nationality that represents the canoe as a symbol of Canadian unity subsumes First Nations under the general category of 'Canadian,' and thereby elides the histories of assimilation and cultural genocide that attempted to erase these beliefs and to instil in First Nations peoples an attitude of instrumentalism towards the landscape they had created as spiritual.

The third premise upon which the symbolism of the canoe rests is the premise that canoeists were the founders of Canada. This argument is repeated by most canoeing advocates, often through direct reference to Innis, Creighton, and other historians. James Raffan states in *Bark, Skin and Cedar* that 'Scholars like Harold Innis and his protegés Donald Creighton and Marshall McLuhan have amply demonstrated that the east-west axis of commerce from Lachine to the Lakehead, extended west by the mighty Saskatchewan River, and subsequently the Canadian Pacific Railway (established with canoes during the fur trade, with its voyageur agents responsible to a company and government in the East and ultimately across the Atlantic) created a unique pattern of development, and intercontinental communication ... Creighton's writing, for example, establishes the central role of the canoe and its attendant services to the Canadian way of doing business.'[44] Bruce Hodgins argues: 'to a considerable degree, much of this country was put together, in the early years, by the canoe and by people who canoed. The canoe was the principal mode of travel, and the main inland commercial activity of the time involved a critical role for the canoe and the complex travel network built around it. The fur trade empires were canoe-based ones.'[45] John Jennings reiterates that 'Canada is not an artificial creation ... The essential shape of Canada was determined, above all, by canoe exploration and the fur trade.'[46] Eric Morse recounts in his autobiography, *Freshwater Saga* (1987), how during his tenure as a student he 'became aware of the work of Harold Innis' and read his 'classic book, *The Fur Trade in Canada: An Introduction to Canadian Economic History* [1930].'[47] Morse quotes Innis in 'Canoe Routes of the Voyageurs: The Geography and Logistics of the Canadian Fur Trade' to argue that Canada's east-west political and geographic orientation was determined specifically by the east-west movement of goods along the canoe routes established by fur traders. 'The fur trade thus stopped "Manifest Destiny" at the border; and long before Confederation, it ensured that the foundations of Canada as a nation had been securely laid.'[48]

A vital part of the argument that the canoe made Canada is the contention that the fur trade canoe routes of Canada determined the location of its border with the US. This contention rests on the negotiations over the location of the border in the area between Lake Superior and Lake of the Woods. Innis argues that 'la Verendrye had laid down the boundary of Canada in the search for the better beaver of the Northern areas,'[49] referring to La Verendrye's promotion of the route through the Grand Portage to the Pigeon River from Lake Superior to Lake of the Woods in the early eighteenth century. The Canadian Canoe

Museum website similarly declares that 'The canoe determined national boundaries,'[50] and Eric Morse, in *Fur Trade Canoe Routes of Canada Then and Now*, states that 'The Border Lakes route [to Lake of the Woods from Lake Superior] follows the international boundary to Lake of the Woods. More accurately, the international boundary follows the lakes, for the Commissioners in settling on a line through this complicated country adopted as their working principle the "customary waterway" of the early voyageurs.'[51] Indeed, in the 1783 treaty signed between Britain and the US in the wake of the 'Revolutionary War,' the boundary to the west of Lake Superior was to follow the Pigeon River to the canoe route, and the canoe route to the Lake of the Woods, continuing from there along the 49th parallel to the headwaters of the Mississippi River (reserving for Canadians the fur trade country west of the Mississippi and forbidding US settlement in the North-West). However, this left Grand Portage, a vital part of the route, in the United States. Further, it soon became clear that the headwaters of the Mississippi might not actually reach the 49th parallel; Jay's Treaty in 1794 stipulated that a survey would be performed to ascertain whether or not this was the case. The survey was completed in 1797 by David Thompson, who discovered the inconvenient fact that the headwaters of the Mississippi were located far south of the 49th parallel. Rather than renegotiate the treaty, Canadians lost access to the water route for trade into the Mississippi valley and west. With the Canada-US border reconfirmed, local American officials decided to enforce their exclusive right of access to the major route west at the Grand Portage. According to John Bigsby, the British member of the International Boundary Commission that surveyed the Lake of the Woods to redetermine the border west in 1823, 'The American Government, properly conceiving that the Grand Portage, the centre of so much commercial activity, was within their territory, signified, about the year 1802, to the amalgamated company, now called the North-west Company, their intention of imposing a duty … The company then built their Fort William, and made the Dog River and other streams and lakes their road into the north-west fur countries, although this route is much inferior in every respect to the old route; so much so, that the voyageurs had to be coaxed and bribed into the use of it.'[52] So while it was undoubtedly true, as Grace Lee Nute avers, that the boundary '*is* the boundary just because the voyageurs made it their highway during the fur-trade era, and the negotiators of the treaty were definitely influenced by the fact,' and it may be true that the original intention of the treaties 'was to preserve the use of the commercial route for both countries,'[53] this was not how things turned out: as Hugh MacLennan wrote in *Seven Rivers of Canada*, 'The boundary to which the British finally agreed was a triumph for the United States and a permanent disaster for Canada.'[54] The part of the international border through what has come to be called the Border Lakes region did follow the canoe routes of the voyageurs, but the major portage into that region, the portage that had been used by all travellers to the west from Lake Superior for many years, was left ten miles to the south of the border in the US and for a number of years was closed to Canadian traffic. Eventually, the Webster Treaty of 1823 mediated between the American and Canadian claims, and 'all these portages along the border lakes route were internationalized,' so that by the time Eric Morse paddled these waters in the late fifties, 'without hindrance or formality, anyone c[ould] camp or lunch in either country as he paddle[d] the international boundary.'[55]

The border also contradicted the traditional canoe routes of the fur trade in the area west of the Rockies. The Hudson's Bay Company was supplying its posts in the interior of BC from the original Fort Vancouver (now Vancouver, Washington) at the mouth of the Columbia River, and eventually developed a cross-continental route over the Rocky Mountains at Athabasca Pass and down the Columbia River to the Pacific. Despite the importance of the Columbia River to the fur trade, the Oregon Treaty of 1846 extended the border at the 49th parallel west of the Rockies and blocked access to the lower Columbia. The Hudson's Bay Company was forced to close Fort Vancouver and build a new fort on Vancouver Island (now Victoria) to serve as a supply station for their inland posts, necessitating the creation of a new and arduous route into the interior to avoid the unnavigable sections of the Fraser River. Clearly, the fur trade canoe routes did not determine the location of the border in this case, either. W.J. Eccles is flatly contemptuous of Innis's claims about the border, stating that 'In fact, if the fur trade were to have determined the border in the Great Lakes areas then it would presently run from the western end of Lake Erie south of Lake Michigan to the Mississippi' (440), and 'Had the western boundary been determined by the fur trade it would today run along the Saskatchewan river to the Rocky Mountains, rather than along the 49th parallel of latitude, for the fur trade country lay to the north of that river, and west of the Rockies it would follow the lower reaches of the Columbia River' (440–1).

While academic historians like Innis and Creighton foregrounded the roles of First Nations in the fur trade (and thus in the making of the nation), popular canoeing writers in the 1950s and 1960s were as racist as their times. As far as Eric Morse was concerned, the First Nations people constituted the market for European goods and had little part in the trade itself beyond 'becom[ing] dependent' (14) on trade goods. While in the early fur trade years, Morse stated, 'Indian middlemen' removed the necessity for white men to travel inland by taking goods to trade with their neighbours, when organized transportation to the North-West began around 1778, their participation in the fur trade was reduced to initial guiding and supply. 'The Indian showed the trader *how*' – how to travel, fish, acquire and preserve food – and 'showed the trader *where*' by serving as guides, but clearly the Indian and the trader were not the same person. Neither was 'the Indian' a voyageur: according to Eric Morse 'the voyageur employed by the North West Company was the Canadien – tough, gay and carefree,' (8) while the Hudson's Bay Company employed the 'Orkneyman voyageur' (9).

Indeed, Morse's remarks on the fur trade repeat many of the patronizing stereotypes that reduced 'Indians' to childlike people who needed to be managed by non-indigenous Canadians: he wrote that 'A special rapport, in fact, existed between the Indian and a good fur trader – cemented by many a casual alliance with a chief's daughter while wintering at a trading post' (19). While Morse admits that 'Quite obviously the Canadian fur trade, regularly plying the broad emptiness between the St. Lawrence and the Rockies, could not have been carried on without basically friendly relations with the Indian tribes along the way,' his comment that 'Indians caused no serious interruptions of the trade in Canada, after the pacification of the Iroquois in the late seventeenth century' (19) seems to recall the stereotype of the 'savage Indian' in order to replace it with another stereotype, that of the defeated and the 'pacified,' of negligible importance.

Both Morse and Grace Lee Nute, an American historian and author of numerous books on the fur trade, were writing out of a set of cultural assumptions that determined that the 'heroic' voyageur 'Knights of the waterways' were 'French Canadians, and [only] occasionally Indians and part-Indians.'[56] This assumption has long since been contradicted by historical evidence. Indeed, not only was Sir George Simpson's famous express canoe paddled solely by Mohawks from Kahnewake, but 'Between 1790 and 1815, approximately 350 men'[57] from Iroquois communities were hired by the Montreal fur companies. According to Timothy Kent, in the 1840s and 1850s 'the majority of the voyageurs who paddled in the brigades on the St. Maurice River system from Trois Rivières were hired from Kahnawake and Oka.'[58] Many of Franklin's voyageurs, most of whom perished on his foolishly planned first expedition to the Arctic Ocean by way of the Coppermine River, were indigenous, including the infamous Michel, who is clearly identified in the published text as Mohawk.

C.E.S. Franks in his book, *The Canoe and White Water* (1977), is the first popular canoeing writer to include Creighton's argument that First Nations were necessary to the fur trade, and to provide a popular history that takes greater account of their continuing presence. He argues that there is a 'discontinuity' in the tradition of canoeing caused by 'the gap between the explorers and fur traders on the one hand, and the farming pioneers on the other.'[59] While 'the fur trade was the first white intrusion over most of the country,' by the time settlement occurred, 'the fur trade had long since left. Settlement in the wilderness of Upper Canada did not follow from the children of the fur-trade frontiersman; it came from immigration … There was little continuity between the fur trader who had travelled by canoe and the settler coming by road or ship' (54). For Franks, while the fur trade and the canoe 'established the geographical logic of Canada as a nation,' it 'did not lead to settlement' (54). Thus 'the majority of Canadians who lived in the settled south lost contact with the heritage of the fur trade era' (56), which, for Franks, included canoeing techniques and experiences. This discontinuity can be partially overcome, according to Franks, by recovering the techniques of white-water canoeing, which can serve to link 'Canadians of the present to the age of the voyageurs' (65).

Franks suggests that the 'frontier of resource extraction' can coexist with First Nations peoples, while the 'frontier of settlement' cannot. The fur trade and other early resource extraction industries relied on the maintenance of First Nations peoples on the land, where they could serve as a guides and independent contractors who located and harvested the resource and then transported it to a central location for processing and transportation to foreign markets. Franks acknowledges that 'Although the French Canadian voyageur has received the most attention, many canoe brigades were manned by Indians and Métis who worked just as long and hard' (136). Franks states that 'the one group which might have provided continuity between the fur traders and the settlers was the Métis, the cultural and blood descendants of the voyageurs and the Indians' (55), but also notes that the Metis were unable to provide a sense of cultural continuity between the indigenous and non-indigenous communities because they 'were defeated in war, had their settlement pattern destroyed by the surveyor's grid, and retreated into cultural isolation and economic impoverishment from which they have not yet emerged' (55–6). From a contemporary perspective, Franks's use of the passive voice begs the question of who did the defeating and destroying; the Metis may have been pushed, rather than voluntarily 'retreating.' Nevertheless, Franks directly confronts the role of First Nations in the canoeing history that he recounts, and accounts for the way in which that history frequently fails to foreground a contemporary First Nations presence.

While Morse and Nute provide examples of historical narratives that marginalize or ignore First Nations, and Franks accounts for their absence by the destruction of their cultures by settlement, more recent canoeing histories of Canada figure First Nations as 'partners' in the fur trade, and the canoe as a 'heritage' that has been left to 'us' by them. This perspective informs McNab, Hodgins, and Standen's article, 'Black with Canoes,' which represents First Nations as active participants in the fur trade and active resisters of settlement, and the canoe as an aid to both activities that was nonetheless 'bequeathed to the European newcomers.'[60] James Raffan proposes that the canoe 'connects us ... first to the land, to the Aboriginal people, [and] to the explorers,'[61] suggesting that these three elements of nationality are of equal importance and that the various interests of all three can be reconciled through the canoe. Craig MacDonald writes that the portage trails created and maintained by the Anishinabe in the Temagami district 'represent an important remnant of Canada's cultural heritage,'[62] implying that these are trails that non-indigenous peoples inherit as much as the Teme-augama Anishinabe First Nation. According to John Jennings, the canoe is 'one of the greatest gifts of the First Peoples to all those who came after'[63] and is thus an appropriate symbol of the nation.

According to Elizabeth Furniss, in her book *The Burden of History: Colonialism and the Frontier Myth in a Rural Canadian Community*, the depiction of First Nations peoples as 'helping in the process of colonial economic expansion and settlement'[64] is a common component of what she calls the frontier myth. 'Histories commemorating the arrival of early explorers, settlers, missionaries, and industries in remote regions of Canada constitute the master narratives of Canadian nationalism' (53), and thus popular regional histories as well as the everyday lives of ordinary Canadians are 'permeated by the values and identities of a selective historical tradition that celebrates European expansion, settlement and industry' (53). 'Aboriginal perspectives on these events remain inaudible and unavailable to the general public' (65), and instead 'the lands of Canada are seen as being acquired through an 'inheritance,' a term that suggests the rightful transfer of wealth and equates the Canadian nation with a 'family' in which all members share equally the national patrimony' (144).

The contradictions within this argument should be obvious: if the fur trade was the vanguard of the Canadian state, then it laid the basis for the destruction of First Nations. If, as Innis and Creighton argue, the fur trade forts became the basis for settlement, and the pattern of communication pioneered by the fur trade canoe routes supported this settlement, then the fur trade was the beginning of the end of a way of life for First Nations. If the early profits from the fur trade underwrote military and civil governments in New France, and later trade was pursued by Europeans in order to maintain political and military advantage, then the fur trade participated in the conquest and settlement of Canada. Even if, as Eccles states, much of the country was not suitable for agricultural settlement, 'staples' such as lumber, pulp and paper, and minerals took the place of fur, and their development required technologically educated workers and the extinguishment of Aboriginal title through treaties.[65] To represent First Nations as active agents in the fur trade, within the historiographic tradition that sees the fur trade as the determining element in the formation of Canada, is to suggest they participated in their own destruction. Or to put it another way, would they have 'bequeathed' the canoe to us if they had known what we were going to do with it? This perspective makes it difficult to see how the narrative of nationality that holds that 'Canada is a canoe route' can be compatible with justice for First Nations.

The failure of the canoe narrative has sparked many popular attempts to reconceive master narratives of Canadian history in a way that provides for justice for First Nations. John Ralston Saul, in his book *A Fair Country*, has recently argued that 'Canada' and Canadians can justly claim to be an indigenized, 'métis' nation because Canadians are characterized by 'egalitarianism, a proper balance between individual and group, and a penchant for negotiation over violence,' which are 'all aboriginal values that Canada absorbed.'[66] According to Saul, Canada is based on an egalitarian society that existed in the northern part of North American during the eighteenth century, in which Europeans were of necessity partnered with First Nations in the attempt to survive, and in which mixed-race marriages were the norm and little distinction existed between the lives of First Nations peoples and their poverty-stricken immigrant neighbours. Yet, contradictorily, he also points out that the Canadian state that succeeded this egalitarian society in the nineteenth century was hierarchical, racist, imperialist, and, overall, vitally opposed to the very values of equality and inclusivity that characterize the 'true' Canada. This regime derived from European (mainly British) ideas about the economy, politics, and race and perverted the course of national development towards the exploitation of First Nations peoples and resources, so Saul argues. Paradoxically, it seems that according to Saul the project of Canadian sovereignty contradicts its essential nature as an egalitarian society. In order to identify Canada with its 'aboriginal roots' Saul is forced to alienate the last century-and-a-half of Canadian history and condemn much post-Confederation theorizing about Canadian society as un-Canadian. In his attempt to indigenize Canada, Saul, like his predecessors, is creating a history whose claim to literal truth is intended to allow it to function as 'arbitrator of the realism of contending political programs' in the present. As a plausible genealogy for an inclusive Canada in the present, Saul's book is emotionally inspiring; but his explanation that racism is un-Canadian seems to elide and evade the consequences of actions taken by the Canadian state.

The history of the canoe purports to demonstrate the power of the canoe to heal the split between the land and the nation. This power is held to inhere in the canoe, firstly, because the canoe is indigenous: its materials are identical to the landscape; its shape is based on the potentiality of those materials and on the requirements of the landscape; and its designers and original fabricators, 'Indians,' are both indigenous and associated with/identical to the landscape. These arguments are contradicted, however, by the practice of recommending and using canoes commercially made of artificial materials such as fibreglass and Kevlar. The value of a metonymic relationship with the land, originally attributed to the canoe because of its materials, has been transferred to the canoe itself: this is a textbook example of Marx's idea of fetishization. In addition, the activity of paddling a canoe is held to promote identification with the landscape because it brings the paddler into direct contact with the natural geography and the physical limitations it imposes, as well as the desirable scenery and animal life accessible by no other means. This is contradicted by evidence that shows that direct experience of nature is never direct: it is mediated by European ideologies, even in the case of the early-nineteenth-century Euro-Canadians who are often cited to prove it. Attempts to adopt First Nations beliefs about the land in the form of the stories that explain its topography and spiritual significance are mediated through non-indigenous sources. If indeed the fur trade underwrote European military ambitions, settlement, and the formation of the state – which ultimately required the extinguishment of Aboriginal title – it cannot be innocent of the effects of these on First Nations. The argument that the canoe determined Canada's borders is not sustained by the evidence.

The historical narrative of nation that places the canoe at the centre of Canadian history is, finally, contradictory. It purports to include First Nations as partners, but frequently relegates them to origins or identifies them with the landscape. It promotes the heroism and strength of European voyageurs and explorers and claims them as the vanguard of the Canadian state, yet absolves them (and their spiritual descendants) from any responsibility for the actions of that state. It also embraces a direct and felt relationship with the land, but does so by constructing that land according to European ideas of landscape or by appropriating First Nations technologies and knowledge. Instead of creating an identity between the nation and the geographical space it occupies, it merely expresses the desire for that identity. This narrative, which constructs canoeists as the 'folk' who are the closest to the land, conveniently obscures the originary violence that laid claim to the land and forced it to yield up its resources at our bidding – 'what we are, and what we did.' The claim that 'Canada is a canoe route' merely indulges the imperialist nostalgia that longs for what it has already destroyed.

'The Anglo-Saxon idea of pleasure': Eric Morse and Recreational Wilderness Canoeing

An important aspect of the 'ideology of the canoe' as described by Daniel Francis is the belief that by paddling a canoe we make ourselves Canadian. Canoeing, and especially wilderness canoe tripping, allows paddlers to take up the subject position of the explorer or the voyageur (or even the 'Indian') in order to feel a vicarious identification with the founders of the nation and to find in that experience the historical and geographical continuity of the nation. Eric Morse is a central figure in the popularizing of wilderness canoe tripping as a recreational pastime. The founder of an informal group of wilderness canoeists who called themselves the 'Voyageurs,' Morse undertook to rediscover and retrace the fur trade canoe routes, at that time mostly unmarked and neglected. Morse researched the routes in the journals of early explorers, acquiring copies of government maps and aerial photographs and planning yearly trips for the group throughout the 1950s and 1960s. He publicized the activities of the Voyageurs and often submitted diary accounts of their trips to newspapers and popular magazines. He eventually published his research as *Fur Trade Canoe Routes of Canada* (1969), which offered detailed maps and how-to information for the growing number of Canadians and tourists who wanted to recreate his journeys. Morse's fame as a canoeist and his practical, historical, and geographical knowledge made him in later life an 'expert' whose lobbying on behalf of the preservation of fur trade canoe routes and canoeing rivers had important consequences. He advised on the Centennial Voyageur Canoe Pageant; he was instrumental in having many accessible portages and canoe routes identified with historical markers; he lobbied to create a park in the Slave Lake-Artillery Lake region of the Northwest Territories and spoke up for wilderness preservation in Algonquin and other provincial parks.

Perhaps even more than his publications, however, his friendships and acquaintance with many important federal politicians and civil servants helped shape both the public and the political will to promote the canoe and canoeing as a symbol of the nation.

The example set by Morse and his companions as recreational canoeists inspired generations of Canadians to emulate their project of 'retracing' the routes of explorers and fur trade brigades. In the wake of Morse and his group, these canoeists often suggest that the feeling of identification with their historical forebears is a necessary part of their canoeing experience, and perhaps even its goal. Indeed, as Beverly Haun-Moss recounts in her analysis of the motives for recreational canoeing: 'So compelling became the desire to recreate the experience of the wilderness explorations of early Europeans that paddlers have continually retraced their voyages as those rivers became accessible to recreational canoeists ... This aspect of recreational canoeing is so pervasive, and so well recorded by the canoeists themselves, that Bruce Hodgins and Gwyneth Hoyle were able to compile a chronological record of many of the trips taken on major Canadian Rivers, *Canoeing North into the Unknown: A Record of River Travel, 1874–1974.*'[1] Eric Morse himself is important to this study, but his activities are also important as they provide an opportunity to investigate the meaning of the recreational pastime that he introduced and popularized, that of retracing the fur trade canoe routes in a quest to re-experience and thereby metonymically understand the experiences of early Europeans in Canada.

Eric Morse was born in 1904 in Naini Tal, India, where his father farmed jasmine for the perfume trade. His family immigrated to rural Ontario when he was five, and Morse attended Trinity College School and spent summers at a family cottage in Haliburton. He recounts in his autobiography, *Freshwater Saga*, his discovery of Haliburton County when he was twelve: 'I had never known, till I went to Haliburton, that such country existed, where one could travel for weeks going from lake to lake. Not only were its rock-bound rivers and lakes themselves scenic, but the rock inhibited both farming and settlement, and the forest everywhere hid and protected wildlife.'[2] He began recreational canoe tripping as a teenager, using the family cottage as a base, and continued throughout his early career as a schoolmaster and office worker. Deciding on a career in teaching, he attended Queen's University, completing an MA in history after a scholarship semester spent working at the School of International Studies in Geneva, and returned to Trinity as a master in 1936. In 1939 he enlisted in the RCAF and was posted to Ottawa.

The move to Ottawa was fortuitous. Morse wrote in his autobiography: 'I had access to canoe country close at hand, for the Gatineau, Coulonge, Lièvre, Rouge and their tributary rivers all drain southward off the Shield into the Ottawa River' (10). By the end of the war he had decided he wanted to stay. He had also decided he did not want to return to teaching, which he now considered 'a dead end' (10). He applied for a job as national secretary of the newly formed United Nations Association, based in Ottawa. This led to his appointment in 1949 as the national director of the Association of Canadian Clubs, a position he held until his retirement in 1971.

The first Canadian Club was founded in 1893, and the organization quickly sprouted branches in most major Canadian cities; they amalgamated as members of the National Association of Canadian Clubs in 1939. By 1949, when Morse was hired, they boasted over 40,000 members in 100 clubs across Canada. Their stated aim was to promote Canadian culture and pride in Canadian citizenship; their submission to the Massey Commission (The Royal Commission on National Development in the Arts, Letters and Sciences) in 1949 advocated, among other things, increased support for national art and history museums and the adoption of a national anthem. They organized and funded projects such as travelling art exhibits from the National Gallery and the designation and preservation of heritage sites and buildings. They were best known, however, for their speaker's series. Club branches in Toronto, Montreal, and Ottawa featured well-known politicians and government figures, often making major policy statements. 'Before instantaneous [news] coverage, Prime Ministers used the Club to reach out to Canadians'[3] at their luncheon meetings in the confident expectation that important business people and political allies would be in the audience. Morse's job included producing national publicity material for use by all the clubs and promoting and coordinating cross-Canada tours of important speakers.

While the clubs have no official political affiliation, in Morse's day ties with the federal Liberal party were strong. The local Ottawa branch included William Lyon MacKenzie King on its executive, and frequently invited speakers suggested by 'Mr Pearson' (Lester Pearson, then Liberal minister of External Affairs, and later prime minister). Their speakers in 1949–1950 comprised an A-list of elected politicians and important international figures: Premier Joey Smallwood of Newfoundland; Byron Johnson, Liberal premier of British Columbia; Liberal MP David Croll, the first Jewish member of Parliament; Lawrence Steinhardt, US ambassador to Canada; and Andrew McNaughton, general officer commanding of the Canadian Army from 1942 to 1943, former defence minister and subsequently Canada's representative to the United Nations. The volunteer executives of individual clubs included prominent business people, political figures, and academics; the diplomats of all foreign embassies and high commissions in Ottawa were invited to join their local club at a special membership rate.[4]

The 1950s and 1960s were an exciting time to be involved in Canadian culture. The experience of two world wars had promoted debates about the role of Canada in relation to the Commonwealth and prompted Canadians to begin to think of themselves in terms of their independent place in the world. Officially, Canada was no longer a colony of Britain; however, the postwar economic (and population) boom as well as the Cold War had brought the nation even more closely into the orbit of the United States. An election was fought over the US plan to locate nuclear missiles in Canada, and American soldiers came onto Canadian soil to build the Alaska Highway and participate in the Distant Early Warning system. Canadian national cultural institutions were founded, the CBC expanded into television production with the express mandate to counter US domination of Canadian airwaves, and legislation to limit foreign ownership of Canadian companies was contemplated. After much debate about the nature of the nation and its place in the world, Canada acquired a national anthem and a flag. The wildly nationalistic celebration of the Canadian centennial in the Expo '67 World's Fair showcased Canadian culture and technology, and prompted debates about the future of the nation and definition of its culture. The Canadian Clubs and their members were positioned to take part in these debates, and Morse to guide their direction.

Morse's dedication to his job, and his success at it, indicate many of his strengths and interests. He was committed to and supported a nationalist view of Canada, and he worked tirelessly in both his professional and canoeing lives to promote knowledge and preservation of Canadian culture and history. He was also an inveterate schmoozer, a man who created and cultivated a network of like-minded men, mainly liberal in both ideology and party affiliation, who were his friends and allies. These two characteristics reinforced each other: he was able to use his network of friends and acquaintances to promote his view of Canada, and reciprocally his view of Canada helped to make him friends and allies. These qualities, plus his administrative abilities, his lively writing style, and his meticulous and accurate research, helped to make him an enormously influential person.

Morse recounts in *Freshwater Saga* that he was initially attracted to canoe tripping because of his love of wilderness landscapes and his enjoyment of the feeling of independence that came from 'the ability to make one's way through the country by unmechanized means' (6). However, his studies in the history, culture, and geography of Canada added depth and breadth to his cherished pastime. While his MA thesis had been on the immigration of Indian citizens to Canada[5] (an interest that grew from his family experiences), in the course of his studies he encountered Harold Innis's *The Fur Trade in Canada*, and the book 'struck an immediate chord.' He 'began to read all [he] could of the journals of the early fur trade, of explorers, and of other travellers by canoe or dog team, and began to build up a library of those early journals' (9). The effect of this reading became apparent when, at an Ottawa dinner party in 1951, he challenged a group of diplomats to join him on one of his canoe expeditions: 'some of the Canadians were asking the diplomats present how much they could possibly learn of the true Canada on the cocktail circuit. They should experience what it was like to paddle Canadian lakes and rivers, trudge over portages, feel the spray of rapids, camp among pines, and face the insects. In the end the diplomats said, "OK, show us." So it was agreed that three Canadians, Omond Solandt, Blair Fraser, and I, would take three diplomats on a canoe trip' (11).

This challenge, and the way it was taken up, was an important moment in the development of 'the ideology of the canoe.' Morse's suggestion conflated the geography of Canada with the nation as an ideological construct and suggested that both were available through the experience of canoeing; it identified the nation as a whole with canoe travel undertaken not for any useful purpose such as trapping, surveying, exploration, or even simply for recreation, but with the express (and only) purpose of understanding the (symbolic) nation through (metonymic) experience. The challenge was expressed in exactly these terms: the fact that it was taken up by a group of influential, educated men with access to power in Canada suggests not only that these men accepted its premises (that canoeing would instil a sense of Canadian nationality in canoeists), but that this point of view could and would become a dominant way of understanding both the nation and recreational canoeing.

The resulting trip in 'attractive, if undemanding' canoeing country near Ottawa was a success, and the group was eager to repeat their experience. 'Thus was born an informal, congenial and strong wilderness canoeing group ... The summer trips became longer, the personnel changed from year to year as members came and went, but the asso-

ciation [was] lasting' (11). Ongoing members of the group included
Tony Lovink, Netherlands ambassador to Canada; Omondt Solandt,
chair of the Canadian Defence Research Board; Blair Fraser, Ottawa
correspondent for *Maclean's* magazine and frequent contributor to the
Ottawa Citizen; and Elliot Rodger, vice chief of general staff of the Canadian Army. In 1952 the group took their first trip to Quetico Park in
the north-west corner of Ontario, and in the middle of the park kept an
appointment to meet Sigurd Olson, an American conservationist, nature
writer, and president of the American National Parks Association. Olson
joined the group as 'bourgeois,' in 1953 (Morse became the 'research
department') and became another long-term member. Other members
of the Voyageur group[6] in the fifties and sixties included Dennis Coolican, president of the Canadian Bank Note Company and membership
secretary of the Ottawa branch of the Canadian Clubs; Tyler Thompson, a high-level diplomat in the US embassy; and Frank Delaute, then
secretary to Governor General Vincent Massey. Occasional paddlers
accompanying Morse and his friends at the time included 'Terk' Bayley,
assistant deputy minister of Lands and Forests in Ontario; John Ende-
man and 'Woody' Woodward from the South African embassy; Major
General J.M. 'Rocky' Rockingham, general officer in command of the
Canadian Armed Forces in Quebec; Angus Scott, executive director of
the Canadian Parks and Wilderness Society; and Pierre Trudeau, then
parliamentary secretary to Prime Minister Lester Pearson, later Liberal
minister of Justice, and after 1968, prime minister.

This group was typical of the wilderness canoeists who preceded and
followed them in that they were white, male, and well-educated, with
middle-to-upper class backgrounds. In addition, 'most were of English,
Scottish or Irish descent' and urban based.[7] While the group may seem
to contain a high proportion of men who held politically and culturally
powerful positions in Canada, this too is not unusual: Bruce Hodgins
and Gwyneth Hoyle have identified cabinet ministers, future and former
prime ministers, television and print journalists, and university professors among the many who have canoed Canada's northern rivers in the
wake of the Voyageurs group. The circle of influential people who supported 'the Voyageurs' extended well beyond actual paddlers: a party
held on 13 March 1959 to celebrate the exploits of the group included
among those invited the Honourable George Hees, minister of Transport and former president of the Conservative party; E. Davie Fulton,
minister of Justice in the Diefenbaker government; Davidson Dunton
and Albert Truman from Carleton University; Lionel Massey, son of Gov-

ernor General Vincent Massey; Alvin Hamilton, minister of Northern Affairs and Natural Resources; and Lester Pearson (soon to be prime minister); as well as the presidents of Canada Packers and Steep Rock Mining.[8] In addition, the many private school and summer camp groups that undertake wilderness canoe trips are composed of the children of the rich and urban, and contain many future lawyers, politicians, and members of the business elite.

The Voyageurs' trip to Quetico Park in 1954 marked a turning point for the group. They decided to enter the park by way of Grand Portage and the Pigeon River, following the traditional route of the historical voyageurs. In *Freshwater Saga*, Morse describes the experience: 'We knew from Alexander Mackenzie's and other early journals that the Montreal fur traders headed west around Lake Superior's North Shore and that, when they reached the Grand Portage, they followed it up to the plateau where the continental divide lay and where the waters flowed westward. On the way up the nine-mile portage next morning we came upon a large sign erected by the Minnesota Historical Society. This sign, which had a tremendous impact on us, informed us that the path we stood on, circumventing the unnavigable cataracts and canyons of the lower Pigeon, had first been trodden by La Vérendrye in 1732. Soon after that time it had become the way by which the voyageurs of the North West Company surmounted the plateau west of Lake Superior, 1000 feet above the lake, carrying westward the trade goods and bringing back the beaver pelts from the Athabaska country. The sign made clear, too, that Mackenzie, Fraser, Thompson, and other explorers of the west had used this very path. The words of the sign and the path itself were inspiring. We were for the first time travelling the route of the voyageurs ... We decided, then and there, that next year we would start to retrace the rest of this celebrated fur trade route, but starting from its western end, coming mainly downstream. This pattern now became a theme for our canoe trips in the fifties and sixties, retracing historical Canadian rivers – historic in the sense of having been used in the fur trade or by early explorers' (14–16).

Morse and his group repeatedly describe the experience of personal identification with their historical forebears as a motivation for their trips as well as an emotional benefit they gained from their activity. In his account of the Grand Portage trip, written for the Ottawa Ski Club newsletter, Morse states that 'the lure' of the border lakes route 'was history': 'we were projecting ourselves back into the eighteenth century, trying to live for seventeen days a luxury-diet version of the life of the early explorers

Sig Olsen, Tony Lovink, and the Voyageurs at Grand Portage, 1954.
Image number WHi-74087. Courtesy of the Wisconsin Historical Society.

and voyageurs.'[9] Journalist Blair Fraser, one of the Voyageurs, wrote of Grand Portage in a feature article for *Maclean's*: 'Here as nowhere else men of the twentieth century can feel the charm and some of the challenges the makers of Canada knew.'[10] About their 1958 trip over Methye portage, Morse wrote: 'The whole trip was fascinating for its historical atmosphere: the voyageurs of an earlier day were with us constantly.'[11] Sigurd Olson wrote in *The Lonely Land* that 'Ghosts of those days stalk the portages and phantom brigades move down the waterways ... those men were with us and when the haze of our campfire drifted along the beach, it seemed to join with the smoke of long forgotten fires.'[12] These moments of identification with early European explorers are a defining aspect of the practice of recreational wilderness canoeing, and become a pattern for recreational canoeists who come after.

Such moments of identification represent the process of interpellation as Canadian: the canoeist takes up a subject position created discursively through history and popular representation, and in so doing inserts himself into the narrative of nationality. According to the historiographic tradition, the explorers and voyageurs made Canada; through identification with them by means of undertaking the same trip, and battling similar obstacles, individual canoeists prompt themselves to 'feel' Canadian. This assumption is implicit in Morse's suggestion that his audience of diplomats and civil servants in the embassy in Ottawa could only understand 'the true Canada' if they 'paddle[d] Canadian lakes and rivers.' Members of the group repeatedly wrote explicitly that identification with explorers and voyageurs made one more Canadian. In 'We Went La Verendrye's Way,' Blair Fraser comments that the Grand Portage trip 'gave us all a new awareness of Canada by bringing us into a kind of personal contact with Canada's past.'[13] The very name of the group (which Morse says was coined by the press[14] but which the group was using to refer to itself as early as 1954) and their adoption of fur trade brigade terms ('bourgeois' for trip leader; 'boisson' for a celebratory rum; 'pipe' for a short rest stop) suggest that the level of identification with historical figures was self-conscious and intense. Stuart Hall has written: 'identities are the names we give to the different ways we are positioned by, and position ourselves within, the narratives of the past';[15] these paddlers were assuming an identity by self-consciously positioning themselves in relation to a specific narrative of the past.

The group paddled historic rivers throughout the remainder of the 1950s: the Churchill in 1955, the Hayes in 1956, Reindeer Lake (north of Frog Portage) to Lake Athabasca in 1957, the Clearwater River and Methye portage in 1958, and the Camsell River through Great Bear Lake to the MacKenzie in 1959. They bought three wood and canvas Prospector canoes from the Hudson's Bay Company (HBC) in 1955, which they named for their owners (Moro for Morse and Rodger, Solo for Solandt and Lovink, and Cool for Coolican and Olson), and had them shipped during the winter months to the post that would be the 'put-in' point for next summer's trip. They tried to set aside three weeks of holiday for each trip and frequently flew in and out of the more isolated locations, booking hotel rooms and charter flights months in advance and ensuring that the HBC post supplying their comestibles was stocked with their preferred overproof rum.[16] Morse researched each route meticulously during the winters, issuing periodic bulletins soliciting feedback on his progress and providing typescripts of excerpts from explorer narratives to each paddler (with correspondence and typing handled by his office staff). The routine was interrupted in 1960, when Morse took a trip along the north shore of Lake Superior with his wife, Pamela, whom he had married in 1959.[17] From 1961 onward, Pamela Morse accompanied him on all of his major canoe trips, organizing the food and frequently keeping a log of their journey. She was usually the only woman in a group of three to six men.

The group had varying levels of experience as paddlers, and all of them initially found white water challenging. Morse (in *Freshwater Saga*) and Frank Delaute (in a series of articles written for the *Ottawa Journal*) describe their attempts to learn about white-water techniques by observing other canoeists. On their first challenging trip on an unfamiliar river, the Churchill in 1955, the Voyageurs pulled in behind 'four canoes of Indians' and followed them down the river, carefully imitating their path through any navigable rapids (*Freshwater Saga* 20). 'Our greatest difficulty was learning to back-paddle and steer at the same time, but we got the message: a canoe in a rapid is not meant always to be paddled forward, but often sideways, or sometimes even backward' (20). Eventually they came to love white water, and teased each other about the occasional dump; when Pierre Trudeau paddled with Morse for the first time in 1967, he and Angus Scott hung up on a rock and ended up completing their run in reverse.[18] Despite incidents like this, the Voyageurs were generally cautious in wilderness situations where rescue would be unlikely. They split the provisions among the canoes in case of upset and asked for advice from locals along the way. An infallible rule, Morse wrote, was to check the state of the portages at either end of a set of rapids; if they showed evidence of constant use, both up- and downstream, then you had better portage, he advised.

Travelling with Eric Morse was strenuous. Angus Scott, who participated in several trips in the far north in the 1960s, recounts Morse's focus on keeping to a schedule that frequently required rising at 4:00 am to take advantage of good weather.[19] Keeping to a schedule was practical: the group would inform the local RCMP where they were going and when they expected to arrive so that if they were late, someone would come looking.[20] But wading up rapids in freezing water and portaging double fifty-pound packs might have made the required daily mileage seem like an egregious burden to the average paddler. The group would celebrate the beginning of each trip with a good steak dinner and red wine at the first campsite; the provisions for the rest of the trip would be a mix of canned and dried food. Some of the men enjoyed fishing, but the group never relied upon 'the land' for provisions, and their packs were consequently weighty. A luxury never neglected, however, was overproof rum and various mixes to make it palatable. Morse preferred lemon powder, water, and a little sugar, and the resulting concoction was optimistically called a 'daiquiri' (Terk Bayley was convinced that the drink was an effective mosquito repellent). The overall experience of travelling with Morse may be gauged by a joking postscript to a letter he wrote to Elliot Roger dated 11 February 1957. Morse quotes from G.M. Grant's account of his trip across Canada with Sanford Fleming's railway survey party in 1872, *Ocean to Ocean*: 'July 23 Rose at sunrise ... An hour later, L. and M. came in by canoe; they were travelling for pleasure. Since they had travelled all night and were tired, seedy, and mosquito bitten, they represented, in their own persons, the Anglo-Saxon idea of pleasure.'[21]

Grant's (and Morse's) little joke turns on the popular belief that the 'WASP' (white Anglo-Saxon Protestant) is incapable of enjoying himself because it makes him feel guilty; he can only really have a good time if he is suffering for it. Certainly, it sounds as though the pleasures of travelling with the Voyageurs were well-tempered with discomforts. However, the term Anglo-Saxon suggests other associations as well: the turn-of-the-century idea of the British Empire and the accompanying belief that the 'Anglo-Saxon Race' was naturally energetic and hard-working, and so destined to govern lazy, comfort-loving 'lesser races.' Morse and his canoeing friends would have been horrified by this association, being good liberals in their own historical context and supporters of Canadian independence from Britain. But their identification with the 'explorers and voyageurs,' whom they believed were the vanguard of the Canadian state, suggests their identification with the goals and aims of that state, including the extinguishment of Aboriginal title and the establishment of Canadian sovereignty. Their project of retracing the fur trade canoe routes and experiencing the associated hardships, challenges, and triumphs suggests that their motivation included what Beverly Haun-Moss has called a 'desire to master the land,' to 'explore, codify and control' it, to map and stabilize Canada's claim to the geographical space occupied by the state.[22] Morse's project represents a response to the cultural anxiety of the various debates about Canadian 'identity' and Canada's future taking place in the 1950s and 1960s: an attempt to stabilize the cultural narrative of nationality and prove its legitimacy by literally going out and performing it. This kind of 'Anglo-Saxon pleasure' might be

derived from physically verifying the supposed 'historical roots' of the
nation in the land and reclaiming the land in a gesture of not British,
but Canadian imperialism.

Cultural historian Christy Collis argues a similar thesis in response to
what she calls the 'Footsteps narratives' of adventurers and recreational
travellers in central Australia in the 1970s and 1980s. These narratives of
expeditions designed to 'follow the footsteps' of early explorers involve
'not just remembering – through reading Empire's documents – historical imperial spatiality, but also activating it in the present tense.'[23] The
emptiness of central Australia is what makes this process of continual
reclaiming both possible and necessary: while settlement with its 'het-
erogenous fences, roads and houses' represents one form of 'colonial
spatiality'(5), only 'emptiness' can 'guarantee a space in which imperial
exploration can be prolonged, a site in which the rituals of possession
and originary spatial production can continue' (5). Undertaken in the
context of contemporary Aboriginal land claims and frequently including the grandsons of explorers among the party, 'what is at stake in Footsteps expeditions is ... the reinstatement and reactivation of imperial
spatiality' (12).

Morse's expeditions took place in an era of similar anxiety about the
nation, an anxiety prompted not so much by Aboriginal land claims
as by a clash between a postwar conservative nationalism, represented
by thinkers like George Grant and Donald Creighton, and a capitalist
bourgeoisie that was willing to see the nation more integrated into the
growing US empire.[24] Throughout the period from the late 1950s to
the late 1970s the 'identity' of the nation was called into question: its
independence required to be justified, its essence defined, and its 'roots'
recovered. As part of this process, Canadian literary critics attempted
to identify the specifics of Canadian literature; historians delineated
the elements of history that had created unique Canadian political
and social institutions; schools of Canadian Studies were founded; and
debates took place about teaching Canadian materials in elementary
and high schools. Ordinary Canadians took up recreational canoeing
and the practice of retracing historical canoe routes in this period partly
because it was represented as a way of stabilizing their identity as Canadians. By positioning themselves within the particular narrative of the past
identified by canoeing enthusiasts, and popularized by writers like Morse
and his colleagues, canoeists were 'remade as Canadians.'

If, as Tony Bennett suggests, 'The unity of a nation ... [is] the unity of
a people who share the same space and time, the occupants of a territory

which has been historicized and the subjects of a history that has been territorialized,'[25] then the kind of canoe trip undertaken by Morse and those who came after constitutes a strategy for historicizing the territory of the nation and creating the canoe tripper as the subject of a territorialized national history. Like the history museums and heritage sites that are arranged in narrative form, the canoe trip that retraces historical canoe routes coercively positions the paddler in relation to the past and invites them to take up a specific identity in relation to it. As Carol Duncan puts it in relation to museums, 'the museum [makes] manifest the public it claim[s] to serve: it could produce it as a visible entity by literally providing it a defining frame and giving it something to do.'[26] Like Duncan's historical museum displays, the canoe trip includes the elements of 'following a prescribed route,' 'recalling a narrative,' and 'engaging in [a] structured experience that relates to the history or the meaning'[27] of the physical landscapes paddlers pass through. In order to historicize the landscape through which it passes, the canoe trip must be conceived of *as* a canoe trip, rather than merely as a journey to somewhere you need to get to; the fact of canoe travel to some extent determines the route of the trip, rather than the other way around. The goal of such trips is recreational, and so canoe trips don't really begin to happen until the 1880s with the vogue of outdoor recreation as an antidote or a cure for urban malaise and the supposed feminization of the urban man's life. These trips follow the routes laid out by previous white explorers/ travellers, including frequent reference to published accounts of earlier travellers in the region and often a ritual visit to, or touching of, the signs of previous travellers (Back's chimneys at Reliance, Hornby's grave, the cairn on the Hanbury River, Methye portage), which indicate the way that the landscape is preconceived as historicized. In addition, paddlers often participate in the rehistoricizing of landscape by creating markers such as cairns and lobsticks to mark their own passage.

The activities of the Voyageurs group were publicized in newspapers and magazines and on CBC radio and television. Morse professed surprise in his account of the 1955 Churchill trip that national media were interested in a 'mere vacation trip,' positing in *Freshwater Saga* that only the novelty of the Voyageurs' mature ages ('we averaged, as a group, nearly fifty years of age') justified a front-page spread in the *Toronto Star* 'with big headline and photos!' (21). However, Morse's papers reveal that he sometimes invited press coverage, and often facilitated it, while other members of the Voyageurs contributed in their own way to publicizing the activities of the group. In a 'Memo to the Voyageurs' dated

19 June 1954 about the 1954 trip from Fort William to Fort Frances, Sigurd Olsen laments: 'sorry *Time* and *Life* decided against coverage. I really think they did not realize the historical importance of the expedition. On the other hand, if their feeler convinced *Macleans* [sic] to have Blair do a feature, perhaps it is all to the good.'[28] Blair Fraser's feature, 'We Went La Verendrye's Way,' appeared in the 1 October 1954 issue of *Maclean's*, and news reports about the trip appeared in the *Chisholm Free Press, Winnipeg Tribune, Fort William Times-Journal, Ottawa Citizen*, and *Saskatoon Star Phoenix*. This level of coverage was not unusual: other trips were reported, usually at their beginnings and endings, in both national and local newspapers. Morse sent background information, including details of the route and personnel, to the chief of the Ottawa bureau of the Canadian Press wire service, Clyde Blackburn, and coordinated posed photos of the paddlers to accompany the resulting wire-service copy. Morse recounts that on most trips the newest paddler was designated to produce a daily log, and diaries of almost all of the trips after 1954 were published in the *Ottawa Journal* by participants like Frank Delaute and Dennis Coolican. Sig Olson was a well-known nature writer, and he published his version of the 1955 Churchill river trip as a book, *The Lonely Land*. Terk Bayley wrote up manuscript diaries of the trips he took and circulated them. 'Rocky' Rockingham wrote up the 1958 trip for the *Canadian Army Journal*. Eric and Pamela Morse were interviewed on the CBC television program 'Take Thirty' after their 1965 trip on the Rat River and over McDougall Pass. Morse was the featured speaker at the annual dinner of the Arctic Circle in 1962, on the subject 'Paddle and Portage across the Barrens.' Morse also contributed his own accounts of their trips to *Sports Review* magazine, the *Ottawa Journal*, *Canadian Geographic Journal, Arctic Circular*, and numerous government publications on wilderness travel and tourism, in addition to publishing *Fur Trade Canoe Routes of Canada* (1969), which appeared with University of Toronto Press.

   In writing about their adventures, Morse and his friends contributed to a genre of recreational wilderness canoe-trip narratives that pre-existed them. Wilderness canoe-tripping accounts include a number of elements that might be considered generic conventions: lists of supplies and equipment, with discussions of their merits and defects; historical research into the intended route and excerpts from accounts of earlier explorers and travellers; attempts to identify historical sites along the way, such as campsites, landmarks, or cairns mentioned by previous explorers/travellers; a declaration of the way that the route or the landscape is 'unchanged'; a moment of identification with previous travellers or explorers; and frequently a new 'discovery' that represents the contemporary travellers' contribution to knowledge (the best way to run a rapid; a rapid unmarked on the map). Contemporary travellers usually encounter, and sometimes compare themselves to, Native people, especially with the intent of representing themselves as indigenized Canadians. Recreational canoe-trip narratives as early as Ernest Thompson Seton's *The Arctic Prairies: A Canoe-Journey of 2,000 Miles in Search of the Caribou* (1911) contain all of these elements, as do contemporary accounts posted on websites or published in the wilderness canoeing magazine *Che-mun.*

The narratives of the Voyageurs (Morse, Bayley, Delaute, Coolican, Olson, and Rockingham) also describe lengthy preparations for their trips; they include lists of food and equipment with commentary on their suitability. The groups compare the written accounts of fur trade explorers with their own experiences, quoting specific passages and reading excerpts around the campfire in the evening. Morse attempted to identify the historic voyageurs' camping places along the shore of Lake Superior in 1960; they searched 'for the remains of Sir John Franklin's Fort Enterprise' (115) on Winter Lake; in 1972 they 'spotted some faint writing made long ago by scraping off the black lichen' and identified the initials of Guy Blanchet, who had paddled the Taltson in 1924. Everywhere they combed the landscape for stone steps, log landing places, and navigational landmarks they shared with the historic voyageurs; as much as possible they tried to ensure that they saw the landscape from those earlier perspectives. When they stood at the top of Methye Portage, they did not merely marvel at the view; they recalled Alexander Mackenzie's famous description of the view and marvelled at Alexander Mackenzie marvelling at the view. They considered the techniques of white-water canoeing as in themselves a historical artefact to be recovered and preserved. They treated the whole country as if it were an experiential museum, filled with authentic artefacts in the forms of landmarks, topographical features, ruined buildings, and fireplace chimneys, all of which could be experienced to materialize and legitimate the Canadian national narrative.

Morse and his party also inaugurated the practice of writing notes to subsequent paddlers and enclosing them within a stone cairn built to mark their passage. In 1962 they inserted a note into a coffee can buried inside a stone cairn they encountered on the Hanbury River, a cairn that has since become a ritual place of pilgrimage for wilderness travellers, who open the cairn, read the notes it contains, and insert their own contribution. The cairn contained seventy-nine messages by 1991 when the notes were retrieved and published in the book, *Arctic Cairn Notes*. The messages were signed by Prince Andrew and his then-wife Sara Ferguson, former Prime Minister John Turner and his family, journalists Craig Oliver and Jean Pelletier, former Prime Minister Pierre Trudeau, MP Peter Stollery, and cabinet minister Judd Buchanan, along with paddlers from Japan, Sweden, the United States, and Canada. While Morse was careful to point out to anyone who asked that the cairn had been created by John Kelsall in 1951, Kelsall's original note has long since disappeared, and Morse is usually credited with making the landmark. The note from David F. Pelly, author of a book on the history of the Hanbury and Thelon river systems, states: 'This cairn is perhaps the best testament to Eric [Morse's] contributions to recreational canoeing in the Canadian wilderness. He was the pioneer that we are all following.'[29] The Voyageurs also built a cairn on Jolly Lake in 1964 during their trip from Clinton-Colden Lake through the Snare River canyon: 'We built a cairn to house the firewood, and also inserted a bottle with a paper saying who we were and when we had passed. We gave the name and address of our youngest member, Angus, for we were curious to know if there would ever be any other traffic on this route' (*Freshwater Saga* 114). The cairn was rediscovered several years later by Morse's friend A.C. [Bert] Hamilton, the well-known Spenserian and Queen's University English professor, with his sons.

Like many canoe-trip narratives before and since, the Voyageurs' canoe-trip diaries often claim that the landscape looks identical to the way it did when first encountered by Europeans. As Christy Collis points out, only by imagining themselves in an unsettled place can adventurers perform the acts of endurance, suffering, discovery and claiming that create their identification with the historical figures they emulate.[30] Grand Portage, according to Morse, 'still looks exactly as it did before the white man came,'[31] and in this unmarked space Anglo-Canadians can elide their own urban experience and the history of conquest and settlement, and fantasize an Eden before 'the fall' represented by the conquest of First Nations and the industrialization of Canada. By taking up the position of voyageur, they elide their actual positions of power in the nation and 'forget' the way that they have benefited from this 'fall.' Moreover, they can present themselves, educated white middle-class urbanites, as the founders of Canada and the inheritors of a tradition that constructs them as indigenous.

The encounters Morse and his party had with actual First Nations peoples are revealing. While the group always deferred to local knowledge when travelling in unknown waters, and frequently wrote to HBC posts to ask the manager to consult the local 'Indians' about the level of the river and the state of the portages, they present themselves as the true indigenes by virtue of their choice to travel by canoe. Morse writes in *Freshwater Saga* about the people they encountered on the Churchill in 1955: 'Those Indians less practised in guarding their real thoughts expressed surprise at seeing a group of white men, all paddling, and more of the Indians seemed quite puzzled by the complete reversal in our roles: the Indians with outboard motors, the whites paddling. So used had they become to regarding the canoe as a vehicle of work that its recreational use seemed beyond their grasp. Not only on this Churchill trip but also in subsequent years it became apparent that the absence of an outboard motor was regarded among them as an indication of lower economic status' (21). Morse repeats the phrase 'reversal of our roles' in his account of their 1958 Churchill trip from Île-à-la-Crosse to Waterways,[32] indicating its importance for him. The reversal was not merely that the 'whites' were using muscle power and the 'Indians' modern motorized technology: instead, given the way that the Voyageurs identified canoeing with closeness to the land and performance of nationality, their persistence in canoeing indicates the way that the Voyageurs identified themselves as having become the new indigenes.

Sigurd Olson is even more direct in his account of canoeing with the Voyageurs, *The Lonely Land*. He describes the local Cree people they encounter as 'childlike' and 'primitive,' but seeks to emulate their 'happy carefree air,'[33] which he associates with freedom from 'time, schedules, and the seriousness of life' (107). He anticipates that after a few days on the river his own group of white men 'will fit into the scenery like the Crees themselves' (37). During the trip, they consider they are 'living in harmony with the land, and like the Crees, [they] made no great changes in the terrain' (157). Olson has little to say about how the leisure, income, and equipment that facilitated their trip depended upon the very lifestyle he sought to escape, while his association of the Cree with 'the land' and a happy carefree life is contradicted by the obvious poverty and hunger he reports encountering among them. Yet, like Morse, he claims a strong identification with the land by identifying with First Nations peoples.

Eric Morse's achievements did not end with the publication of *Fur Trade Canoe Routes of Canada, Then and Now* in 1969. He was also instrumental in suggesting and setting up the Hudson's Bay Company U-Paddle system, a program designed to facilitate recreational canoeing in remote locations. The Hudson's Bay Company acquired a fleet of Grumann aluminium canoes at Morse's suggestion, which they located at various of their posts in popular paddling country. The canoes could be reserved in advance for a specific location and dropped off at a convenient post at the end of a wilderness trip. This system remained in operation until 1985, when it was cancelled in a downsizing operation that would eventually see this venerable Canadian company sold to US buyers. Morse also rediscovered the Second Chaudière portage and arranged for a marker to be erected by Historic Sites and Monuments Board of Canada. He subsequently became a member of the Capital Regional District Historical Sites and Monuments board. He shared his research on the 'La Vase' portage between the Mattawa and French River systems: 'The Ontario Archaeological and Historic Sites Board was able to confirm these findings from their own early documents, and in 1961 erected a small monument near the pond, beside the Trans-Canada highway, with a small plaque setting out the facts' (72). He designed markers to be placed on the Trans-Canada highway at the locations of historic portages and waterways, and he worked with local Chambers of Commerce and branches of the Canadian Club to have them erected. He also contributed to the debate on which channels of the French River had been used by the voyageurs and published scholarly articles attempting to identify locations referred to in Samuel Hearne's *Narrative*.

In his later life, Morse was disgusted by the predictable results of the new popularity of wilderness canoeing. He experienced the 'irony' identified by Bruce Hodgins that canoeing in the wilderness makes it less wild and that the more canoeists in the wilderness, the less desirable it becomes as canoeing country.[34] The ambivalent legacy of settler expansion is perfectly expressed in an article on the Camsel River trip that Morse wrote for the *Ottawa Journal*, in which he reproduced a parody of a historical marker that greeted the canoeing party in Norman Wells: 'Upon this stone, August 1789, sat Alexander Mackenzie whilst fighting mosquitoes and planning this present refinery. Since that date this stone has been a saluting point for dogs, foxes and wolves in honor of the man who led the missionaries, fur traders, tuberculosis and tincans down this great river to the sea.'[35] While Morse declines to comment, this paragraph illustrates succinctly the ambivalent legacy that he celebrates; the explorers and voyageurs were the vanguard of an invasion by Anglo-Canadians that resulted in the destruction of the landscape (the refinery), the First Nations peoples (tuberculosis and missionaries), and the resignification of the northern part of North America as a field to both supply and consume commodities of use to modern capitalist cultures. Morse and his Voyageurs do not self-consciously identify themselves with the Alexander Mackenzie who was racist or the profit-motivated companies that employed him; however, their trips were constructed as retracing the fur trade routes and therefore as reinscribing the expansionist drive of empire that deprived First Nations of their lands, livelihoods, and in many cases their lives.

Bruce Hodgins and Gwyneth Hoyle point out that identification with 'living heritage' remains one of the most important motivations for wilderness canoe tripping. Even though, as Hodgins and Hoyle point out, Harold Innis's contention that 'Canada had been made by the fur trade' is an oversimplification, paddlers still find identification with 'the myths and history of fur trade transportation' a satisfactory way to justify their activity.[36] The formation of the Voyageurs to enact Eric Morse's project of identifying and paddling the historical routes of the voyageurs was an important moment in the development of 'the ideology of the canoe.' Morse attempted to overcome the sense of 'being alien in Canada' by conflating the geography of Canada with the nation as an ideological construct and suggesting that both were available through the experience of canoeing. According to the historiographic tradition, the explorers and voyageurs made Canada; through identification with them by means of undertaking the same trip, and battling the same obstacles, individual canoeists prompt themselves to 'feel' Canadian. Repeatedly in writings by Morse and the members of his canoeing expeditions, the assumption that identification with explorers and voyageurs made one more Canadian is explicit. These paddlers assumed an identity as Canadians by self-consciously positioning themselves in relation to a specific narrative of the past; their point of view would become a dominant way of understanding both the nation and recreational canoeing.

Chapter Four

The Centennial Voyageur Canoe Pageant as Historical Re-enactment

In 1967, the Canadian Centennial Commission sponsored a canoe race across Canada as part of the national centennial celebrations. The race, from Rocky Mountain House (near Edmonton) to the site of Expo '67 in Montreal, followed a route that had been used by the North West Company in the eighteenth and nineteenth centuries to transport trade goods and furs between Montreal and the isolated commercial outposts on the Saskatchewan and Winnipeg Rivers and in the north. Canoes representing eight provinces[1] and the two northern territories, and paddled by all-male teams of six (along with spare paddlers and a support crew), left Rocky Mountain House on 24 May and arrived at Expo on 4 September, to be welcomed by the chair of the Centennial Commission, John Fisher, and Secretary of State Judy Lamarsh in a live, nationally televised ceremony. The Voyageur Canoe Pageant was one of the most successful national centennial events, with extensive radio and television coverage and 67 front-page stories, 76 editorials and columns, and four-colour supplements in local and national newspapers.[2] The arrival of the voyageurs in small communities was also a successful catalyst for local celebrations; sporting headbands and bright red centennial sashes, team members participated in countless official welcomes, historical re-enactments, bison barbecues, sprint races, beauty pageants, parades, and other centennial events organized specifically to mark their passage.

From the perspective of forty years later, the Centennial Voyageur Canoe Pageant seems an obvious, even inspired, choice for an event that would celebrate Canadian history, represent cultural diversity and 'the three founding peoples' of Canada, highlight the foundational role of the landscape in Canadian identity, and emphasize Canadian unity. The canoe becomes mythic because this shift is in the interests of the 'elites'

The Centennial Voyageur Canoe Pageant on their way to Expo 67, 1967.
© Government of Canada. Reproduced with the permission of the Minister of
Public Works and Government Services Canada (2011).
Source: Library and Archives Canada/Credit: Frank Grant/Centennial
Commission fonds/PA-185522.

that 'use [myths] to reinforce the status quo and further their claims
to privilege,' as Daniel Francis argues.[3] In the case of the 'ideology of
the canoe,' this 'tradition' was invented, popularized, promulgated, and
underwritten by specific individuals in a specific time period, from the
mid-1950s and into the nationalist 1960s and 1970s. The Centennial
Voyageur Canoe Pageant was a central event in the creation of this 'ideology of the canoe,' as Francis calls it, serving to dramatize and embody a
particular historiography of the nation and to display it through popular
spectacle as a kind of proof or demonstration of the historical and affec-
tive claim to the land that constitutes Canada as a nation.

    While the Centennial Canoe Pageant is widely remembered among
Canadians of a certain age, the details of its proposal and performance
are not well known. James Raffan makes several references to the event
in his books *Fire in the Bones: Bill Mason and the Canadian Canoeing Tradi-*

tion (1996) and *Bark Skin and Cedar: Exploring the Canoe in Canadian Experience* (1999), and Jamie Benidickson also describes it in *Idleness, Water, and a Canoe* (1997): both authors get most of their information from an unsigned article published in the Summer 1967 issue of *The Beaver* (which itself is almost wholly indebted to a government press release.)[4] Pierre Berton includes a chapter on the race in *1967: The Last Good Year* (1997), which relies heavily on the memories of Manitoba team member Don Starkell.[5] Copious documentation concerning the event is preserved in the records of the Centennial Commission at Library and Archives Canada, and information about provincial teams is held in respective provincial and territorial archives; these allow a clear view of the nationalist rationale and the specific version of Canadian history that was used to justify government sponsorship of the event.

In 1964 Norm Tyson, an avid canoeist and canoe race organizer from Flin Flon, Manitoba, submitted a proposal for a race he called the 'Canadian Centennial Canoe Classique' to the planning branch of the Centennial Commission, a federally funded bureaucracy in charge of the preparations for the Canadian centennial celebrations.[6] In honour of Canada's hundredth birthday, Tyson proposed a race for 100 paddlers in conventional two-man canoes that would last for 100 days and offer a prize of $100,000 to the winners. The race would follow fur trade canoe routes, to the extent that they were known and passable, and travel approximately 3,300 miles from Edmonton to Montreal in the summer of 1967. The project officer who received Tyson's proposal, A.J. (Arnie) Charbonneau, immediately forwarded the brief to Eric Morse for comment. In written comments, Morse suggested that Tyson's project be reconceived as a historical pageant rather than a race *per se*, with costumed teams from the various regions or provinces of Canada re-enacting the lives of the fur trade voyageurs, and with a drastically reduced budget for prizes. Charbonneau joined these two proposals together in a memo he wrote to the executive committee of the planning branch on 27 August 1964, proposing that they consider organizing and sponsoring the 'Canadian Centennial Canoe Classique.'[7]

Charbonneau's memo is worth quoting at length because many of the points he makes justifying the canoe pageant are repeated in subsequent documents (sometimes in the same words). Charbonneau states that the purpose of the race would be 'to *re-enact history* and produce a *unique*, colourful and thrilling attraction that will capture the imagination of Canadians.' He goes on to situate the history of the fur trade and the role of voyageurs as originary and definitive of Canada itself.

'Starting with Champlain, in the early 1600s, and ending with Mackenzie in 1793, a line of communication was established across the Atlantic,
across a continent and on to the Pacific Ocean ... For the *canoe half* of
the route the explorers and fur merchants depended on the *Voyageurs'*
(italics in original). 'In fact,' Charbonneau quoted from Canadian historian A.R.M. Lower, '"the whole system rested on the skill of the voyageurs
with paddle and packstrap." "One hundred and eighty pounds a man
over a portage, twenty hours travelling a day if necessary, salt pork, corn
meal, dried peas and pemmican, infinite amounts of strong tobacco:
these were the pillars of internal exploitation"(A.R.M. Lower, page 139)
[sic].' Charbonneau highlighted the meaning and purpose of the race
as a re-enactment of the founding of Canada:

> *This is what the Canoe Classique is attempting to portray.*
> It will be a natural and fitting tribute to the courage and stamina of the
> explorers, voyageurs and fur traders, the founders of Canada. Since the
> canoe was the original means of transportation and is a symbol of Canadian
> exploration, this event will be a reminder of the colour and pageantry of
> Canadian history.

In two appendices, Charbonneau proposes 'Plan A' for the conduct of
the race, which is essentially Tyson's idea, and 'Plan B,' Tyson's idea mod-
ified by Morse, in which canoes representing provinces combine a race
with a historical pageant, travelling in voyageur costume in 24-foot cedar
freight canoes with six to eight paddlers each. Morse considered Tyson's
suggested budget unrealistic, and thus Charbonneau's 'Plan B' advised
that paddlers should receive a modest *per diem* payment and only token
cash prizes for winning and placing at the end of the race in Montreal.
      Charbonneau's situating of the fur trade and the role of the voyageurs
at the centre of Canadian history, as well as his copious quotation of
Lower, is almost certainly the result of suggestions by Morse. Morse was
a graduate in Canadian history with a Master's degree from Queen's
University at Kingston,[8] and he recounts in his autobiography, *Freshwater
Saga* (1987), how his background in Canadian history and his reading
of Harold Innis's *The Fur Trade in Canada* influenced his subsequent recreational canoeing. For him, the system of fur trade canoe routes was
the historical skeleton of the nation, and their geographical orientation
both the explanation for and the proud assertion of our independent
sovereignty as a nation. Lower's early work as an economic historian had
been strongly influenced by Innis's interpretation of the fur trade as a

model for a staples-based economy, but in his later career he became much more interested in the formative effect of wilderness on Canadian institutions and identity. Lower was a personal friend of Eric Morse; a copy of Morse's 1958 pamphlet, 'The Voyageurs, Canoe Trips, Methye Portage' in the Queen's University library is inscribed to Lower from Morse. They shared a strong commitment to nationalist historiography and to the centrality of the voyageurs and canoeing to the history of the nation. Lower's work would provide both historical evidence and an intellectual framework within which to present the proposed canoe race as a 'natural' centennial event, nationally symbolic, fundable, and uncontroversial.

Morse's (and through his, Charbonneau's) adoption of an Innis-and-Lower perspective on the fur trade was to have a determining effect on the interpretation of the pageant re-enactment. As Alan Filewod has argued, 'Because history can only be accessed through the structures of historiography, what is brought to "life" in living history is not the lived experience of the past, but the *reading* of the past.'[9] Historical re-enactments offer a 'highly selective history,' cautions historian Michael Dawson, which often chooses to 'finesse awkward issues, either by reinterpreting them ... or by ignoring them altogether'[10] in order to attract participants and to represent the goals of organizers and promoters.[11] In this case the goals were those of the centennial celebration itself: to represent a unique Canadian identity that could include all three supposed 'founding races' (Aboriginal, French, and British), to situate this identity as issuing directly from history, and to link this identity in a continuous relationship with the land, conceived of as the geographical nation. In this particular reading of the past, contemporary Canadian independence of the United States and Canadian geographical unity issue directly from the trading practices of the North West and Hudson's Bay Companies in the eighteenth and nineteenth centuries; anglophone Canadians, French Canadians, and Aboriginal peoples participated in the trade, and their work in the wilderness fundamentally influenced the composition of our institutions and community practices; and the fur trade laid the foundations of the transportation routes and settlements that remain important to present-day Canada, as well as inaugurating a tradition of recreational canoeing by which contemporary Canadians remain in touch with values of Lower's wilderness. This view of the fur trade emphasized its collaborative nature, in the process 'finessing' the issue of the disparities in power and status of indigenous peoples and French Canadians within Canada. It assumed the importance of private profit in the creation of the modern state and ignored those who conceived of economic development along other lines. And by advocating canoeing as a way of connecting both with history and the land, it both 'finessed' the awkward realities of the urbanization of Canada and the loss of undeveloped forest spaces and ignored the persistence of Aboriginal title and sovereignty.

For those Canadians who followed the progress of the Centennial Voyageur Canoe Pageant on television or in print media, participated in the associated events, or paddled along, the pageant functioned as what Anne McClintock calls in *Imperial Leather* a nationalist 'commodity spectacle.'[12] Discussing a 1938 re-enactment of the South African 'Great Trek,' McClintock argues that contemporary 'nationalism takes shape though the visible, ritual organization of fetish objects – flags, uniforms, airplane logos, maps, anthems, national flowers, national cuisine and architectures as well as through the organization of collective fetish spectacle – in team sports, military displays, mass rallies, the myriad forms of popular culture and so on' (374–5). The canoe originally functioned as a simple means to get from one place to another (sometimes the only means); however, since its economic use value has been diminished by the internal combustion engine, it has become an object, and a pastime, that is assumed to have meaning and significance in itself.[13] Because objects are material, and they seem to be literally a part of events in the real world, this materiality functions as a kind of alibi for, or 'proof' of, the reality of whatever symbolic meanings they accrue from being positioned in narratives, or myths. From this perspective, the material fact that the canoe has persisted as a means of transportation in some isolated communities, and remains widely used in recreational canoe-camping, is material proof of the mythic meanings of continuing Canadian independence, of the continuing cooperation and mutual respect of the 'three founding races' in the project of nation-building, and of the continuing importance of wilderness in Canadian society. Thus, like McClintock's re-enactment of the Great Trek, the Voyageur Canoe Pageant is an example of a state-sponsored spectacle designed to mobilize a commodity fetish in a ritual performance to 'create the illusion of collective identity' (373). The Canoe Pageant provided a model for the interpellation of thousands of Canadians as nation-builders through their participation in subsequent holiday trips that retraced the routes of the explorers by canoe. Historical discourses like those mobilized to explain and justify the Centennial Voyageur Canoe Pageant create subject positions that re-enacters are invited to take up and perform, not only for the limited period of the public event, but in their everyday lives. Up until 1967, it was possible to paddle an open canoe in Canada without being aware of the association of the canoe with patriotism; certainly after the Centennial Voyageur Canoe Pageant, it was not.

Charbonneau arranged an initial organizing meeting held on 14 May 1965 at the Fort Garry Hotel in Winnipeg; Morse was among those who attended, as was Bill Mason, well-known amateur canoeist and filmmaker. Copies of Morse's 1962 pamphlet, 'Canoe Routes of the Voyageurs: The Geography and Logistics of the Canadian Fur Trade,' were distributed to the provincial representatives (some provinces had sent 'commodores,' or team coaches, while others had sent civil servants representing their provincial centennial administrations), and the NFB film 'Les Voyageurs' was shown during the course of the two-day meeting. Mason had served as historical consultant and cameraman on 'Les Voyageurs'; according to James Raffan in his biography of Mason, Mason felt he 'knew everything about the voyageurs,' and one of his ambitions was to 'paddle the whole route.'[14] Committees were formed to advise on dress for the canoe race (chaired by Bill Mason, including Eric Morse), on the selection of an appropriate canoe (chaired by Morse, including Bill Mason), and on rules for the race (chaired by racing advocate John Nikel). To the extent that the race would become a historical re-enactment, its justification and ideology from the beginning was that of Innis's nationalist fur trade history and the work of amateur canoeist-historians like Morse, Lower, and Mason.

The race was initially to be funded by provincial and federal contributions centrally administered from Ottawa. This plan proved impractical, however: teams found the travel arrangements, equipment, and food provided for the 1965 trial run from North Bay to Gananoque inadequate, complaining that the dehydrated food was inedible and some of the supplies provided unsuitable for canoe travel. The final contract between the Centennial Commission and the participating provinces specified that each province was to select, train, and equip their team at their own expense, as well as contribute cash to a central fund, the amount to be determined by provincial population (for example, Ontario contributed $40,000, while Manitoba was asked for $15,000). The Centennial Commission was to organize and run the race, providing the canoes, a vehicle for each team, and the *per diems* and prize money for the participants. While subsidies above and beyond the *per diem* amounts were banned, in practice many of the participants, notably the provincial commodores or team coaches, were effectively paid to participate by being given paid leave from the provincial government jobs or by being hired by the provincial governments or centennial organizations to run their teams. John Nikel turned down the opportunity to become chief organizer of the race ('Gouverneur de la Route'), pointing out that he was already being paid more to be commodore of the Alberta team; Carl Monk of Ontario and John Murrant of New Brunswick were provincial government employees (Lands and Forests, and Youth, respectively). In addition to choosing, equipping, and training the teams, provincial centennial administrations committed to send teams to the trials held in 1965 and 1966, and to send representatives to participate in survey expeditions to explore and recommend the route. Some provinces also provided personnel for route navigation and safety; Ontario put its Lands and Forests personnel at the disposal of the pageant as soon as it crossed the provincial boundary.

The strong participation of the Lands and Forests ministry in Ontario underlines the way that personal relationships and a sort of old-boys network facilitated the administration of the race, and partly explains the wholehearted commitment of time and resources devoted to it by both federal and provincial centennial administrations. The deputy minister of Ontario's Lands and Forest ministry was G.H.U. 'Terk' Bayley, an avid canoeist who had undertaken a month-long wilderness trip with Eric Morse in 1965.[15] Bayley signed a ceremonial 'blanket permission' for the pageant to travel 'through the waters of Ontario.'[16] Sigurd Olson of Minnesota, a nature writer and former president of the American Parks Association, facilitated the passage of the canoe pageant across the border;[17] he was an alumnus of Morse's Voyageurs canoe group. Numerous civil servants who undertook to organize or publicize the race knew each other through their service in the Canadian army; the original 'Acting Chief Commodore,' Major-General Elliot Rodger, former Vice Chief of the General Staff and another friend of Morse, as well as the eventual Chief Voyageur, Colonel Bill Matthews, and the original race organizer, Major A.J. Charbonneau, were retired army officers. Many of the men who were in a position to facilitate, promote, or make decisions about funding the race were male, white, anglophone recreational canoeists, some of whom were friends and colleagues already, who already subscribed to the nationalist history that saw the voyageurs as 'the founders of Canada.'[18]

Yet the adoption of Morse's suggestion that the race become a re-enactment created practical problems with the administration of the event from the beginning. While the organizers and civil servants adopted and

promoted the race as a re-enactment of a pre-existing history and a dra-
matic 'pageant,' many of the participants were established canoe racers associated with boating and canoe clubs across Canada. Many of the
teams were made up from two-man canoe racing teams who had com-
peted against each other numerous times at established meets, and they
brought with them a testosterone-fuelled competitive ethic and a determination to beat the other teams.[19] Arnie Charbonneau, who by late
1965 was the head of the newly formed sports division of the Centennial
Commission, further confused things when he adopted the language of
boat racing from Tyson's proposal, identifying the team coaches as 'Provincial Commodores,' and race officials as 'Technical Commodore' and
'Head Timer.' The confusion over whether the event was a race or a pageant was evident as early as the trial held in the summer of 1965, when 'a
continuing dispute' arose over which portions of the route from North
Bay to Gananoque were to be timed. In reports written after the trial's
conclusion, Alberta Commodore John Nikel and Ontario Commodore
J.A. Mitchell mutually accused each other of being confused about the
aim of the trial: as Mitchell put it in his 'Commodore's Report' of 11 September 1965, 'Alberta had come to the trials prepared to race whereas
none of the other teams were prepared to do any more than follow the
route.'[20] For his part, Nikel complained in his 'Commodore's Report on
the 1965 Trial' that the Ontario team had decided 'that the entire trials
will be judged on four 1000-meter sprints' and that 'the policy of the
Ontario team was to take it as easy as possible during the daily laps but
to try to win the sprints' using their allegedly numerous spare paddlers.[21]
The Alberta team considered the slow pace of the trial to be an inadequate test of the paddlers and pulled away from the rest of the canoes
to reach Gananoque hours before the others. Mitchell concluded 'the
desirable blend of pageant and race seems to be the root of the problem.
Only after this fundamental agreement has been reached can Ontario
decide if participation in the 1967 Pageant is to be worth the expendi-
ture.'[22] The issue was again debated after the two trials held in the summer of 1966, the first from Fort St. James down the Fraser River and
across the Georgia Strait to Victoria from 6–15 August, and the second
from Lachine to New York City on 23–30 August. These trials were run
by Nikel as 'Technical Commodore' and Tyson as 'Chief Timer,' and the
western one, in particular, was marked by almost daily disputes about
alleged fouls (canoes running into each other), unmarked start and finish lines, and issues of right of way. At a Commodores' meeting held 6–8
October 1966 in Regina, the issue was raised at a round-table discussion

by the newly appointed head of the Canoe Pageant division of the Centennial Commission, Bill Matthews, who stressed that many of the small communities on the pageant route, as well as the provincial governments who were footing the bill, put more emphasis on a pageant. The provincial commodores were divided as to whether an all-out race for 3,300 miles would be safe, feasible, or desirable. They decided to stress the pageant aspect of the event, but the debate was far from over. Nikel wrote to Matthews in a letter dated 11 December 1966 that it would be a mistake to remove the race element, for the paddlers would not stay motivated without it: 'If you ruin the competitive aspect in the 1967 Pageant you will arrive with less than five teams in Montreal.'[23]

In practice, the tension between racing and pageantry was resolved by Matthews's meticulous organization of the 1967 event. A retired army colonel who had assisted Arnie Charbonneau in organizing the 1966 trials, Matthews created a detailed itinerary of each day's travel, based on the route surveys undertaken by paddlers from various provinces in 1965 and 1966. Each leg of the trip was designated a lap (a timed movement from point to point along a required course), a sprint (a short race on flat water before a crowd), a brigade (untimed travel from point to point in which the group stayed together for safety, usually on large bodies of water like Lakes Winnipeg and Superior), or a transit (untimed travel from point to point, during which crews could make their own way in their own time). Matthews organized a support crew of trucks, trailers, and spare paddlers, as well as safety boats contributed by the military, coast guard, and provincial lands and forests personnel. Each start line, finish line, and camp-site were specified, and an advance crew liaised with local organizers and identified laundry and shower facilities and grocery stores in the tiny communities along the route. Lists of local medical facilities were supplied, and the crews were assured that they would never be more than two days between hot showers. All of this information, along with lists of events along the route at which paddlers were expected to appear, was gathered together in a handbook distributed to each of the 'Chief Voyageurs' (as the provincial commodores were renamed). Even with these clear instructions, however, most of the teams failed to show up at their first major scheduled event, an official welcome to Edmonton by the premier of Alberta,[24] prompting Matthews to write a terse memo reminding the team coaches that the paddlers were expected to attend the organized public events.

Surprisingly, in the course of the debate between pageant and race, the question of historical authenticity never arose. While the race was

justified to funding agencies and publicized as an authentic re-enactment of the voyageurs' journey, the day-to-day operation of the event
was never put into this context. Crews might have cited evidence from
George Simpson that the real voyageurs did frequently 'race' for portions of their journey, challenging rival crews as a way of relieving the
monotony of daily travel; and certainly the historical voyageurs had to
reach distant goals before winter weather made travel by canoe impossible, and therefore 'raced' the weather. However, neither of these arguments seem to have been articulated by the participants, nor are they
recorded in extant documents. For the participants, the Voyageur Canoe
Pageant was definitely a present-day affair.

   Despite the participants' focus on racing (and winning), the promo-
tional material associated with the pageant consistently promoted the
race as a re-enactment of the founding of Canada as a nation. This interpretation is reiterated in the records of the pageant from start to finish,
from letters sent to the provinces in 1964–1965 designed to solicit their
participation in this national event, to the publicity material distributed
by the Centennial Commission during the race itself. Charbonneau's
initial proposal designated the voyageurs 'the founders of Canada.' A
'Centennial Report ' signed by Centennial Commissioner John Fisher
refers to Morse's 'Canoe Routes of the Voyageurs' to argue that 'as
much history can be learned from a canoe as from a history book': by
'follow[ing] in the wake of voyageurs and fur traders along the early
inland waterways,' the pageant 'will remind us how some of our colourful pioneers travelled and developed the early economy of Canada.'[25]
The publicity pamphlet distributed during the pageant in 1967 declared
that the voyageurs 'were all brave men of vision' who by participating in
the fur trade helped 'create Canada.' An article that appeared in *Hunting and Fishing in Canada* in March 1966, in the run-up to the pageant,
declared that the canoe was 'The Boat that Built Canada,' and the voyageurs the men who built it. It attributed Canada's independence from
the US to the 'abundance of waterways [that run] in general, east and
west' and to the opportunities they offered for commercial trade.[26] The
status of the race as a re-enactment was emphasized at key geographical
locations with ceremonial and public re-creations of the rituals of the fur
trade. At Rocky Mountain House, the race began as Secretary of State
Judy LaMarsh stood before a one-dimensional mock-up of a trading post
(dubbed 'Fort Facade' by the press and the paddlers)[27] at the site of the
original Rocky Mountain House and charged the race participants with
a reproduction of a fur trade era 'licence' containing their instructions.

At the Height of Land Portage, each of the paddlers was initiated with a sprinkle of water from a cedar branch and a drink, in imitation of the traditional Height of Land ceremony, while logger and BC paddler Harry Schwartz shinnied up a tree and lopped off its lower branches to create a monumental lobstick in honour of Minnesota fur-trade historian Grace Lee Nute. As the pageant arrived at the Expo site in Montreal, the paddlers presented their 'licence' to their *Gouverneur*, Judy LaMarsh, along with a beaver hat and a buffalo robe fashioned into a cape, which she modelled for the cameras.

The publicity and descriptive material is explicit about what kind of meanings these re-enactments were supposed to signify. The essential and explicit meaning is continuity through time and through space, a theme asserted in the discourse of the pageant in three aspects: continuity of the 'voyageur' as subject position, continuity of the land as wilderness, and continuity of the geographical and political nation as Canada. The publicity materials define the voyageur as a person marked by stamina, adventurousness, strength, initiative, and hard work, and they suggest that 'we' as Canadians are the same people as the voyageurs – 'we' share with them the qualities necessary to build a nation. In this material, gender, race, ethnicity, and class have no place; the fact that the workforce in those voyageur canoes was differentiated hierarchically,[28] or that most voyageurs were of indigenous or Metis origin, is not mentioned. The Centennial Report issued by Commissioner John Fisher claims the voyageurs as 'our forefathers'[29] without accounting for the discrepancy that allows a white man (or woman) to (metaphorically) claim indigenous and mixed-race ancestry for Canada, and for all Canadians.

All of the press materials stress that the modern-day voyageurs would face the same conditions as their historical models: the land is the same place that was visited by the historic voyageurs and, the publicity materials claim, is an isolated wilderness space 'still untouched by civilization.'[30] Bill Matthews is quoted in a press release asserting that the race required 'a unique combination of stamina, endurance and courage as the paddlers will face difficulties similar to those encountered by their predecessors.'[31] Centennial Commissioner John Fisher's Centennial Report emphasized challenges faced by the voyageurs, both then and now: 'This includes portages over slimy rocks, up mountain sides – lifting their canoes and heavy loads of equipment – sleeping outdoors – soaked hundreds of times – tired, worried, stormbound; plagued by black flies.'[32] An article in the *Cariboo Observer* suggested that the Canoe Pageant participants faced 'the same treacherous rapids, backbending portages, drenching rains and thunderstorms, blackflies and four-engine mosquitoes as did the ancient ones.'[33] However, the theme of the continuity of the land was also subject to contradiction and subversion. While the publicity materials asserted that the land was still untouched wilderness, the participants had been assured by Bill Matthews that they would never be more than two nights from a hot shower. Press coverage of the route included an article about the necessary release of water from Squaw Rapids dam by the Saskatchewan Power Company; the Saskatchewan River had been dammed in order to provide water for the generation of hydroelectric power, and the reduced flow was not adequate for navigation, even by canoe.[34]

The race was also supposed to demonstrate the geographical continuity of the land, according to the press materials. This continuity was indicated simply by reiterating the fact of the extreme length of the race in almost all of the publicity materials.[35] Accounts of the challenges presented by portages demonstrated how this continuity had been created by overcoming the geographic barriers between watersheds. The pageant also offered evidence of cooperation among administrative and political jurisdictions. A ceremony was held at the border of each province, symbolically passing jurisdiction over the race from province to province, emphasizing the permeability of these barriers as well as their contiguity. However, no one mentioned that historically very few canoes ever travelled the entire route from Rocky Mountain house to Montreal in a single season. At the height of the North West Company trade into the interior, the route was divided at the start of the Grand Portage: there the crews of the 36-foot *canots de maître* travelling from Montreal would hand their cargo over to a crew of winterers and return to Montreal; winterers, who had come to the portage from the interior, would hand over their furs, load up with trade goods, and return to their posts before freeze-up. Only on the rare occasions when someone was travelling from Montreal to a permanent posting in the interior would they continue their journey past the Grand Portage; even in such cases, travellers would usually disembark from the larger canoes designed for the Ontario route and continue in the smaller North Canoe. In other words, both the geographical and historical continuity asserted by the Voyageur Canoe Pageant was flawed in practice.

The canoes themselves also disrupted the illusion of historical continuity. They were made of fibreglass and specifically constructed for the race, containing two seats and four thwarts to facilitate the way the six paddlers changed sides. Canvas and cedar canoes constructed by the

Trying out the Chestnut canoes on the Ottawa River, 1965. Bow to stern:
Eric Morse, Blair Fraser, Marcel Joyal, Michael Redford, Arnie Charbonneau,
Rene Bellemare. Reproduced in *Fur Trade Canoe Routes of Canada,
Then and Now* by Eric Morse.

Chestnut Canoe Company were ordered for the trials, but they were
immediately deemed inadequate; they not only increased in weight during the course of the trial as the wood swelled with water, but the seats
broke during use.[36] Fibreglass canoes were chosen to replace them, for
ease of repair and durability, and an order was placed for canoes built
using the discarded Chestnuts as forms. Birch-bark canoes such as the
actual voyageurs paddled were never considered.

The most important symbolic representation of chronological con-
tinuity was the naming of the canoes themselves after canonical explor-
ers associated with the home province of each team. The names selected
were as follows: Northwest Territories: Sir Alexander Mackenzie; Yukon:
Robert Campbell; British Columbia: Simon Fraser; Alberta: David
Thompson; Saskatchewan: Henry Kelsey; Manitoba: Pierre Radisson;
Ontario: William McGillivray; Quebec: La Verendrye; New Brunswick:
Samuel de Champlain; Nova Scotia: John Cabot. These names signal

the way that the pageant conflated the subject position of the voyageur
with the explorer, despite the differing class and racialized status of each.
Certainly not all of the explorers chosen were English-speaking, and they
were not all members of the elite in their home cultures. However, positioned as the leaders of their expeditions, or even as the forerunners of
the Canadian state (as they were in the pageant narrative), they were not
mere voyageurs, either. The naming allowed each province to 'own' their
explorer; although these men actually travelled through unceded First
Nations territories, their names were mobilized by the pageant to legitimate and naturalize provincial boundaries.

Despite the evidence that paddlers of First Nations and mixed-race
ancestry dominated the position of voyageur in the fur trade, no effort
was made to recruit teams that represented First Nations. Indeed, representation according to racial/ethnic or cultural community was not
a priority in recruiting paddlers, as indeed it was not a perceived cultural priority at all in 1967. In Manitoba, as in other provinces with an
active canoe-racing scene, paddlers were chosen by the team captain
based on points awarded for competing on the largely white two-man
canoe-racing circuit.[37] Those Metis and First Nations paddlers who did
participate (notably Roger Carrière of Cranberry Portage, an almost
legendary figure in northern Manitoba and Saskatchewan who regularly
won 'trapper' competitions as well as canoe races, and his paddling partner Joe Michelle) participated as representatives of their provinces, not
as representatives of ethnic, racial, cultural, or reserve communities. The
effect of subsuming the indigenous identities of these paddlers under
the provincial banner was, again, to naturalize the political divisions of
present-day Canada and to symbolically convey the legitimacy of Canadian sovereignty. In contrast, the 2005 Saskatchewan Canoequest held
in honour of Saskatchewan's centenary featured teams named for their
indigenous and Metis communities. These teams claimed the canoe
routes themselves, and the landscapes through which they travelled,
as the territories of their own ancestors, specifically de-legitimizing the
idea that the routes originated with the fur trade, or were even primarily
important because of their fur trade history.[38] While many First Nations
paddlers have taken up the legacy of the Voyageur Canoe Pageant by
organizing and participating in subsequent canoe journeys, these have
been re-signified as part of a community healing process and as a strategy for continuing to assert Aboriginal sovereignty, and specifically not
about national (that is, Canadian) identity.

The assumption of First Nations identities under the rubric of provincially organized canoe teams was only one element of the general way that the pageant reiterated the colonial relationship between First Nations and Canada. At The Pas, the paddlers re-enacted the erecting of a cross by Henry Kelsey in 1691 (though because of confusion about their arrival time, no crowd was there to watch). While this event signalled the founding of their town for the residents of The Pas, another meaning of the ritual is implicit: the re-enactment of the appropriation of the lands and natural resources belonging to First Nations and the initiation of cultural genocide. The canoe pageant might be interpreted as signifying not any specific event from the past, but the continuing enactment in the present of Euro-Canadian domination. In Lac du Bonnet, a member of the Quebec team re-enacted a local legend that the explorer La Verendrye named the community by throwing his hat in a tree and kissing 'an Indian princess named Minnewawa.'[39] This re-enactment symbolically claims and names First Nations territory, reinforcing this action by playing out the stereotypical gender roles of conquest and appropriation.

In contrast to the provincial teams, the Yukon and Northwest Territories teams were made up mainly of First Nations paddlers, and their presence revealed the fractures and absences of the popularized version of Canada that the pageant promoted. The most important was the charge of racism levelled by the original commodore of the NWT team, Father Brown, over his team's experiences at the 1965 trial. In a written submission bristling with a sense of insult and offence, Father Brown recounted the racism his team endured during their trip. He stated in his 'Commodore's Report on the NWT Team's Participation in the Eastern Trials of the Centennial Canoe Pageant during August 1965'[40] that despite having confirmed seats booked by the Centennial Commission in Ottawa, when he arrived with his team members to board the airplane in Edmonton he was told there would be no seats available. After some argument, the group was flown to Toronto, where again the team was denied access to previously booked seats on the flight to North Bay and in desperation decided to take the train. Father Brown recounted that the team members were picked out of the line-up waiting to board the CN Dayliner and escorted to seating in a rear car (an older coach without reclining seats), where they were told that they would not be allowed to enter the smoking car (the car where alcohol was being served) and if they wanted to smoke they could get off the train at a scheduled stop and smoke on the platform. Their problems did not stop when they arrived in North Bay: team members used to a traditional diet wanted fresh fish to eat, and while like the other teams they were prepared to catch them, they were used to nets and were not prepared to use the fishing rods supplied by the Commission. During the re-enactment portions of the race, team members were offended by comments made by municipal officials, in particular a speech given by Mayor Post of Orillia in which she recounted playing the part of an 'Indian Maiden' in the re-enactment of Champlain's arrival. Father Brown recounted the response of his paddlers to the mayor's speech: 'See that white woman over there? She shook the hand of Champlain when he arrived, but she was a squaw then.'[41]

Documents in the archives show that CN Rail categorically denied any racism;[42] in a contradictory move, the CPR granted paid leave to Roger Carrière, who was a CPR sub-foreman, declaring their pride in his career as a paddler.[43] Father Brown resigned as commodore and was replaced by Jack Adderley. But instead of recognizing the First Nations paddlers as simply Canadians, the exoticizing discourse of race tended to dominate press coverage of the Yukon and Northwest Territories teams. When the paddlers arrived in New York City at the end of the 1966 trial from Lachine, the New York press focused their coverage on the real 'Eskimos and Indians' among the group and photographed them eating ice cream (presumably intending an ironic joke on 'Eskimos' and the cold).[44]

Relations between the pageant participants and staff and First Nations peoples seem to have been marked by anxiety. Pageant staff were warned to provide security for paddlers and their effects when camping on the Duck Bay Reserve: in a letter to Bill Matthews dated 4 April 1967, Ken Ouellette, the regional liaison officer for Manitoba, warned that 'Duck Bay is an Indian Reservation, and a very rough one, I spoke to a couple of Mounties in the area and they said that it would be advisable for the Voyageurs to stick right by their tents and equipment at all times while they are in Duck Bay. The reason for this is that there could be a fair amount of vandalism should this equipment not be watched closely.'[45] Some First Nations participated in local events welcoming the pageant to their communities; notably, Chief Richard Malloway of the Skwah First Nation welcomed the participants in the 1966 trial when they arrived at Minto Landing in Chilliwack after being guided in by the Skwah Reserve Canoe Club, headed by Burn Mussel. While the press called this a re-enactment of Simon Fraser's arrival in 1808, Fraser had actually arrived downstream at the present location of the Skwah Reserve. This change of venue was significant; the Skwah Reserve was not considered an appropriate place to welcome the voyageurs, even if historically accurate, and the community of the Skwah First Nation as a whole did not take part. The cursory level of participation seems even more marked as the Skwah First Nation has a longstanding tradition of canoe racing and has had a canoe club, paddling dugout racing canoes, since the 1900s.[46]

The roles of women in the founding of the nation were similarly elided, not just by the history that determined that the nation was founded by voyageurs (which notoriously ignored the important role of First Nations women as guides and interpreters in the fur trade, as well as alternative narratives in which women might have figured more centrally), but also by the administration of the pageant itself. Not only were women excluded from becoming paddlers, but, incredibly, they were specifically barred from jobs as 'stenos' (typists and clerical staff) for the pageant by vote of the provincial commodores.[47] Anne McClintock points out that women are typically represented in discourses of nationalism as guardians of purity and the domestic hearth, static and essentialized in contrast to dynamic and progressive masculine agency; women's involvement with the pageant was almost entirely limited to feeding and providing support for the paddlers.[48] The Centennial Commission publicity staff even solicited recipes from the volunteer cooks for the food the paddlers ate along the way and contributed to an article by food editor Helen Gagen in the *Toronto Telegram* on how to create an authentic voyageur meal.

The exception to the almost complete exclusion of women from central roles in the Pageant was the honouring of Minnesota fur trade historian Grace Lee Nute at the re-enactment of the 'Height of Land' ceremony. However, the documents make it clear that the priority for the pageant organizers was that a lobstick should be created at this ceremony; the spectacle of a paddler (or paddlers) climbing a tree and removing most of the branches by hand, creating an enduring landmark, was too crowd-and-press pleasing to pass up. A lobstick was supposed to honour a single individual; the commission staff wracked their brains for a suitable individual who would guarantee to attend the ceremony. Centennial Commissioner John Fisher and other race officials were considered for the honour. Grace Lee Nute, as an American and one of the first historians to write popular books about the voyageurs, was eventually chosen in order to appeal to the local crowd from the US border town of Ely, Minnesota. Her gender was not a factor in the choice.

The unity that the pageant was supposed to signify also broke down over language. The Official Languages Act would not become law until 1969: not surprisingly, 'most of the Centennial staff in Ottawa was not bilingual.'[49] The original project officer, A.J. Charbonneau, was; he had been involved, while an officer in the Canadian military, in efforts to recruit francophone soldiers and in programs to teach English to potential officer candidates to prepare them to function in an English-speaking command structure.[50] However, Charbonneau was promoted to head of the Sports Division, and his replacements, Chief Voyageur Bill Matthews and Project Officer Vic Chapman, were not bilingual. In a letter to Quebec provincial representative Simon-Pierre Rainville dated 1 mai 1967, Matthews recognized the Quebec team's anxiety about being understood during the race and promised that all safety staff would be bilingual. Another letter from Matthews, dated 26 April 1967, apologizes for his inability to have the operating manual translated in time for the race. A letter from Chapman accompanies 'a brief on canoes' in English, apologizing because an incompetent French translation had caused 'misunderstanding.'[51]

For many Canadians, as for many of the race participants, the Centennial Voyageur Canoe Pageant was an emotional high, a participatory moment in which they sensed themselves to be part of something bigger, something meaningful that was symbolized not only in the race itself but also in all of the events of the centennial year. Margery Fee's analysis of the function of representations of Native peoples in Canadian literature provides an interesting way to account for the emotional force of the canoe as a Canadian myth. Fee identifies a common narrative pattern in contemporary Canadian writing, whereby a white Canadian 'is confused and impelled by a strong desire to know more about the past: personal, familial, native or national.'[52] This crisis of belonging, or of identity, is resolved though an encounter with an object or person associated with indigenous people. 'This resolution is often a quasi mystical vision of or identification with, Natives'; frequently an indigenous person, figured as a ghost or ancestor, passes on an artefact or object that symbolically figures the protagonist as the legitimate inheritor of the land. The protagonist positions himself within a narrative of Canadian identity that includes indigenous cultures as the ancestral cultures of modern-day Canada. Through this narrative trope, Fee argues, Canadian literary works resolve issues of reconciliation with the past and naturalize white Canada's 'appropriation of their land' (24) while avoiding the vexed problem of justice for actual, present-day indigenous communities. The Centennial Voyageur Canoe Pageant performed a similar function of naturalizing Canada's land claim though an encounter with the canoe, enacting a narrative of Canadian 'nation-building' that figures First

Nations as willing partners in an economic enterprise that specifically prefigured the Canadian state and subsumed their cultures under the banner of Canadian nationality.

As Fee reminds us, the ideology of romantic nationalism 'was used to support the argument that [rulers] should come from a local elite rather than a foreign aristocracy' (17–18). The 'ideology of the canoe' did not arise naturally or neutrally from the events of the past, but was created and promulgated in part by a group of Anglo-Canadian men in positions of power in government and other public organizations, operating through their friendships and through the institutions of academic history, recreational infrastructure, and government-sponsored public spectacle, as part of an ideological project to promote a hegemonic unity in Canada and to position the Canadian state as the legitimate sovereign power within a specific geography enclosed by political borders. Within the historical moment of the Centennial year, and extending beyond it, this project was understood to be an anti-colonial one, one that opposed the political and economic domination of Canada by foreign powers by asserting its historical roots, its unity, and its legitimacy as a nation. However, in retrospect it is easy to see how it also functioned to secure the power of local elites and subsumed indigenous cultures under the banner of continuing white privilege. As McClintock writes, 'fetishes embody crises in social value, which are projected onto and embodied in, what can be called impassioned objects.'[53] The object that Daniel Francis identifies as representing the Anglo-Canadian desire for unity with the land, the fetishized canoe, continues to obscure the gap between settler-invader culture and the legitimate rights of First Nations, disguising their incommensurability by evoking the vagueness and emotional force of myth.

Chapter Five

Reading/ Writing the Wilderness Canoe Trip

from a canoe the landscape is always rising. You paddle flooded folds in the surface
of the Earth, in a quest for closure, the completion of a line to be sketched across the
lowest courses of encountered terrain. But the landscape is prophetic; in its contours,
your journey is predetermined. You follow, rapt in romance; the land does not follow
you. On a map, you run the lines from noun to noun, as you extend the boundaries
of the landscape you imagine traveling.

John Moss.[1]

In *Enduring Dreams* John Moss suggests the ways that a canoe trip and
reading/writing about a canoe trip are activities that overlap and inter-
penetrate. Both follow an inevitable route: the 'folds in the surface of
the earth' that all waterways must follow are like the discursive pathways
in the cultural landscape that make stories possible. Both predict their
own ends; paddler and reader, action and story are rapt/wrapped in the
romance plot that leads inevitably towards closure, the completion of the
trip/story. Neither paddler nor reader can choose direction once the
trip has been initiated: 'You follow … the land does not follow you.' Just
as the paddler traces the route on a map, the reader progresses 'from
noun to noun,' both 'extend[ing] the boundaries of the landscape
[they] imagine travelling.'

In the spring of 1926, three men loaded up a 20-foot Chestnut canoe
and put in to the Athabasca river at Waterways. One was John Hornby,
an English trapper and adventurer who had lived and travelled for some
years in the North; the others were his 17-year-old nephew, Edgar Christian, and a young British war veteran, Harold Adlard. The group told
their friends they intended to paddle to the eastern end of Great Slave

Lake and ascend Pike's Portage to Artillery Lake and the Casba River, up the Hanbury and down the Thelon. They paddled into the Barrens, and they didn't come out. The story of John Hornby has haunted both writers about the North and wilderness canoe trippers since the bodies of Hornby and his companions were discovered by a party of prospectors in a cabin on the Thelon River in 1928. Despite Hornby's experience as a hunter and outdoorsman, the group had starved to death; their last few months were documented in a pathetically short and naive diary left in the cabin by Edgar Christian, which was published ten years after his death.

The diary and the story it adumbrates have inspired multiple literary treatments: Malcolm Waldron's *Snow Man*, published in 1931; George Whalley's *The Legend of John Hornby*, published in 1962; a radio play by Whalley broadcast in 1966; a novel written in 1976, also called *Snowman*, by Thomas York; the 1993 stage play *Who Look in Stove* by Lawrence Jeffrey; *Out of the Whirlwind*, a literary fiction by M.T. Kelly in 1995; a nonfiction adventure book, *Cold Burial*, by Clive Powell-Williams (2003); and most recently, Elizabeth Hay's Giller Award-winning novel, *Late Nights on Air* (2007).[2] These literary retellings of Hornby's journey occupy the liminal space between two of Beverly Haun-Moss's motivations for canoeing, those of conquest and of submission to the land. Waldron and Powell-Williams describe a Hornby who wants to conquer, to live in, the masculinist North, where physical endurance and strength ensure survival, and to go down in the history books as the 'first white man to …' Whalley, York, and Jeffrey create a Hornby who submits to the land, who lives and dies according to its dictates, and who feels an uncanny emotional affinity for the Barren Grounds. What makes these interpretations of Hornby's life and death compelling is the way these characterisations blend into each other: the conquering Hornby is on the verge of madness, and the Hornby who is rapt by the mystery of the Barrens is also the leader who risks all for some kind of fame. Numberless parties of canoeists have retraced Hornby's trip, making the pilgrimage to see the three wooden crosses, the ruined cabin, the axe-marked trees, and the hunting blind that mark the spot where the three men died. The texts that retell his story are literally haunted by their foregone conclusions, by the ghosts of Hornby, Adelard, and Christian. What are those who retrace his journey looking for? And what do they find? Each of these retellings is a map that charts the cathexis of desire for the land, for rootedness, that Hornby represents; like the son in Margaret Atwood's 'Death of a Young Son by Drowning,' his body is planted in the Barren Grounds 'like a flag.'

John Hornby in 1919. Courtesy of Library and Archives Canada, PA-213986.

These treatments share little enough: merely a series of documented events with no obvious meaning. Christian's primitive diary conveys his British 'Boy's Own' world-view as pathetically inadequate to the eventual circumstances of his death, but only suggests motives, relationships, histories, significances, and his is the only written record of the trip. John Moss speculates that it is the very lack of information, the lack of an *explanation* for what happened, that makes the events of Hornby's life and death so compelling for wilderness travellers and wilderness writers. 'It is the words that Hornby did not write, did not publish, the account he neglected to offer of himself and the harrowing years in a wilderness he embraced with ferocity ... it is his absence of voice that makes Hornby's vision the ineluctable limit for others, writing of their own adventures to the edges of the same terrain' (56). Hayden White points out that a satisfying story requires a 'social center by which to locate [events] in respect to one another and to charge them with ethical or moral significance.'[3] This is what the Hornby story lacks, and what each writer and reteller, what each paddler who retraces Hornby's trip, creates. Writers, readers, and paddlers, compelled along a predetermined route towards an inevitable ending, in each retelling find a new way to give meaning to the series of events that led to the three wooden crosses, the ruined cabin, the axe-marked trees, and the caribou blind on the Thelon River.

Malcolm Waldron's book *Snow Man: John Hornby in the Barren Lands* (1931) is a popular account of Hornby's life cobbled together from the diary and notes written by James C. Critchell-Bullock, a fellow Englishman who had spent the winter of 1923–4 trapping with Hornby at the east end of Artillery Lake. Critchell-Bullock had intended to write Hornby's biography, but in the end turned his material over to Waldron, a professional writer. The resulting book appeared three years after the deaths of Hornby and his companions had been front page news in Canada, and the version of Hornby's character it articulates stands in the shadow of those deaths.

Waldron's Hornby is driven by the easily understood motive of masculine competition: he wishes to 'outdo all others in the Barrens.'[4] He proposes the trip to Artillery Lake in order to 'be the first white men ever to winter in the Barrens' (17): Hornby declares the Barrens are 'virgin! I can name on the fingers the men who have really penetrated beyond the timber. Most of the country is unexplored. Most of it no man has seen' (16). Hornby persuades Critchell-Bullock to accompany him by implying he is too soft for the trip. C-B angrily replies, 'you think I'm just another one of those damned remittance men' (20) and immediately commits to accompany Hornby. Hornby's competitive spirit is an aspect of his overwhelming masculinity, along with his strength, endurance and energy. Hornby is 'a man so much a man,' (11) writes Waldron, that he can portage 90-pound packs on his 5'4", 140-pound frame and jog barefoot in the snow. Hornby's 'astonishing energy and virility' (290) are the basis of his biography, Waldron declares, and he praises 'the unconquerable and boundless spirit of the man, that spark that lived behind his eyes, and drove him on to feats that have become legend. That was his glory' (288).

Waldron's *Snow Man* is the source of the eccentric theory of starvation attributed to Hornby in most of the subsequent written accounts of his life. Waldron's Hornby argues that starving people in cities cannot properly be said to be starving: 'An incompetent, languishing in civilization for lack of food or money to buy it, is really not starving at all. He is merely dying for want of nourishment. Starving is an active, not passive, process' (230–1). Hornby challenges C-B by declaring that 'Starving is a luxury reserved to a few' (230) and that perhaps Critchell-Bullock is among the lucky few who 'can be taught' (11). In Waldron's book, C-B accompanies Hornby partly to obtain such uncomfortable knowledge and partly to prove himself worthy of it.

Waldron's Hornby is driven by a kind of misanthropy to find a spiritual home in the Barren Grounds. According to Waldron, Hornby had 'an infatuation for snow' (6) and only truly felt at peace when he had glimpsed 'Back's chimneys' at Reliance, the historic landmark that showed the canoe route into the Barrens (42). Summing up Hornby's life, Waldron writes: 'Hornby and the Barrens were inseparable. Without the Barrens there could have been no Hornby. The lone lands were his life and his love' (287). The misanthropy Waldron describes derives from the turn-of-the-century ideology of the 'New Romantics,' who rejected the city as artificial and feminized. Waldron's Hornby contemptuously declares that he will not go back to 'civilization': 'Back where the man with the cleanest shirt is the most respected' (278), back where strength of mind and body have no value. In contrast, he appreciates the way that the Barrens force him to concentrate on essentials rather than ephemeral social rituals: 'I can wake up in the morning here and know I have no troubles beyond keeping alive' (53). For Waldron, Hornby's love of the Barrens is less a psychological state than a physical one, a craving for freedom, independence, challenges, and triumphs, in short, the desire for a field upon which to exercise his masculinity. 'For Hornby's dream was simple. To be alone, with Nature at her bleakest; to roam with the wind, and be as free; to seek hardship as other men seek comfort, and for the same reason' (287).

Waldron's assessment of Hornby's character and the meaning of his fatal canoe trip was too Victorian to be fully convincing even in 1931; more typical of the modernist treatments of the story are Whalley's and Jeffrey's, which both in their different ways find the starvation deaths of Hornby and his companions meaningless and almost trivial. George Whalley's biography of Hornby is one of the great texts of Canadian modernism, neglected perhaps by literary scholars so far because it is non-fiction. But it is well worth critical attention: beautifully written and meticulously researched, with a characteristic and approachable narrative voice. The book evokes and modifies some of the major themes of modernism – order and chaos, madness, meaninglessness, and the redemptive power of art – and represents them though a uniquely Canadian form of the modernist quest: the one-way canoe trip. It is also a succinct demonstration of Whalley's theories of the creation and function of symbol in literature. The book self-consciously situates itself within a historically limited but important critical discourse – 'myth criticism' – and gives substance and specificity to the casual way we talk about myths of the North and of nationality.

Whalley was an eminent professor of Romantic literature at Queen's University in Kingston who specialized in the Romantic poetic process and the works of Coleridge and Yeats. A poet himself, Whalley was described by his friends as a 'renaissance man': he was a professor, writer, musician, recreational canoeist, and former Navy intelligence officer, involved with the Boy Scouts and interested in northern exploration. In *The Legend of John Hornby*, he set out, on the one hand, to debunk the myth of the North, carefully challenging the idea of heroic endurance for the noble love of Queen and country, and to create a figure who conformed instead to the image of the despairing and aimless modern man whose basic lack of conviction makes him fundamentally unable to summon the strength of the Victorians to 'strive, to seek, to find, and not to yield.' Yet Whalley also strove to represent Hornby as a mythic figure, using the techniques and the motivations he had detailed in his recently published study of the poetic imagination, *Poetic Process* (1957); for Whalley, Hornby was mythic in the sense that he represented something chaotic and empty at the heart of the human soul.

Two recent books that address the idea of myth in representations of the North are Sherrill Grace's *Canada and the Idea of North* (2001) and Renee Hulan's *Northern Experience and the Myths of Canadian Culture*

(2002). Both of these books provide an interesting context for a reading of *The Legend of John Hornby*. Grace's comprehensive survey of representations of the North identifies the common theme of 'the North
as a place of extremity and masculine adventure': 'the North is a place
that men go to escape what they believe women represent: the comfort
of home, civilization, safety, and boredom — in short, the feminine.'[5]
Grace's North is an ironized version of Waldron's, and her assessment of
Hornby is very like his; Hornby wanted to 'conquer the barrens,' but was
prevented by tragic chance, a 'fatal mistake' in calculation: 'the caribou
did not pass by the cabin that year; the spring came late, and one by one
the men died' (286n29). Hulan's book addresses myth as national ideology: she suggests that evocations of the 'myth of the north' 'focus on the
nordicity of national identity as part of a broader tendency in Canadian
cultural history that seeks to unify and shape collective experience and,
in so doing, to smooth over differences.'[6] While she does not specifically
comment on the Hornby story, her approach focuses on what these stories have in common, the fact of the predominance of stories of the North
in the creation of a nationalist narrative, rather than on the complexities
of an individual representation. In general, she concurs with Grace on
the way the North is represented as 'a place of extremity and masculine
adventure.'

In contrast, *The Legend of John Hornby* seems at first to self-consciously
depart from these representations of the myth of North in order to
debunk the idea of heroic adventure in unpopulated places. Like the
New Romantics and the paddlers described by William Closson James,[7]
Hornby may have run away into the North to get away from a civilization
he though of as tainted, but Whalley points out in the very first line of
the book that the person who runs away to the wilderness to find solitude
or emptiness is merely foolish. 'Fifty or sixty years ago, a man travelling
by canoe and on foot in the North-west territories could be certain of
very little except that wherever he went others had been before.'[8] Even
as early as 1904, a traveller who ventured beyond Fort Resolution 'had
moved into the company of people as yet unknown to him although ...
they already knew about him' (1). In Whalley's book, Hornby runs away
to a place that is everywhere marked with the evidence of human habitation, and in which he is necessarily required to live in close quarters with
the travelling companions he seemed to despise and wish to evade. Place
names, portages, abandoned cabins, camp-sites – all represented evidence of human habitation and should have demonstrated to him that
'with luck, a man might survive; with skill – which is perhaps the logic

of luck – he might be comfortable and live long' (1). Hulan points out that the word myth not only signifies 'a story that articulates a particular world view,' but also 'an untruth, or false notion' (3), and Whalley sets out to suggest that the myth of the North is just that – an invention, a construction, a lie.

Whalley wrote in an essay that what attracted him to Hornby's story was 'the kind of experience it implied rather than expressed; a sense of high adventure ineluctably decaying into desolation and perplexity.'⁹ He begins, as his title suggests, by considering the legend of John Hornby as legend; he gives the details of Hornby's arrival in the Edmonton area in 1904, the educated younger son of an upper-class British family, and his initial employment as a packer, trapper, and guide. The legend 'is mostly to do with Hornby's feats of strength and endurance' and partly to do with his eccentric behaviour: Hornby habitually travelled miles over mountain trails at a jog-trot, and once ran '100 miles from Edmonton to Athabaska Landing in under twenty-four hours for a wager of a bottle of rum' (7). He was also solitary, taciturn, and refused to travel with any man who had brown eyes. He 'lived like an Indian,' said Whalley's sources, and departed for a winter alone in the bush with little more than a gun, an axe and a sack of flour; he knew more about the country and the game animals than any one other than the native inhabitants, and yet with all his experience and knowledge, he starved to death. 'I knew there was a Hornby myth in the North,' writes Whalley; 'Stefansson for one had said so' (3), and Whalley dutifully recounts the verifiable and the fantastic, pointing out that 'heroic elaboration of the truth is one of the chief forms of emotional release in the North, and a good story travels quickly and has a long life' (8). The book begins with the project of gently debunking these myths, seeming to put in their place 'the real Hornby,' the result of careful scholarly research and judicious sifting of fact from exaggeration.

Whalley has written that he did not want to do anything as simplistic as to represent Hornby as an 'anti-hero': to do so, he thought, would be to prejudge the complex issues that arise from Hornby's life. Instead, he wanted to 'withhold judicious comment – the curse of the omniscient – about the only things that matter: if they matter they cannot be fully known or categorically stated; they can only be allowed to come before our attention in their full complexity and in their just simplicity.'¹⁰ The only explanation that Whalley claims he can offer for Hornby's death is the patient accumulation of the facts he had derived from his research, free of the moralizing omniscient interpretations that he calls 'the curse' of fiction. The resulting book, appropriately, conforms to Frye's mythos of winter, stressing 'the humanity of its heroes, minimiz[ing] the sense of ritual inevitability in tragedy, suppl[ying] social and psychological explanations for catastrophe, and mak[ing] as much as possible of human misery seem, in Thoreau's phrase, "superfluous and evitable." This is the phase of most sincere, explicit realism,' according to Frye.[11]

In place of the intrusions of an omniscient narrator, Whalley offers a technique he calls 'naming,' a process he describes as 'evocatively, rehearsing with liturgical care and reiteration those things felt, touched, with the sense, remembered.' He compares this technique to the discourse of lovers, who have created between themselves an alphabet of symbols and allusions 'already intimately and uniquely known between them' that, because of their familiarity, 'call back into felt reality moments of heightened recognition and profound feeling.'[12] In this way *The Legend of John Hornby* creates its own intrinsic system of symbols in the manner of the imaginative poetry Whalley had analysed in *Poetic Process.*

Whalley believed that symbols constituted a kind of 'alphabet of human experience' held in common by all human beings and that 'The same clusters of images tend to persist simply because man is constituted as he is and is embedded in a Nature which has not altered substantially within human memory.'[13] Myth is 'an articulated structure of symbol or narrative,' 'primitive, communal and religious in origin' and therefore 'an indispensable principle of unity in individual lives and in the life of society.' A successful symbol evokes in the reader an 'incredulous sense of recognition – "almost," as Keats says, "a Remembrance,"' though this 'remembrance' is not created by distance in time, but rather it suggests the sense of wholeness and inevitability that the symbol creates through its evocation of a whole pattern of previous usages and meanings (169).

Strangely enough, for a book that focuses on men escaping the domestic, one of the most evocative of the pairs of symbols Whalley creates are two shelters that Hornby frequented at different times in his life. The first was a cabin built in 1911 by the Douglas brothers, George and Lionel, whom Hornby travelled with in 1912. Built with a combination of skill and deliberation, the Douglas house at Hodgson point on Great Bear Lake was infused with the love and respect of the brothers for each other, and with the sense of order and discipline that Whalley associates with their common background in the British Navy. Set in contrast is Hornby's 'cave,' the shelter dug into a gravelly esker on the shore of Artillery Lake that he shared with Critchell-Bullock in 1924. The roof was held up by poles wedged between the floor and the ceiling, with additional supports added as the jerry-built structure shifted; by Christmas there were so many poles the inhabitants could hardly navigate between them. The roof was waterproof only when frozen; Hornby and Critchell-Bullock spent the winter with sand in their beds, their clothes, and their food, and they were flooded out when the snow melted. These two extremes represent the binary of order and chaos: George Douglas, an 'always admirable figure in a corrupt and positivist world' (76) with 'a keen sense of occasion and an exquisite sense of order' (75), and Hornby, 'disorganised, irrational, living according to the whim or impulse of the moment, relapsing as suddenly into apathy as into action, incoherent, without demonstrable purpose' (76).

In *The Legend of John Hornby*, as in many other modernist texts, the protagonist's experience of the First World War is an important cause of his alienation from others and his loss of purpose. Hornby enlisted and, like many Canadian northerners, may have become a sniper. According to Whalley, information about Hornby's military record is sparse; he was awarded the Military Cross in 1916, and soon after he was wounded badly enough to be sent to England for treatment. While the wounds were officially described as 'superficial,' Whalley notes that 'those who saw the scars of the wounds later did not think the wound can have been trifling' (11): his informants variously describe 'a crushed breast bone and a big sunken place between his shoulders' (116) and 'seven machine gun bullets right through his body under his ribs' (117). Whalley takes hold of the narrator's omniscience with both hands when he details Hornby's postwar physical and mental state in language that places Hornby in the tradition of Siegfried Sassoon and Wilfred Owen: 'The noise of the guns, he told Peggy Watt, had nearly driven him crazy. The war had sharpened and deepened all his worst suspicions. His skill as a hunter had been turned to predatory killing, the murder of men. The civilized world had gone mad; civilisation was in suicidal decay and all its ways were unclean. Now that he was officially released from the army and the world, he came out of hiding, and like a wounded animal finding a quiet place to die, he turned toward the North' (114).

But Hornby found nothing in the North that could console him, according to Whalley. His common-law wife, Arimo, had married another man; his trading area at Great Bear Lake had been usurped; his friends among the First Nations people had left the area. His trips to the North became more and more disorganized, and Hornby became more and more unprepared for the everyday challenges of feeding and sheltering himself. Early in the book, Whalley attributes Hornby's stubborn determination to make a life in the Barrens to a kind of romantic obsession, a 'fatal devotion to the Barren Ground' that 'in the end ... would steal Hornby's reason' (50). But by the end of the book, Hornby's repeated statements that he would take just one more trip North before retiring seem to have no justification at all. His death, and that of his companions, Harold Adlard and Edgar Christian, seems almost anticlimactic, for Whalley resists no occasion to point out that their expedition was badly equipped, stupidly scheduled, and doomed to failure from the outset: aimless, pointless, meaningless.

In *Poetic Process*, Whalley identified the motive for poetry as 'symbolic extrication,' a process whereby the poet is overwhelmed by the strong feelings provoked by an encounter with 'the Real,' an insight that he wishes to rid himself of by embodying that meaning and those feelings in a structure. The resulting pattern of symbols, a 'mythic structure,' both purges the poet of his unbearable feelings and becomes the means whereby readers gain insight. The process of symbolic extrication becomes important in *The Legend of John Hornby* in two senses. Hornby himself is mute; because he produced no writing besides his scattered notes for an autobiography, he was unable, in Whalley's vocabulary, to 'extricate' himself from the intense and debilitating feelings that the Barrens evoked in him. The poetic process of symbolic extrication – the creation of a powerful pattern of symbols, a myth – as a method of ridding oneself of a kind of obsession, is delegated to Hornby's biographer, Whalley himself, who self-consciously makes this process clear in his account of the writing of the biography: 'And there is another kind of naming, more muted and incoherent, that is literally, in desolation, a piecing together of a world that threatens to slip away into nothingness – the swift rehearsal of a lifetime in the instant of drowning, the sharp laconic pattern of classical elegy.'[14] Hornby was unable to save himself through art, but Whalley could and did.

In this sense, Whalley considers his main character mythic. Not because he represents the Victorian explorer conquering the North, and not because he is a strong and capable man who earns his masculinity through trials and challenges. Instead, the Hornby myth for Whalley represents 'a sense of high adventure ineluctably decaying into desolation and perplexity,' the triumph of chaos and meaninglessness over the strength of character and 'sailor-like' discipline and neatness that characterized his own life. 'The central figure in a myth or tragedy has a stature and power that not even accurate history can confer,' Whalley writes in the conclusion to *The Legend of John Hornby*, 'and through the blurring and distorting vehicle of his own legend certain features remain clear and distinct: something enigmatic and puckish about the man; a passionate sense of the integrity of the country; a birdlike inconsequence of purpose' (325). Finally, the myth has a 'stature and power' because it evokes what Whalley considers universal discourses of the human spirit: the disciplined struggle against emptiness of mind and loss of purpose, the desolate loss of value attendant upon war, and the epic encounter of men with the conditions of their own existence. Hornby was, for Whalley, merely 'a very unheroic, confused, and evasive though likeable man, not typical even of himself, a man who stumbled sideways into whatever tenuous immortality his death had accidentally presented him with … it all just happened; haphazard and yet as horrifyingly inevitable as the stealthy onset of a bad habit.' Yet Whalley suggests that Hornby 'would find his life reverberating at times to the echo of other lives whose history was obscure and dark and to be guessed at only from allusive evidence as though from the dim traces of buried meander rivers' (1).

Whalley summarizes a philosophy that he thinks Hornby would have endorsed: 'In civilisation there is no peace. Here, in the North, in my country there *is* peace. No past, no future, no regret, no anticipation; just doing. That is peace' (325). In Whalley's book, Hornby is less contemptuous of 'civilisation' and more a victim of it; he flees into the timeless present of action, away from memories, regrets, obligations, and demands. He and his companions could have survived, even thrived, in their wilderness cabin with only a little forethought; it was Hornby's refusal to take that forethought that doomed them to death. For this reason, I think of Whalley's biography of John Hornby as a kind of Canadian 'Death of the Ball Turret Gunner' or a non-fiction *The Wars*,[15] the story of idealism destroyed on the battlefields of France and buried by the rise of industrial capitalism. The themes of international modernism are made native to Canada in Whalley's book through the use of the metaphor of the one-way canoe trip.

Thomas York's *Snowman*, published in 1976, appropriates the figure of Hornby and the events of his final canoe trip to perform an allegorical function in an avowedly fictional story. The main characters, Bartholomew and Christopher (known as Bard and Claus) are employees of a mine in Yellowknife; they are suspected in the death of a Native woman, Louise (whom Bard has abused, but not killed, and Claus has returned to her community only to be beaten for his pains), and flee by boat to the east, where in the final section of the novel they encounter Hornby at Pike's Portage and accompany him to the cabin on the Thelon. York

appropriates much of the dialogue, description, and incident in this section from Waldron's *Snow Man* (without acknowledgment), assigning
Bard the role of Adlard and Claus that of Edgar Christian. The ending,
like that of all canoe trips, is predetermined.

York's Hornby is introduced in an earlier section of the novel when
Bard and Claus encounter a Catholic priest who shows them records
relating to the deaths of Fathers Rouvière and LeRoux, missionaries
whom the historical Hornby guided in the years before he enlisted.
Claus reads the correspondence (quoted at length by York, presumably
from Whalley's *The Legend of John Hornby*) and wonders about Hornby's
presence in the North: 'Which of the several motives was his main one:
to live like an Indian, to get musk-ox skins, to find the Copper Mountain
(presumably at Coppermine?) Certainly it wasn't to convert – was it to
cozen – the Eskimos? What, then?'[16] York picks up on a theme mentioned by both Waldron and Whalley: the idea that Hornby was a 'White
Indian' (Waldron 158) or 'wished he had been born an Indian' (Whalley
325); supposedly his habit of jog-trotting when he portaged was adopted
from 'Indians,' he despised 'White man's grub,' and he had posed as
an Indian on treaty day and would have got away with his money except
for his blue eyes (Whalley 6–7). For York, Hornby becomes a kind of
indigenized white man, a European who has gone native and who represents a bridge between the Euro-Canadian and the land.

For in York's novel, Native people, especially Native women, are identified wholly with the landscape. Claus refers to Bard's Native sex partners
indiscriminately as 'wildee,' which York explains is a short form for 'wilderness.' The starving Hornby dreams of Great Slave Lake as the body of
a huge woman who suckles him. The apotheosis of this symbolic pairing
of the feminine wilderness and the masculine self occurs when Hornby
encounters Arimo, remade in York's novel as an embodiment of pas-
sionless acceptance of the land.[17] Arimo, recognizing her long-lost partner, rushes toward him, unaware that intruders from Yellowknife have
their rifles trained upon him. She is killed on the beach while embracing
Hornby, sacrificing herself for him in a form of 'sacred marriage' (109),
as York terms it. Before he dies, Claus has a vision that the union of
Hornby and Arimo will cause a kind of blooming in the desert, creating a
homeland for the dispossessed in the Arctic: 'Hornby was Patriarch, and
Arimo the barrengrounds' Abbess, spiritual mother of all living there: all
whom the world did, or death does, exile – they would find succor there'
(227). Interestingly, the only person in the novel who could legitimately
represent the union of white and Native cultures, of human and natural

worlds, is the mixed-race miner Watmough, who instead commits the sexually perverse and violent murder of the Bard's sexual partner, the Dogrib girl, Louise.

In York's novel, the death of Arimo seems to forestall the possibility of paradise, but Hornby carries on. Indeed York borrows thematically from both Whalley and Waldron to create Hornby as an organic figure whose goal is merely to exist physically, to represent life and the natural at its most basic. York defines existence narrowly as the continuance of life by means of the natural processes of eating, digestion and elimination, and he metaphorically or symbolically locates each of his characters in relation to these basic processes. Bard, who operates the primary crusher, is overseer of the mine's digestion, and Claus, the bulldozer driver, is the lord of its waste; Louise feels connected to the natural world, even in the city, when she sits on the toilet; Summers, the white civil servant, is constipated. Both Hornby and Arimo, in York's novel, find peace and each other only when they cease to strive and are satisfied merely to perform daily tasks, without reflection. Hornby explains the goal of his invented game, 'barrengrounds chess,' is 'To endure … As long as you can, and with what you've got, to endure' (212). Early in the novel, Claus wonders about Hornby: 'Did he have a motive, did a person need to have a motive other than merely to survive, and to survive under the most pitiless conditions?' (39). Finally, Claus comes to understand just before his death that eating, digestion, and elimination are the only things that matter: 'Civilization with its comforts and codes [is] neither alluring nor oppressive, just remote – the scaffolding around the centre, which is here. This is the long-awaited and much-dreaded ring of famine: only we are on the inside, though it is not the side that wins' (226).

By representing Hornby as a 'white Indian' who has a special relationship to the wilderness, York's *Snowman* situates itself firmly in the context of the Canadian literary critical discourse of the 1970s, which was strongly influenced by the ideas of Margaret Atwood and Northrop Frye. Like Atwood in her influential book *Survival*, the novel sees Canadians in general as afflicted with a fear of the body and a sense of alienation from the landscape; like Frye, it looks to 'Indians' to 'symbolize a primitive mythological imagination which may be reborn in us, resulting in the "immigrant mentality" being replaced by an "indigenous mentality"' that can heal this alienation.[18] Hornby's ability to 'live like an Indian' makes him a model of a 'natural' life, life stripped of all inessentials, yet it also gives him the symbolic significance of the masculine agent of fertility and spiritual rebirth in a traditional Christian mythic structure. He becomes a kind of touchstone that brings self-knowledge for the characters who, like Claus, come to understand him. Yet in York's *Snowman*, Hornby also remains enigmatic; Claus's starvation-induced vision is undercut by Hornby's sudden appearance at the cabin door, 'so that, gradually falling prey in the stifling cabin to the little man's inane and incessant chatter, and his crazy scrambling among the fox entrails for a bladder for his enema bag, Claus forgot his benevolent assumption of Hornby and Arimo together spanning the Arctic, forgot his beatific vision of the Free Forest and the Fertile Barrens' (228). The deaths of the whole party finally question the ability of the 'white Indian' to heal Euro-Canadian alienation from the land and its original inhabitants.

Lawrence Jeffrey's Hornby is nothing like York's; paranoid, even suicidal, he speaks rarely and attempts to quash communication among his companions. Jeffrey takes his inspiration mainly from Edgar Christian's diary, as his title, *Who Look in Stove*, suggests; before his death, Christian had left a note that read 'Who[ever finds this] Look in Stove' to ensure that the diary placed in the cold ashes of the stove to protect it from the elements was found. The real-life diary is the work of a not particularly literate young man; its stumbling and inadequate language becomes the theme of Jeffrey's play, *Who Look in Stove*, which portrays the relationships among the three companions through ambiguous and sketchy dialogue characterized by miscommunication, non-communication, reticence, and lying.

The theme of language and the way it constitutes human experience is introduced early in the play. Jeffrey's Hornby is trying to keep the other two from talking, and he terrorizes Edgar into tears. Confronted by Adlard about his behaviour, Jeffrey's Hornby explains:

'Words are dangerous things.'
'It's all we've got lots of, Jack. Words. Lots of words.'
'Naming something makes it real. Doesn't matter if it exists or not, naming makes it as good as real.'
'Like what? Hunger? Fear?'
'Shutup!'[19]

Hornby seems aware from the beginning that the group faces death by starvation; in silence he hopes to prevent the canoe trip/narrative from proceeding, from moving forward from word to word, and in this way he hopes to evade the predetermined ending. But he can't control Edgar's diary, and the fact of the diary's existence obsesses and irritates him throughout the play. Edgar explains that he tries to include in the diary what gets left out of conversation; he uses the metaphor of a bad telephone connection: 'You try and get across the distance, you shout what you mean to say. And then when you're finished ... when you hang up ... there's this silence ... There's suddenly this odd silence' (46). The silence between the characters is occasionally broken – as when Edgar confesses that he had never loved his father, but he loves Hornby, and when Hornby challenges Adlard to examine his own motives for joining what was, from the beginning, essentially a suicidal expedition. Sherrill Grace comments on the languagelessness and silence of the North in her discussion of *Who Look in Stove*, but it seems to me that the silence in the play owes less to the mythology of the North and more to modernist playwrights like Samuel Beckett and David Mamet. The theme of the impossibility of true communication is expressed throughout the play; indeed, Hornby complains that most conversation is mere ritual (62) and that even romantic love fails to bridge the distance between two people (61). The dialogue in the latter part of the play consists mainly of the repetition of names as the dying men attempt to reach out to each other with language, and fail.

M.T. Kelly's *Out of the Whirlwind* similarly seems to confound communication, as the four characters, Albertans on a recreational canoe trip along the Thelon River, speak to each other in one-sentence challenges, aphorisms, and non-sequiturs. Their diverse motives and goals, their vehemently held moral values and intellectual prejudices, as well as their opposing genders, seem to make communication impossible. The group loses most of their food in what at first seems to be a camping accident and head down the Thelon River to the site of Hornby's cabin in the hope that a rescue party will locate them easily at such a well-known landmark. However, the rescue plane never appears; they are not equipped to hunt or fish, and no other canoe-campers come down the river. Despite their conviction that 'There'll be other people; there's always other people. This is the twentieth century' (128), they starve to death in isolation.

Kelly grasps the mythical significance of Hornby's story and uses it to evoke many of the central symbolic narratives of English literature. His title comes from the Book of Job, and implies both the malevolence and the sublime terror of a face-to-face encounter with the Old Testament God. Chapter titles also come from Ecclesiastes and from Shakespeare. But Kelly places these chapter titles among others that evoke the literature of exploration: 'The Land of Feast and Famine,' the name for the North coined by Hornby; 'A Journey to the Northern Ocean,' from Samuel Hearne; and 'The Country of the Musk Ox in Summer,' from the beautiful description of heaven in the last paragraph of Warburton Pike's *The Barren Ground of Northern Canada.* Chapters are also named for 'The Dismal Lakes' and the 'Rapids of the Drowned,' places that actually exist. These choices suggest that Kelly anticipates a reader who will recognize both sets of cultural references, as well as the depth of the themes of confrontation with God, nature, and the self that his novel evokes.

One of the central issues in Kelly's version of the Hornby trip is the human relationship to the animal self. Two of the characters are biologists who experiment on animals; a third is an animal rights activist. In the opening chapters, Claire performs microsurgery on a rat, which is rendered immobile while its spine is exposed; Malcolm points out that despite the layers of anaesthesia, the rat appears to be starving. The implied parallel between the starving people on the Thelon and the rat in the university lab suggests that the people's predicament is the result of a bizarre and seemingly pointless experiment. Claire and Daryl are obsessed with their bodies, with Daryl obsessively touching his abdominal muscles, as if to reassure himself that his 'sixpack' is still there, and Claire devoted to 'working out' with the guys. But this obsession seems to blind them both to the mere facts of their bodily existence: Daryl insists he can 'run down' a caribou, and Claire finally confesses to throwing away the food, justifying her act by her desire to lose weight. Claire's urban understanding of her body and its requirements is so distorted that it causes the deaths of the entire party. The group's eventual struggle with starvation (during which the animal rights activist, Malcolm, admits to a lifetime of hunting) recalls Waldron's Hornby and his theory of active starving. Like Hornby, they demonstrate the truism from *King Lear* recalled by Malcolm: '"Unaccommodated man," Malcolm said. "A poor, bare, forked animal"' (71).

Clive Powell-Williams's popular account of Hornby's death, *Cold Burial: A True Story of Endurance and Disaster* (2002), is haunted by none of Whalley's scruples about omniscience or Kelly's interest in body consciousness. Powell-Williams, a British schoolmaster, is particularly interested in Edgar Christian and in the way his 'Intensive training in moral character, team activities, leadership and cheerfulness'[20] at Dover College prepared him for the challenges he faced in the north. He situates Edgar's story in the context of the 'cult of heroism' of the time, discussing Leigh Mallory, who died in an attempt to climb Everest, and noting that a survivor of the Scott Expedition to the South Pole gave a talk at Edgar's school. Powell-Williams amply demonstrates his own investment in the same ideas he attributes to his historical subjects, blithely repeating the sort of statements that have given the British a bad reputation in Canada for generations – for example, alleging that Edgar was sent to Canada by his relatives because 'an immature young man of no great intellect or savvy was generally thought most suitable for the colonial life' (25) (I wonder how the colonials felt about that), and referring to Native people as nomads and squaws: 'the air thrummed with tom-toms and was torn by the weird screeching song that accompanied the Indians' long gambling sessions' (97). Powell-Williams perhaps did not anticipate how his historical references to *Boy's Own* magazine would supply a context for his own writing.

Powell-Williams's Hornby is the villain of the piece – a British expat who had 'gone native' and, as a result, was 'dangerously close to insanity' (41). Hornby's extraordinary generosity to those he met and his 'ideas about travel in the barrens were derived from Indian thinking' (99). As a result, he holds life cheap and 'stak[ed] his life, and that of his friends, on the toss of a coin' (86). Edgar becomes the hero of the piece, the evidence of his diary that the group had remained 'cheerful' to the end cited as proof of the values instilled in the British upper classes: 'What had failed was unimportant – the mortal body. In terms of the spirit, and as a testament to comradeship, mutual help and struggle – to human love itself – Edgar could see only what was positive and honourable ... even in failure, it honoured their family and their nation, turning physical defeat into a moral victory and justifying everything' (243–4). In Powell-Williams's book, Edgar Christian's Britishness is the central fact; the Canadian myth of the North and the Canadian obsession with telling and retelling the story of the wilderness canoe trip as disaster have no place.

The experience of wilderness readers/writers and paddlers comes together in the most recent literary retelling of the Hornby story, Elizabeth Hay's *Late Nights on Air*. Hay's novel creates a palimpsest of traces across a map of the Canadian north; the canoe route taken by the four main characters in the book – Harry, Ralph, Gwen, and Eleanor – retraces the route Hay herself followed when, as a young woman, she retraced Hornby's final trip, following the route created by the explorers and surveyors whose maps and written accounts her characters consult as they paddle, the route made famous by the deaths of Hornby, Christian, and Adlard. But while the route is predetermined, both geographically and narratively, its meanings are not, as Hay's book demonstrates: each character makes a different story from the events of Hornby's life, and its meaning changes as their trip progresses.

Gwen and Harry initially become friends over a shared interest in Whalley's radio version of Edgar Christian's diary, broadcast as 'Death

in the Barren Ground.' Gwen first heard the story as a child in her parents' house, and she associates it with escape from the restrictions her
father had placed on the household: she felt 'locked in' to a home with
no TV or newspaper, but when she heard 'Death in the Barren Ground,'
'she entered somebody else's life and saw it from beginning to end ... A
blue-eyed, soft-voiced, lucid madman who courted hardship and seemed
absolutely fearless.'[21] Inspired by the story, Gwen goes to Yellowknife
to experience the North as Hornby saw it. When she reaches Hornby's
cabin, she wanders off alone, feeling that 'In her mind she was with
Hornby and Edgar and Harold Adlard' (299); instead of encountering
an inspiring ghost, however, she meets a grizzly bear and barely escapes
being mauled. Afterwards, she realizes that she associates her fear of the
bear with her fear of her father (300) and his eyes with the eyes of Eddy
(302), the violent and abusive partner of her friend Dido. Eleanor speculates that the grizzly represented the spirit of Hornby, come to warn
Gwen away from his paradise (310). What all of these associations have
in common is violence, fear, unexpected peril, and they impress upon
the naive Gwen that in her encounters with others, be they in the South
or the North, she may risk violence and death. Gwen later realizes that
she has left her tape recorder and her precious audio record of their trip
behind with the bear, a metaphoric substitution for her innocence.

Harry identifies with Hornby strongly, to the extent that his interpretation of the events of Hornby's life is completely personalized. At the
beginning of the novel, when Harry is in love with the unresponsive
Dido and content to hide the wreck of his broadcasting career in Yellowknife, he believes Hornby was motivated, like him, by 'an enormous
appetite for doing without' (128). In rereading Whalley's *The Legend
of John Hornby* after Dido has left him and his employees have assailed
his actions as station manager, Harry almost offers special pleading for
Hornby, whose characterization in Whalley so much resembles his own
life: 'if you saw [Hornby] as a distillation of his shortcomings, then you'd
call him a loser, feckless, under-prepared, dangerous. If you saw him
instead, in all his complexity, in the fullness of his extraordinary life,
then he was no less irresponsible, but he was also astonishingly vivid,
driven, solitary, intense, endearing. Harry was all for seeing people in
their complexity and having them return the favour' (230). But by the
end of the novel Harry has regained much of his self-confidence and is
prepared to move on to other career paths and other loves; like Hornby,
and like the fictionalized characters of Whalley and Thomas Berger in
the novel (231–2), Harry sees his life as being like the caribou migration,
'sideways, backwards, forwards, a passage enlivened with indecision in

the face of real and imagined danger ... He felt attuned not to the God within but to the uncertainty within' (306).

Eleanor and Ralph both write the meaning of Hornby's story differently, but their experience of retracing his journey brings them together. Eleanor has begun to be interested in spirituality, especially the tradition of Christian mysticism that she encounters in the life of St. Teresa. She places Hornby in the context of ecstatic visionaries: 'Hornby's description of the Barrens as sudden, featureless, endless, as land ground down and scoured by glaciers, put her in mind of the holy men of the desert starving themselves in order to have visions' (131). Ralph intuits the uncanny spirituality of the Barrens as well, and describes it as a place 'Where seen and unseen meet' (294). However, Ralph's main understanding of Hornby grows from his own recognition that he wants to settle down: 'Ralph set down the book, understanding an aspect of Hornby for the first time: he had been seduced by the idea of a well-built home ... The tiny, extraordinarily tough, self-destructive Englishman had actually been seeking a wild kind of comfort. In himself something similar was going on' (295). Upon coming to this realization about Hornby, Ralph determines to ask Eleanor to marry him on the last night of the canoe trip, but like Hornby's their trip is predetermined to end in tragedy, and Ralph is killed in a canoeing accident immediately after Eleanor says yes.

Hay's narrative structure allows each of her characters to read Hornby in the light of their own lives and to interpret him according to the social context of their own times and ages. In this her book represents what the characters admire most about Whalley's representation of Hornby: its reticence, its refusal of omniscience. Harry says: 'He didn't ridicule Hornby for his mistakes, or excoriate him. He could have so easily. A journalist would have' (298), and Harry is a journalist. In conformity with the codes of literary modernism, Hay and Whalley refuse the luxury of certainty and opt instead for ambiguity and, in Hay's case, a kind of post-modernist awareness of the role of the reader in making meaning from events. Gwen and Harry retain their fascination with Hornby's story partly because it led to the death of their friend; the landscape remains the location of resolved desire and familiarity undermined by death. In an article published in 2004, Elizabeth Hay recommends *Maria Chapdelaine*, the poems of Margaret Avison, and *The Legend of John Hornby* as winter reading. Of first encountering *Maria Chapdelaine* when she was a child, she writes: 'When romantic love is destroyed by a cold country, the love that remains is for the country itself. I didn't buy this when I was 11. Not one bit. But I'm much older now.'[22]

Graves on the Thelon River, 1929.
Courtesy of Library and Archives Canada, e010933330.

The meanings of John Hornby bleed into each other: the conquering imperialist hero, the driven survivor of war, the rapt worshipper of nature, the foolish Englishman 'gone native.' The inability of each of these narratives to stabilize the meaning of John Hornby for Canadian culture demonstrates the way the uncanny governs the meanings of the one-way wilderness canoe trip and recalls other surprising and haunted trips: Leonidas Hubbard's fatal trip into Labrador, the St. John's school disaster on Lake Timiskaming, Franklin's first expedition across the Barrens, George Grinnel's *A Death on the Barrens.*[23] For his readers and writers, Hornby exemplifies the dilemma of the Canadian who is 'alien within Canada,' who is both at home and not at home in the landscape that surrounds him, whose attempt at indigenization fails with his death. For Hornby, the canoe was the vessel in which he was remade as Canadian, neither Native 'Indian' nor native to place, 'caught between two worlds, one dead, the other powerless to be born.'[24]

Chapter Six

Return to Eden: Bill Mason, Canoeing, and Environmentalism

As a young man Bill Mason liked to imagine he was a voyageur, and he 'dreamed about re-tracing all of the voyageur routes.'¹ But by the time he was making his *Path of the Paddle* series of instructional films for the National Film Board, his idea of the value of the canoe had changed: 'The canoe is no longer a vehicle of trade and commerce. It has become instead the means of exploring, or re-discovering, what is left of the natural world.'² Mason's shift of focus is typical of the way that the motives for canoeing changed in the 1970s and 1980s; canoeists, canoeing scholars, and guidebook authors began to advocate canoeing as a way to educate the public about environmental issues and to suggest that the supposed benefits of recreational canoeing and wilderness canoe tripping should be a reason to preserve wilderness.

Beverly Haun-Moss points out that recreational canoeing finds its motivation at the overlap of two conflicting desires: the desire to dominate the land and the desire to submit to it. While the first motivation governs early twentieth-century recreational canoeing, more recent trips emphasize 'a more widely held attitude of becoming attuned to rather than dominating nature. Negotiating rather than conquering rapids and river, and celebrating and harmonizing with the environment, is moving to minimize if not erase the adversarial stances.'³ Bill Mason is the icon of this change: the author of two influential canoeing guides (*Path of the Paddle* and *Song of the Paddle*), writer/director of some of the most popular and most successful films about canoeing and environmentalism,⁴ he is identified by his admirers as one of the most influential environmentalists of his generation of Canadians and as an embodiment of the Canadian identity. He 'helped shape Canadians' understanding of their own land'; '[his] vision of the wilderness as benign, beautiful and precious effectively offered a meaningful alternative to the accepted cultural perception of wilderness as something to be feared, conquered or exploited.'[5] He is remembered in the Bill Mason Memorial Scholarship offered by Paddle Canada, the Bill Mason Outdoor Education Centre operated by the Ottawa-Carleton School Board, and the Waterwalker Film and Video Festival in Ottawa. The Canadian Canoe Museum displays his favourite canoe and features quotations from his books and films. Canoeing outfitters and canoe manufacturers advertise that they carry equipment manufactured to his specifications; canoeing websites from around the world carry quotations from his work; and canoe trippers reference his ideas, even his spirit, in their descriptions of their own experiences. Kevin Callan calls him 'Canada's guru of canoeing.'[6] His biographer James Raffan calls him 'a Canadian hero … a mythical character, larger than life'[7] and 'Canada's quintessential riverman.'[8] He is central to the (re)construction of 'canoeing … as a pleasure without guilt that does not pollute, make noise or alter natural space … actively facilitating an appreciation of the environment, healthy exercise, and self-definition.'[9]

Like most Ontarians of my generation, I knew *Paddle to the Sea* long before I knew of Bill Mason; I saw it numerous times at school and on CBC television, and I cheered for the little carved figure that made its way through waterways I recognized and landscapes I cherished. I saw *Waterwalker* in the late eighties, at a screening in Southam Hall at Carleton University, and found it moving and surprising; with a soundtrack by Bruce Cockburn, glorious images of the Canadian Shield and Ontario lakes and rivers, and the voice of First Nations peoples, it seemed to validate my memories of childhood canoeing and to place them in a political context in which they had meaning – as signs of my nationality and signs of my hope for a more just and environmentally responsible future for Canada. But as James Raffan's biography of Mason shows, this impression was created in spite of Mason's own sense that the film was a disappointment, a failed attempt to express something he felt strongly but had difficulty conveying, and the voices of the First Nations elders that formed part of the commentary were in some ways an afterthought. Bill Mason felt that the goal of his work, and *Waterwalker* in particular, was to overcome the alienation of white Canadians from the land; the film seems to embody the dilemma of the Canadian who is alien within Canada by directly addressing the contradictions inherent in the idea of Canadian nationality, and just as surely failing to resolve them. The fact that I couldn't see that then shows how completely people like me live inside those contradictions.

Terry Goldie suggests that white Canadians respond to their alienation from the land through appropriation, impersonation, and incorporation of indigeneity. Mason appropriates the canoe as the privileged means whereby Canadians can create a link with the landscape that comprises the nation; while paddling his canoe and trying to assume the point of view of First Nations peoples, Mason borders on Goldie's practice of impersonation, trying to become indigenous to the land; and by assuming ownership of the canoe and stewardship of the land itself, he practises Goldie's idea of incorporation, swallowing up the rights of First Nations and their cultures within a new, ethically and environmentally responsible Canada. Eva Mackey shows how in nationalist discourse First Nations cultures are transformed into the 'heritage' of all Canadians, which 'enables the culture of the colonized to be appropriated by the colonisers and put to service in building national and international identity.'[10] The narrative of incorporation elides the long history of colonization and produces what Mackey calls 'settler innocence': 'The celebration of Canadian national "heritage," made possible by appropriating Aboriginal culture, entails no less than the erasure of a history of *conquest*. Aboriginal people become the ancestors of a nation who pass on an inheritance, not the survivors of conquest and colonization.'[11] Mason's implication in the ideology of the wilderness sublime similarly erases the violence of history from the landscape and creates it as a timeless place 'from which human beings had to be ejected before the fallen world of history could properly begin.'[12] By taking the canoe as the symbol of this new environmental awareness, Mason participates in that erasure, even as he is haunted by 'what we are, and what we did.'

Mason was born in Winnipeg in 1929. According to James Raffan in his biography, *Fire in the Bones* (1996), Mason was often ill as a child and suffered from a condition that kept him from growing; as a result he developed a love of solitude and the habit of working alone. Precociously talented as an artist, Mason was indulged by his family and never seriously considered any other career. He was introduced to canoeing during family vacations at Grand Beach on Lake Winnipeg, and as a teenager he was an enthusiastic paddler at Manitoba Pioneer Camp. There he discovered Calvin Rutstrum's camping manual, *Way of the Wilderness*, and he took to heart Rutstrum's advice on camping equipment and paddling techniques. As a young teenager he began his lifelong practice of wilderness camping, developing his own favourite routes and learning the best techniques for white-water paddling by trial and error.

Mason was a commercial artist by profession in 1956 when he was asked by filmmaker Chris Chapman to assist in making a film about the Quetico/Boundary Lakes region, an area that had been the focus of struggles between developers and wilderness advocates since the 1940s. His experiences as the canoeist/second cameraman on Chapman's film introduced Mason to the basics of filmmaking, and his conversations with Chapman convinced him that the wilderness areas he loved to canoe were under threat. This experience determined the new direction of his career: Mason became a filmmaker, using the techniques and approaches he learned from Chapman to embody his belief that the wilderness and its animal inhabitants are under threat, and to attempt to rally support for wilderness and animal protection. He moved to Ottawa and secured employment with the National Film Board of Canada (NFB).

The first film Mason directed for the NFB was a dramatization of Holling Clancy Holling's picture book for children, *Paddle to the Sea* (1966). The journey of the little wooden canoeist carved by an 'Indian' boy was a novel way to teach children about the geography of the Canadian Shield and the Great Lakes Basin and introduce them to the commercial importance of the St. Lawrence Seaway, which was opened to deep water traffic in 1959. But in Mason's interpretation, the theme of the 'wilderness under threat' was front and centre with shots of 'Paddle' negotiating the scummy brown waters of Lake Superior near Marathon, Ontario. Mason would return to Marathon to shoot 'pollution' scenes for his second movie as well. In *The Rise and Fall of the Great Lakes* (1968) the time-travelling paddler dips his cup into the pristine waters of Lake Superior in the past, only to sip from the polluted waters of the present. Both movies feature the contrast between the beautiful, clear, and silent waters of wilderness areas and the crowded, loud, and polluted areas near locks and industrial cities. As Raffan puts it, Mason managed to infuse even these early commissioned films with 'subtle messages about stewardship and the importance of caring for the natural world.'[13]

The next three movies were less subtle. The NFB was commissioned by the Canadian Wildlife Service to create a conservation film about wolves that would highlight the importance of wildlife research and management in the context of human incursions on traditional habitats. Mason was assigned this project, and he spent the next few years filming wolves and wolf researchers on Baffin Island and Isle Royale and in British Columbia. While he was away, his wife Joyce and two children undertook to raise a captive pack of wolves at the family home at Meech Lake in order to facilitate close-up shots and analysis of pack behaviour. The resulting three films included the originally commissioned film *Death of a*

Legend (1968), a twenty-minute television adaptation (*Wolf Pack*, 1971), and a ninety-minute feature film, *Cry of the Wild* (1971), that focused on Mason himself and the challenges he faced as a filmmaker working with wolves. All three took the uncompromising stance that the wolf cull programs instituted in the past were based on myths about wolves as indiscriminate predators and that a more enlightened wildlife policy would see wolves as a necessary part of a complete ecosystem and protect them from human depredation.

Mason's take on the history of the North American environment became the introduction to many of these movies. Chapman had taught him the importance of geographically situating his stories of the natural world by beginning his movie *Quetico* with a map; Mason adopted this practice, augmented by a sequence on the history of the North American environment that situated his stories in a fallen world dominated by Euro-Canadians incapable of living in harmony with nature. In *Death of a Legend*, the opening voice-over described 'The face of our continent, before man came into the picture,'[14] in terms that recalled the Garden of Eden, albeit a garden in which carnivores had a place and death was common. When indigenous peoples arrived, 'About 20,000 years ago,' very little changed, according to Mason: 'his [sic] technology was pretty primitive: and there weren't ever very many Indians, and he killed only to supply his own need. He didn't really change the life of the land, he became part of it.' However, while in Mason's view indigenous people became identified with the natural world itself, 'another bunch was on the way, with power to really disrupt the shifting balances of nature.' In Mason's view, 'Everything was fine until the first Europeans turned up. As in *Bambi*, the arrival of man in the forest signalled the beginning of the end.'[15] Europeans are fallen man, according to the movie, uninterested in living in harmony with the natural world and capable of indiscriminately slaughtering both native peoples and animals in order to '[get] rid of whatever was in the way.' Mason elaborates on this view in his canoeing manual, *The Path of the Paddle*: 'the idea of wilderness belongs to the "white man" … [they saw the wilderness as] a hostile environment they had to "tame." It was the "white men" who saw the land as a dangerous place, one that had to be battled; and made to resemble as much as possible, distant homelands.'[16] In Mason's view, the 'white man' is afflicted with the distorted vision that prevents him from seeing the way back to Eden, which lay before him in the form of the harmonious natural world.

The results of that distorted vision are a common theme in Mason's canoeing films. In *Waterwalker*, the commentary often references the incursion of development into the wild places of North America, spoiling the aesthetic beauty of the landscape and poisoning the plants and animals. Mason laments that development of the Dennison Falls on the Dog River seems inevitable: 'Sooner or later these falls will be silenced behind steel and concrete.'[17] He also suggests that even should the falls remain untouched, being able to access them by road would diminish their spiritual and aesthetic value. In *Waterwalker* he also comments on 'acid rain and how the lakes are dying,' pointing out that even in remote areas 'the birches are in big trouble' and the rest of the plant species are affected by pollution generated many miles away.

Even in films like *Death of a Legend* (whose subject was ostensibly wolves) Mason represented the canoe as the way to discover a sense of the wilderness as home, to enter the 'intricate ever-changing web' that was 'the life of the land.' One sequence in *Death of a Legend* features rapidly intercut shots of motorboats, cars, airplanes, all kinds of loud and offensive modes of transportation, ending with a wide shot of Mason and his family camping beside the water, listening to the howl of a wolf, canoe prominently in the foreground. The message is clear: if you want to understand and access the natural world, the canoe is the way to go. This theme of the canoe as not only a 'green' mode of transportation but also a way to an enlightened understanding of the natural world dominates Mason's subsequent canoeing films: the four-part *Path of the Paddle* (1976) series, *Song of the Paddle* (1976), and *Waterwalker* (1984).

Waterwalker opens with a folksy Mason recapping his idea of North American natural history; before 'white man' arrived it was 'a pristine untouched wilderness' despite the fact that 'the native people ... had lived here for thousands of years.' His motivation for canoeing is his desire 'to catch a glimpse of what that wilderness used to be,' and 'the best way to do that is in a canoe.' *Song of the Paddle* similarly features Mason complaining that 'The modern world which we have created has put a lot of distance between ourselves and the natural world' and advocating 'A journey by canoe along these ancient waterways' as 'a pretty good way to re-establish that relationship.'[18]

For Mason, one way the canoe promotes a relationship with the natural world is simply that canoe travel requires time: 'How we see the natural world and the depth of our relationship with it depends to a great deal on how we travel and how long we stay there ... to achieve a relationship with the land one must travel on foot or by canoe.'[19] In addition, the history of the canoe is an object lesson in utilizing resources sustainably: 'The birchbark canoe is made entirely from materials found in the forest: birch bark, cedar, spruce roots, ash, and pine gum. When it is damaged, it can be repaired easily from the materials at hand. When it has served its purpose, it returns to the land, part of a never-ending cycle. Once you understand the cycle of growth, manufacture, use and return to the land you begin to understand why our modern culture is in such trouble.'[20] Because canoe routes follow the geography of the watersheds, they promote a relationship with the natural world by introducing the paddler to land formations disguised by modern roadways and dams. The canoe is the traditional vehicle of the First Nations peoples in eastern Canada, and so it offers a historical perspective on the land. And because the canoe can be portaged, it leads away from modern built environments and towards a destination that is no destination, but a process of learning through 'living outdoors': 'It is the portages that separate us from civilization. The more portages you can put between yourself and civilization, the greater the wilderness experience … to [the voyageurs], reaching their destination was the only thing that mattered. To today's canoeist, the goal should not be the destination, but the journey itself.'[21]

By the time he wrote *Song of the Paddle*, however, Mason was well aware of what Bruce Hodgins calls 'Canoe Irony.'[22] The more people try to access 'wilderness,' the less 'wild' it is; the lone, environmentally conscious wilderness camper is usually followed by masses of campers who are not so circumspect. In the 'Campsites' section of *Song of the Paddle*, Mason laments that publicizing his favourite camping destinations has 'led to increased traffic and even crowding.'[23] He advises canoeists that it is proper etiquette when travelling a wilderness river 'to choose a campsite that does not spoil the view of a spectacular scene for your fellow travellers' (14) and to practise no-trace camping. He advises against cutting moss to place under a tent, adding that 'Cutting bough beds is a thing of the past' (14). 'With the increasing number of people, the ever decreasing wilderness can't tolerate these abuses any more. The less you disturb the land, the better' (14). Mason's comments demonstrate his awareness that not all canoeists are going to be convinced of the importance of environmental conservation merely by stepping into a canoe; clearly, some of us are more unregenerate than others.

It may seem like a stretch to reference Eden and the idea of a fallen man to explain Mason's account of the role of the canoe in recovering a relationship with nature; it may seem more reasonable to think of Mason as suffering from 'imperialist nostalgia,' defined by Renato Rosaldo in his book *Culture and Truth* as 'a particular kind of nostalgia … where people mourn the passing of what they themselves have transformed.'[24] But Mason's fundamentalist Christian upbringing, and his subsequent search for a less restrictive and more celebratory way to express his faith, puts a particular spin on his nostalgia for a mythical time and place when nature and humans lived in harmony. As a teenager, Mason thrived on the mix of evangelical Christianity and outdoor adventure he found at Manitoba Pioneer camp. Christianity inflected his early enthusiasm for photography as well, which was expressed in a slide show designed to illustrate the presence of God in the natural world. 'God Revealed' included a soundtrack and numerous quotations from the Bible along with Mason's stories about his wilderness trips: it was 'a resounding success whenever and wherever it was shown.'[25] Mason's first commercial film, 'Wilderness Treasure,' was commissioned by the Christian Pioneer Camps organization intended to showcase camp programs; this became another platform for Mason to express his evolving beliefs in the way that wilderness canoe tripping can reintroduce paddlers to Christian spirituality.

For Mason, the wilderness is in itself a work of art, a 'creation' that celebrates the Christian God who made it. In *The Path of the Paddle*, he writes: 'We have become so totally committed to changing our environment that we have become oblivious to the fact that the world around us is a creation in itself – God's creation. Some of humanity's greatest masterpieces have been inspired by this same Creator … I am grateful for the men and women who have created these great monuments, but when I compare these monuments with the natural world, it's no contest … As much as I love and appreciate the great works of art, I know what my choice would be.'[26] Mason's vision of the wilderness as a 'creation' comparable to human works of art argues for its preservation on its own terms. In addition, it implies humans and animals share a common right to exist based on their equality as God's creations: 'I believe we have a moral obligation to preserve and care for the habitat of animals and plant life because, like us, they were created by God and have a right to exist.'[27] Tina Loo calls this Mason's 'ethic of existence' and argues that it represents a major shift in conservation ideology.[28] For Mason, wilderness preservation is not merely instrumental, in the service of creating 'sustainable' recreational opportunities or preserving scarce resources, but an affirmation of the sacredness of all life. While he advocates the preservation of specific places because of the challenge or the pleasure they offer canoeists, he advocates wilderness preservation not for its usefulness but for itself.

Mason's manuscript 'Some Private Thoughts,' which Raffan cites in *Fire in the Bones*, makes explicit the way that Mason identifies modern society's instrumental attitude towards the natural world with alienation from God: in other words, with sin. According to Raffan, in a section of the manuscript Mason retrospectively describes his aims as a filmmaker around the time he made *Cry of the Wild*: 'My films are to the best of my ability an attempt to bridge the gap between ourselves and things natural. I am dealing with things loosely related to the spirit. The spirit of man, the spirit of nature which is for me God. The God who created it and breathed life into it. I am convinced that our problems in relation to nature and also in human terms are because of our alienation from God the Creator. An alienation caused by us. Not God. It is not His fault that we prefer to leave Him out of our lives. To disassociate Him from Nature.' For Mason, the attitudes of 'white men' towards the natural world are the result of our fallen state, our refusal to see the spirit of our Creator in the natural world, and our consequent destructive and manipulative attitudes toward it.

The manuscript goes on to argue against evolution as the sole explanation for the natural world: 'To assume that the world around us is the result of nothing more than a process of natural selection. I just don't buy that.' Instead, Mason argues that the beauty of the natural world, and the way it appeals to the minds and the senses of human beings, implies a conscious design: 'The world around us speaks to me of an incredible mind. A mind that designed it and put it into operation and then gave us the various senses and a mind capable of wonder and awe. We are born to ask questions – why and how.'[29] Mason is not allying himself with conservative Creationism; he is in favour of scientific research on the animals and their ecosystems, as his films show. But his suggestion that the complexity and beauty of the natural world could not be solely the result of natural selection opens up a whole field of speculation. If God made the world and specifically designed it to interact with human sensibilities, are humans a part of that natural world or separate from it; do we re-enter the web of life as just another part of it, an animal, in other words? And if we are not animals, how can we be part of it?

Significantly, when Mason chooses to quote from the Bible in his films and his books, he does not choose to cite the passage in Genesis most often referred to in discussions of Christian attitudes towards the environment. In Genesis 1:20–21, God gives man dominion over the earth, instructs him to rule over and subdue all of the animals, and specifically gives him use of all of the plants, animals, and fish for food. This passage has been used by many ecological writers to criticize Christian ideology for promoting a Cartesian instrumentalism that has devastated the natural world: for example, Carolyn Merchant points out that 'the terms *dominion, mastery, subduing, conquering,* and *ruling* pre-dominate in different translations of the Genesis 1 story' and cites a long-standing tradition of Biblical interpretation that sees humanity as required to re-establish 'dominion' over the natural world in order to recover from the Fall.[30] For many secular deep ecologists, this section of the Bible condemns the Christian approach to the natural world; even for Christians, Genesis 1 is a confusing contradiction to the account of creation in Genesis 2, which seems to promote an attitude of stewardship and cooperation towards nature.

Of course, as a contemporary Christian Mason would have considered himself as governed by the 'New Covenant' represented by the New Testament and not necessarily bound by the statements in Genesis. However, Mason does not as a rule avoid the Old Testament in favour of the New, and he quotes from both. According to Ken Buck in his book *Bill Mason: Wilderness Artist* (2005), Mason resolved this seeming contradiction by believing that 'man did not have "dominion over" but "responsibility for" the world. God did not create the world for man to abuse it, exploit it, to destroy it. Man must nurture it.' Buck attributes this interpretation of the Genesis passage to conversations[31] Mason had with the pastor at Elim Chapel in Winnipeg, Dr. Fred Mitchell, when he was a young man. But even the mission to nurture the natural world implies that humans are somehow above it, separate from it; can Christians ever become part of the 'life of the land,' as Mason believes First Nations peoples did? When Mason quotes the Bible in his films and published works, he chooses passages like Revelations 7:3, 'Hurt not the Earth,' or the affirmation that the natural world demonstrates God's love in Job 12:7–10. These passages are more allusive and less controversial than Genesis, and their poetic diction and syntax make them accessible to non-Christians as poetic and spiritual texts rather than doctrinaire statements of faith.

Mason's environmentalism and his faith joined together in the aesthetic ideology of the sublime, which offered an iconic model for his painting and photography and a philosophical justification for it. For the late-eighteenth-century thinkers who formulated the idea of the sublime, the wilderness was a landscape 'where the supernatural lay just beneath the surface,'[32] and God showed his face 'in those vast, powerful landscapes where one could not help feeling insignificant and being reminded of one's own mortality':[33] 'great cliffs and deep chasms, high waterfalls and tall mountains – which were seen as Nature's grandeur: awesome and emotionally inspiring but unyielding to human control or containment.'[34] Painters who reference the sublime in their art utilize a focus of interest low in the foreground of the painting to emphasize the huge scale of the natural wonders represented and create effects of light and shade (sunsets, dawns) to infuse them with an aura of power and wonder. Carefully composed landscape paintings often included human figures in the foreground to emphasize by contrast the scale of the cliffs or mountains depicted (for a Canadian example, see Lucius O'Brien, *Sunrise on the Saguenay,* 1880). Romantic thinkers in the early nineteenth century suggested that these artworks, and the natural landscapes that they represented, had an emotional effect on viewers; by challenging viewers to comprehend the size and power of the landscapes they represented, they created a sense of wonder, awe, and terror and recalled to mind the power of God. Mason's favourite painter, the British landscape artist J.M.W. Turner, embodied in his landscape paintings the idea of the sublime articulated by Edmund Burke in his influential study, *A Philosophical Enquiry into the Origin of our Ideas of the Sublime and Beautiful* (1757). Following Burke, Turner perceived the sublime not as a characteristic of landscapes, but as an internalized emotional effect located in the viewer. 'Among the best proofs that one had entered a sublime landscape was the emotion it evoked,'[35] and this feeling of sublimity became the subject of Turner's paintings. For Canadian painters like members of the Group of Seven, the canoe was a cultural object of desire because it offered 'a means of fulfilling the desire to interact directly with Nature' and the 'emotional directness of personal experience'[36] in their paintings.

   Mason achieved the effects of sublimity in his films by adopting the point of view of the canoeist, low on the water, and then mimicking his experience by angling the camera up to capture the way rocks, trees, or cliffs towered over the water. In films like *Paddle to the Sea,* long shots show the tiny carving of a canoeist dwarfed by the cliffs of Lake Superior and later by the huge freighters of the St. Lawrence Seaway. In *Waterwalker,* close-ups of Mason's paddling self draw back to reveal a screen dominated by huge Lake Superior swells or towering waterfalls. In his paintings, Mason produces both traditional realistic landscapes that focus on the size and grandeur of his subjects in *Virginia Falls, Nahanni River, Wilberforce Falls,* and *Dry Channel Hood River,* and more impressionistic and Turner-like paintings of sublimity as feeling in *In the Depths of Wilberforce Canon I* or *Surf on Rocky Point, Old Woman Bay, Lake Superior.*[37]

The focus of interest is low in the foreground of many of his paintings of cliffs and waterfalls, and the vivid contrasts of light and shade that suggest rough, broken, and threatening waves or rocks evoke the 'feeling' of awe and wonder as well as the aesthetic pleasure that joined together his three passions: canoeing in the wilderness, Christian faith, and art.

Jonathan Bordo points out, however, that the paintings by the Group of Seven that Mason emulated, unlike Turner's, were premised on the removal of any evidence of human presence. Bordo suggests that this differentiates the 'New World' wilderness painting of Canada, the US, or Australia from the tradition of European landscape painting, which conventionally included some evidence of human habitation, even if only fences, ruins, or gravestones. Bordo suggests that the paradox of the wilderness painting, which is the paradox of the wilderness sublime, is that it implies a viewer, which in itself contradicts its status as wilderness. Bordo suggests that the evidence of First Nations cultures is so systematically removed from Canadian 'wilderness' painting that wilderness itself is nothing more than 'a proper name used instead of inherited place names in colonial situations to justify the violent capture and dispossession of territory.'[38] In other words, you can't have 'wilderness' without internalizing the values of colonialism.

William Cronon agrees that colonialism is constitutive of 'wilderness' as conceived by the sorts of environmental movements that Bill Mason inspired: wilderness preservation societies, for example, or deep ecologists. For Cronon, uninhabited wilderness is nothing more than a creation of the public policy that removed First Nations from their traditional territories, in concert with the 'thoroughgoing erasure of the history from which it sprang.'[39] Indeed, because wilderness refers to 'the original garden, it is a place outside of time ... wilderness offers us the illusion that we can escape the cares and troubles of the world in which our past has ensnared us.'[40] Positioned as the pre-existing state of nature, wilderness becomes the standard against which the environmentalist measures the failings of our human world; 'Wilderness is the natural, unfallen antithesis of an unnatural civilization that has lost its soul.'[41] Cronon suggests that the 'escape from history' is the reason why agnostics and even atheists accept the language of God and spirituality in discussions of the wilderness sublime; it substitutes a critique of modern industrialist capitalism for a critique of current and past policies of genocide and theft, justifying the 'preservation of the wilderness' for the alternative it offers to a violent and valueless modernity and eliding the way that 'wilderness' participated in that very violence: 'Once set aside within the fixed and carefully policed boundaries of the modern bureaucratic state, the wilderness lost its savage image and became safe: a place more of reverie than of revulsion or fear. Meanwhile, its original inhabitants were kept out by dint of force, their earlier uses of the land redefined as inappropriate or even illegal.'[42]

Cronon's analysis reveals the tautology that is built into the idea of wilderness: 'if wild nature is the only thing worth saving, and if our mere presence destroys it, then the sole solution to our own unnaturalness, the only way to protect sacred wilderness from profane humanity, would seem to be suicide.'[43] By idealizing (past) First Nations culture as 'the life of the land' without acknowledging either the reason for their absence or understanding their traditional use of resources, Mason seems to suggest 'that the only way human beings can hope to live naturally on earth is to follow the hunter-gatherers back into a wilderness Eden and abandon virtually everything that civilization has given us.'[44] But Mason does offer a way out of this tautology. By characterizing the desecration of wilderness as sin, he implies that there is a way to live in harmony with wilderness: by following the tenets of a secularized Christianity and respecting the wilderness as 'God's Creation.'

When Mason decided to try to sum up his ideas about the relationship between his faith, his canoeing, and his art in *Waterwalker*, he faced the challenge of trying to get his ideas across not only to a secular audience, but also to the producers of Studio D, the legendary feminist wing of the NFB. Mason had been attached to Studio D at its formation; while his solitary style of working did not particularly mesh with the goals of Studio D, the administrative structure allowed him the freedom to work at his home at Meech Lake, and executive producer Kathleen Shannon knew him and admired his work. However, when Mason screened an early version of *Waterwalker* with commentary that specifically referred to a traditional male Christian God (and no other form of spirituality), Shannon and other members of the unit were appalled. Raffan quotes 'spirited internal memos' that declared, 'Nature is for all of us, including women. The Great Spirit is genderless' and 'Must they bring their male God idols into mother nature's sanctuary?'[45] Mason responded by revising the commentary to remove references to an exclusively Christian God and substituting quotations attributed to First Nations elders culled from a book edited by Terry C. McLuhan, *Touch the Earth: A Self-Portrait of Indian Existence* (1971). Mason chose quotations from the opening sections of the book that talk about the strong identification of First Nations peoples with their traditional territories[46] and refer to a genderless 'Creator' or 'Great Spirit' in order to mitigate identification with a specifically Christian God. Read by First Nations actor and activist Wilf Pelletier, these quotations boom through the woods and over the water as Mason listens, seeming for all the world like the voice of nature itself.

The prominence of First Nations voices in *Waterwalker* highlights the absence of actual First Nations peoples in the film. While Mason's commentary claims that 'because they live close to the land, they're the experts,' no First Nations person appears in the film, and there is no mention of contemporary First Nations issues such as land claims, resource ownership, or treaty violations (even though *Touch the Earth* includes a substantial section on this). Indeed, Raffan points out that Mason's view of Native peoples came from movies and 'his childhood imagination' and that 'he never actively sought to find out if the movie image in any way matched the contemporary reality of First Nations life.'[47] Instead, Mason represents himself searching for historic camp-sites and petroglyphs on the shore of Lake Superior and imagining 'their lives here, how they lived.' The disembodied voice of Wilf Pelletier adds to the impression that 'Indians' are part of the past, not the present. Ironically, when the Friends of Bill Mason tried to have a parcel of land on the north shore of Lake Superior set aside in Mason's memory after his death, the local First Nation demonstrated just how alive they were by objecting and quashing the deal.[48]

From an analytical point of view, Mason's representations of First Nations people seem contradictory and confusing. According to the credits, *Paddle to the Sea* featured Kyle Apatagen as the Native boy who made 'Paddle'; the sequences of his home life were filmed in a cabin rented by Mason's friend and collaborator Blake James, but no other information about this actual living Native person is in print, despite Mason's supposed respect for and idealization of Native peoples. Mason states in *Waterwalker* that the Native peoples he identifies with 'left no written words, only rearranged boulders on the beaches, or pictographs on the rock faces,' yet this sequence is followed by the words of Native elders from *Touch the Earth*, which presumably were written down some-where. And the animal movies feature no First Nations people at all, despite Mason's statement in *Waterwalker* that 'they're the experts.'

The motif of the 'disappearing Indian' in Mason's work is of a piece with his representation of the wilderness as an 'anachronistic space,'[49] a space that is not just physically separate from 'civilization,' but separate from it in time. Mason often referred in his books and his films to a canoe journey as a journey 'back' to the way North America was before it was settled, to 'a world unchanged and unspoiled as God had created it.'[50] The wilderness is defined by 'places that had remained unchanged for centuries'; the Barrens are described in the wolf films as 'a chunk of nature man hadn't touched' and 'a land where ... nothing has changed here for thousands of years.'[51] The implication is that by travelling 'back' to the timeless wilderness, we can 'rediscover' an attitude towards the land that was common to First Nations peoples, that we can '[get] things back into their original perspective.'[52] In looking at the traditions of First Nations peoples or at wilderness landscapes, Mason believes we are looking into the past, and that past is our own.

Despite the way that Mason's work incorporates the tropes of nationalist discourse, surprisingly he does not talk in his films or his books specifically about Canada or Canadian nationality. However, his admirers identify him thoroughly with the debates about 'national identity' that were common in the seventies and eighties. Ken Buck, in *Bill Mason: Wilderness Artist*, wrote that 'Few people have had the influence Bill Mason had in shaping the Canadian identity ... he helped shape Canadians' understanding of their own land, challenging them to love it as much as he did.'[53] Buck declares that his own experience as collaborator and editor on Mason's films helped him to understand 'the role of the artist-storyteller who constructed stories for a nation' and 'the importance of stories in defining who we are.'[54] Producer Bill Brind, who worked with Mason on the wolf films, wrote: 'Anyone who thinks we don't have an identity should spend time with Mason – he couldn't possibly be anything other than a Canadian.'[55] James Raffan states that Mason 'is synonymous with the canoe in Canadian culture,'[56] and Canada Post issued a Bill Mason stamp in 1998, honouring him as a 'legendary Canadian.'

One of Mason's few statements about Canada as a nation defines Canada's uniqueness by identifying the land itself with the canoe: 'In Canada, you can put a canoe into the water at any major city and paddle to the Atlantic, the Pacific, the Arctic, or the Gulf of Mexico ... When you look at the face of Canada and study the geography carefully, you come away with the feeling that God could have designed the canoe first and then set about to conceive a land in which it could flourish.'[57] To a reader who shares Mason's belief in design, this may mean, quite literally, that God was thinking of our pleasure when Canada was made; but to a secular nationalist, the identification of the land and the canoe creates a pathway that, if followed, will lead to a felt sense of nationality, a 'natural' unity of the nation as idea and the nation as geography. By canoeing, and by living in an environmentally responsible way, Mason implies, we not only enjoy the physical pleasure of the clear air and bird-song, the aesthetics of wilderness landscapes, and the joy of freedom, but we can also become part of 'the life of the land' and achieve an identifi-cation with it that overcomes that sense of 'being alien in Canada.'

In the wake of Mason's astonishing popularity and his early death, many canoeists and canoeing writers find in him an iconic figure who represents a bridge between human culture and the land. Raffan writes that Mason overcame the 'garrison mentality,' Northrop Frye's famous characterization of the psychological fear of the natural world that he felt Canadians were doomed to because of their European origins. For Raffan, Mason was 'totally at home in the wilderness. For him the woods were not something against which a palisade wall must be built but a phenomenon to be embraced … Mason, like his tent, was open to the teachings of the wild.'[58] More recent writers take his ideas further to suggest that the canoe can facilitate a kind of mystical union with the land. Bert Horwood writes: 'The canoe is a dialogue with a river, opening opportunities to wonder, both in contrasting the power and tranquillity of the world experienced at first hand, and in the penetration to explore more fully the meaning of that wonder.'[59] Alister Thomas suggests in his article 'Paddling Voices' that 'canoeing is a conduit to heightened per-ception as well as a sense of renewal. There can be a feeling of flow to the wild in the wilderness and to a deep sense of *being* – a spiritual connec-tion, an immersion.'[60] In his analysis of thirty-seven canoeing narratives, Thomas identifies a narrator he calls 'The Poet,' who 'describe[s] a close relationship with the land' and focuses on sensory experiences in the wild that offer a 'revelation of truth about life and sometimes self.'[61] The canoe has become a symbol of harmony with the natural world for envi-ronmentalists, and recreational canoeing a means to a greater awareness of human implication in the natural world: Bob Henderson writes, 'Deep ecology encourages us to ask more comprehensive questions about our place on the earth … As a canoe guide, I ask the question, how can the canoe trip help to bring us "home" within the earth.'[62] If the nation is, as Daniel Francis avers, a group of people who share the same illusions about themselves, Bill Mason and his vision of the canoe is central to Canadians' illusion that the canoe is 'the symbol of our oneness with a rugged northern landscape.'[63]

Chapter Seven

Recapitulation:
The Canadian Canoe Museum

The Canadian Canoe Museum houses over 600 canoes and kayaks, the largest historical collection of its kind in the world. The canoes were collected by Kirk Wipper, a retired professor of physical education and health at the University of Toronto and also the owner and director (from 1957 to 1978) of Camp Kandalore, a private summer camp for boys in Haliburton county north of Toronto. Wipper considered the canoe a Canadian cultural icon, a symbolic object whose material composition and cultural associations represent the meanings of Canada itself and whose place at the centre of Canadian history was self-evident. As his collection grew and part of it became publicly funded, it became for him a legacy that he would leave to the nation. When Wipper retired, the collection was acquired by a group of enthusiastic volunteers in Peterborough, Ontario, who supported Wipper's vision of its symbolic and national significance. Through their dedicated efforts, a museum building was eventually purchased and renovated to display the canoes both as typological icons representing in themselves the symbolic qualities of Canadian nationality and as material evidence of the narrative of Canadian history that placed the canoe at its centre. But despite the museum's commitment to honouring First Nations as the originators of the canoe and as contributors to the building of the Canada, the place of First Nations in the museum remains controversial and the subject of debate and critique among the museum professionals and historians that constructed it. Like the canoe itself, the museum displays seem to exhibit the ideological contradictions that are inherent in the nationalist historiography they depict.

The collection of canoes that eventually became the heart of the Canadian Canoe Museum was initially assembled at Camp Kandalore as part of Kirk Wipper's commitment to experiential education. Wipper believed that 'roughing it' through camping and canoeing was an important formative experience for young men – an antidote for fast-paced, stressful city life – and his rhetoric of camping spoke of instilling in boys the qualities of independence, endurance, teamwork, self-confidence, reverence for nature, and a particular kind of manliness that was also thought to be necessary for success in capitalist enterprise. The practice of canoeing itself was part of the program of increasing physical competence and building confidence for each boy. As Wipper acquired new, interesting, or historical canoes, the boys were encouraged to try them out and to learn the differences among them. The canoes built by the Peterborough Canoe Company, referred to as 'Couchiching Freighters,' were used by groups of very young children: they were stable and safe, yet allowed each boy to paddle and to contribute. The large birchbark canoes were occasionally used by older boys in order to allow them feel a sense of generational continuity and identification with Canadian history. The collection grew and came to include historic canoes that were too fragile for use; Wipper raised money to construct a log museum building on the grounds of Camp Kandalore to house them, and he opened his 'Kanawa International Museum' to the public.[1]

Collections typically serve complex purposes for collectors, helping to signal their class status and their public identities as well as the darker elements of personality like obsession, control, and acquisitiveness. Like most collectors, Professor Wipper had a strong emotional investment in ownership of his collection of canoes; while the nature of and motivations behind his collection can only be speculated, the facts of Kirk Wipper's life support a fairly clear picture. Camp Kandalore, like other historic Ontario summer camps, was the cradle of the Toronto elite; it had an overwhelmingly white clientele, and like most of the private camps in Ontario its fees restricted campers to the upper and upper-middle classes. A list of alumni of private summer camps in Ontario like Kandalore, Ahmek, and Wanipitei is a litany of leaders of business and government, including students from tony schools like Upper Canada College, Rosseau Lake School, and Appleby College and people like former Prime Ministers John Turner and Pierre Trudeau. The VP Academic of my own university attended Wipper's camp. In contrast, Wipper had grown up on what Gwyneth Hoyle refers to as a 'marginal immigrant farm,' was educated in a one-room schoolhouse, and participated in Boy Scouts by correspondence. After his service in the navy in the Second World War, he earned undergraduate degrees in physical education and social work, and on the strength of these and his outstanding work with boys from poor families for the YMCA, he was hired as a faculty member at the University of Toronto in 1950 at the age of twenty-seven. He eventually earned an MA, his only graduate degree. His directorship of Camp Kandalore brought him into contact with the leading and established families in southern Ontario; his status among them would have been enhanced by his engagement in collecting, a pastime associated with the rich and philanthropic. He solicited donations of canoes and money from Kandalore families, which created ongoing social relationships. His choice to collect canoes, which had and continue to have sentimental and nostalgic associations for white, middle-class Ontario families, situated him clearly in a particular web of social relationships. In addition, as a faculty member at the University of Toronto, without a PhD and with few academic publications, his collecting and the occasional publications he issued under the name of the museum may have done service as academic research, protecting his status as a professional and an intellectual as universities became increasingly insistent on scholarly publication.

The collection began to outgrow Camp Kandalore, and in 1975 Wipper formed a non-profit museum corporation with a board of directors drawn from former campers and family members. In 1976 this board successfully applied for funding from the Ontario Lottery Corporation, acquired a significant collection of Aboriginal watercraft (known as the Heye Collection) from the Museum of the American Indian in New York, and began to think about expanding as a significant independent cultural institution. But they received a cold reception from many existing museums and cultural funding agencies. The log building was significantly below standard for a museum: it had no fire exits or sprinkler systems, was unheated, and was otherwise unsuited for modern museum conservation techniques. Yet Wipper was committed to the log building as part of his vision of a Canadiana museum that would represent Ontario canoe culture as he understood it. In addition, many of the canoes had little or no documentation about their histories or even their acquisition; some had sales receipts, but in many cases Wipper was the only source of information, and sometimes he forgot. This made it difficult to positively identify the age of canoes, who had made them, and their cultural contexts, and so the collection was of less interest to established museums. But most importantly, because many of the canoes had little or no information on record, it was difficult to tell which canoes had been donated or purchased with public money, and so belonged to the Kanawa museum, and which canoes belonged to Wipper personally. At this time Wipper had no intention of giving up personal control of the collection, and this was a significant barrier to acquiring additional public funding.

When in 1980 Wipper began to look for another institution to take responsibility for his collection, a group centred at the history department at Trent University began to negotiate with funding agencies, donors, and Wipper himself to move the canoes to Peterborough. The then president of Trent, Donald Theall, was a canoe enthusiast and very interested in setting up the museum as an independent institution on campus, based on the model already established by the Museum of Anthropology at the University of British Columbia. He appointed Bruce Hodgins, history professor and director of Camp Wanapitei, to chair a committee consisting of canoeing enthusiasts from the faculty and administration as well as the community of Peterborough. The committee commissioned a feasibility study from architects MacLennan Associates, who produced a final report in May 1983. When their first choice for a site (near the lift lock in Peterborough) proved to be unavailable, Trent University became the first choice for location. While the estimated costs looked prohibitive, the Trent-Kanawa committee was convinced that the university's record in private and public fund-raising justified their optimism about moving the collection to Trent, even if it was to be housed in a slightly less ambitious building than the one envisioned in the study. However, the plan required Wipper to relinquish his control and ownership of the collection, to donate 'his' canoes to the museum corporation, and initially he was not willing to do so.

Thus began a period of frustration and hard feelings on all sides. Wipper felt that if he was giving up ownership and control of the museum he should be compensated for his out-of-pocket expenses; otherwise he wanted to retain ownership. His personal life and finances were in crisis, and his many friends and supporters associated with the camping movement and the canoe museum were strongly motivated to rally round and support him. For him, the canoes signified a lifetime of financial and personal investment in outdoor education as well as, perhaps, the material proof of his scholarship and his connection to powerful and influential Toronto families. As his situation worsened, he grew more and more attached to the canoes as representative of a personal legacy. Unbeknownst to the Trent-Kanawa committee, he approached the city of Port Hope about displaying his collection (without giving up ownership) and negotiated with the county of Haliburton to continue to display part of the collection there. The Trent-Kanawa committee, composed completely of volunteers who had devoted a great deal of time and energy to securing university support for the project, discovered these negotiations through the newspapers and felt betrayed. For them, the canoes were an educational and national resource that could only serve its proper purpose under public ownership and professional stewardship. Wipper contacted the Museum of Civilization in Ottawa and the historical site at St. Marie among the Hurons and discovered that they were not willing to assume responsibility for the whole collection: they could not display all the canoes, and the remainder would require too much precious storage space. Meanwhile the months passed, and by the time Wipper again called on his supporters at Trent for help in 1988, the administration at Trent had changed and the new president, John Stubbs, was not willing to support the project.

The Trent group was disappointed, but still wanted to bring the collection to Peterborough. On 15 May 1990 they drove to Toronto en masse to attend an annual meeting of the Kanawa Museum board of directors and, with its consent, voted themselves into office. The subsequent events, retailed on the Canoe Museum website in heroic terms, seemed more like a nightmare to the museum professionals who eventually took over. Wipper had already taken some of the canoes to Port Hope, where some donated artefacts had been left outside to rot; others were still at the (unheated) museum building in Haliburton county, and still more were on display in Peterborough. Volunteers took rented trucks, collected the canoes, and brought them to be stored in Alf Cole's barn (Alf Cole was the registrar at Trent) and later in a rented chicken barn outside Peterborough. All the storage spaces were unheated, had no protection against fire, and were occupied by bugs and rodents. When the museum conservators finally got to work on the collection, many of the most significant objects had suffered serious damage. Eventually, through the joint fund-raising efforts of board president, law professor, and former camper Jamie Benidickson and history professor John Jennings, enough money was found to compensate Wipper for his financial outlay, and in 1995 the museum acquired ownership of all the canoes.

The saga of how the museum eventually acquired the canoes from Wipper is not a unique one; it is repeated with variations in the histories of many non-profit and public museums that have their roots in collections assembled by individuals. The history of the McCord Museum in Montreal and the controversy over control of the McMichael Gallery in Kleinburg, Ontario, have involved similar struggles among collectors, professional museum staff, and public funding bodies, often to the detriment of collections and institutions.[2] Wipper was a well-known and loved public figure, rightly celebrated for his achievements in his academic career and his dedication to the assembly of his collection. However, the protracted struggle over the personal and public meanings of his collection, expressed symbolically in the struggle over its ownership, resulted in damaged artefacts, a collection of diminished value, and a legacy of mistrust in the museum community that continues to threaten opportunities for the Canadian Canoe Museum.

In 1996, the Outboard Marine Corporation of Canada donated the site of their former manufacturing business to house the collection, and the museum opened on 1 July 1997 with exhibits constructed by volunteers. Further funding obtained from private donors and a federal government Millennium Infrastructure Grant allowed the renovation of the building in 1999 and funded the design and construction of professional museum exhibits. The original group of Trent professors, many now retired or nearing retirement, continue their involvement with the museum by serving on the academic advisory committee that vets museum text panels and offers suggestions and commentary for displays. The financial position of the museum is still precarious; it was forced to close in 2004 and asked for help from public funding agencies to cover its debts; the final plan for construction, which includes ameliorating the contaminated soil at the rear of the site, has still not been completed. But the museum is open, has received significant support from the press and local volunteers, and recently received a donation of three canoes from the royal family, presented in person by Prince Andrew. The new director, James Raffan, has an extensive history as a canoe enthusiast and is a popular and successful author of canoeing books; if the new museum website is any indication, he is working hard to increase the complexity and seriousness of the museum's mission.

Museum collections, even those that consist of only one kind of type of artefact, are systematically organized by collectors into internal divisions: ordered, as it were, according to categories that have resonance for a given society. In Wipper's original log museum, the Kanawa collection was divided into two categories, Aboriginal watercraft and non-Native watercraft, their difference maintained by their being displayed on separate floors of the two-storey museum. This emphasis on differentiating the Aboriginal and non-Aboriginal watercraft was continued in the early papers of the Trent-Kanawa committee: the original feasibility study listed five categories of canoes in the collection: Aboriginal watercraft;

South Pacific watercraft; fur trade canoes; leisure canoes; other non-Native watercraft (this category included an Irish coracle, for example). This new conception of the collection was based on the priorities of the historians now working to preserve it, who were in the main, fur trade scholars and recreational white-water canoeists. A memo from Board of Trustees Chair Jamie Benidickson to the board[3] laments that Wipper's collection policy seemed to be summed up by the phrase 'gather every-thing that floats,' and it suggests that policy decisions need to be made to govern the 'core enterprise' of the museum: to preserve and interpret canoes related specifically to Canadian history. In the final storage and display of the collection, categories such as 'Aboriginal' and 'non-Aboriginal,' 'leisure' and 'trade,' and 'canoes made in Peterborough' govern how the artefacts are arranged, with galleries designed to highlight what are perceived by the curatorial staff as 'fine,' 'typical,' or 'historically important' examples of the different categories.

Typological displays (displays of one type of artefact) are not currently fashionable in museum studies because they focus on defining a category of artefact and thus prevent proper contextualization of each artefact in relation to its historical period and source culture. However, the typological displays in the Canoe Museum are not merely responses to the categories that order the collection; they are also a response to the problems in collections management, budget, and storage posed by the large number of canoes in the collection and their various states of repair when they finally arrived at the museum. The first priority of the museum staff was to identify and stabilize the most fragile artefacts and move them into climate-controlled quarters. Funds raised in the late 1990s brought the main museum building up to appropriate standards, but the larger building that was to store most of the collection remained unheated. For this reason, one of the priorities of the new display in the main museum building was to get as many canoes as possible, and those of the most fragile type, into the display. This is exactly the opposite of the practices of most museums, which try to shield their most fragile objects from damage due to light, dust, and handling by keeping them out of displays. This priority dictated the look of the 'Origins,' 'It Wasn't All Work,' and 'Peterborough Tradition' galleries, which contain many canoes with little in the way of cultural interpretation or context associated with each individual canoe. Canoes are piled upon each other on storage racks and hang from the ceiling as if airborne. This arrangement makes a kind of sense for the leisure and Peterborough galleries – the canoes look as though they might be stored in overhead racks, the way they would be in a boathouse or a shop – but the effect in the Origins gal-lery seems bizarre, with the canoes suspended from the ceiling at unu-sual angles and spotlights casting shadows that make them difficult to see clearly. The canoes look like illustrations of the famous Quebec folk-tale of the 'Chasse-galerie,' the canoe full of the souls of the damned that flew through the night sky.

The fragile condition of the canoes also contributes to the bizarre 'Chasse-galerie' effect of the Origins gallery. The conservation staff has made it a priority to stabilize the older and more important artefacts rather than restore them (and in doing so replace historic materials with new ones) as might be done with less historically significant examples.[4] The results are not necessarily pretty; hanging the canoes from the ceil-ing, at different angles, sometimes showing the interior and sometimes the exterior, allows the stabilization work to be hidden from view.

The taxonomy of a collection, the way that it is ordered and arranged in categories, reveals much about the values of the society that collects. Eilean Hooper-Greenhill, in her book *Museums and the Shaping of Knowl-edge* (1992), argues that the classification, ordering, and framing of museum artefacts reveals the structure of rationality upon which a cul-ture is based – the assertions that are taken as given, the assumptions that are beyond question for a rational subject in a particular culture. Such a structure is historically determined, and hence unstable and capable of challenge and change: ordering a collection on the basis of categories such as 'Aboriginal' and 'non-Aboriginal' or 'trade' and 'leisure' reveals the assumptions intrinsic to the collectors' society and demonstrates its anxiety to materialize and reinforce these categories, to place them beyond question. The selection of an individual canoe as representative of its category gives it an additional meaning, according to museum the-orist Susan Pearce in her book *Museums, Objects and Collections* (1992). 'Everything that goes into a collection of whatever kind has done so as a result of selection. The selection process is the crucial act of the col-lector, regardless of what intellectual, economic or idiosyncratic reasons he may have when he decides how his selection will work, what he will choose and what he will reject. What he chooses bears an intrinsic, direct and organic relationship, that is a metonymic relationship, to the body of material from which it was selected because it is an integral part of it. But the very act of selection adds to its nature. By being chosen away and lifted out of the embedding metonymic matrix, the selected collection now bears a representative or metaphorical relationship to its whole. It becomes an image of what the whole is believed to be, and although it remains an intrinsic part of the whole, it is no longer merely a detached fragment because it has become imbued with meaning of its own.'5 This final stage is fetishization, the attribution of meaning to the object in and of itself. This meaning is completely irrelevant to the status of the object as an object for use, and it is available only to the collector and his or her own society as material proof of their own world-view, their ideology. For Pearce, museum fetishization occurs in six stages, beginning with sensory discrimination between and among objects, which becomes basis for the collector's choice to accept or reject an object. The resulting assemblage of artefacts is divided into categories, and the categories themselves are reified as 'things' that have an objective existence. Collectors or curators select a single object, an icon, to represent a category and (in retrospect) identify that icon as representing the qualities necessary for inclusion in the category: in doing so they attribute numinous meaning and life to the iconic object.[6]

The series of postcards of canoes produced by the Canadian Canoe Museum represents iconic embodiments of the ideal categories that structure the collection: they are 'fine examples' of Aboriginal canoes and kayaks, fur trade canoes, turn-of-the-century leisure canoes, historical canoes built in Peterborough, and the canvas and wood canoe popular with environmentalists and canoe-campers in the late 1960s and 1970s. These postcards represent the canoes with no context at all: there is not even a representation of a surface that they are resting on; they appear to be floating in air. The lighting diffuses the shadows that would usually occur with single source lighting – the shadows that are everywhere, in fact, in the museum itself. This kind of lighting is associated with fine art objects, and indeed everything about these postcards is designed to make the viewer look at the canoe like it is a fine art object. They focus on the colours, decoration, richness of wood, and elegance of the curved lines of the canoes, as well as the evidence of use and age that confirm them as representations of material objects, real things, that are both beautiful and usable. Cut off from their context, and from their individual histories as artefacts, museum icons are mobilized as an embodiment of the category they are intended to represent; they make the category 'real' by giving it a material 'proof.'

In the final taxonomy of the collection and its embodiment in postcard 'icons,' a new category appears – boats made in Peterborough – and two categories have disappeared – South Pacific watercraft and other non-Aboriginal watercraft. These boats are still owned by the museum, but they are stored away and not on display. While the 1983 feasibility

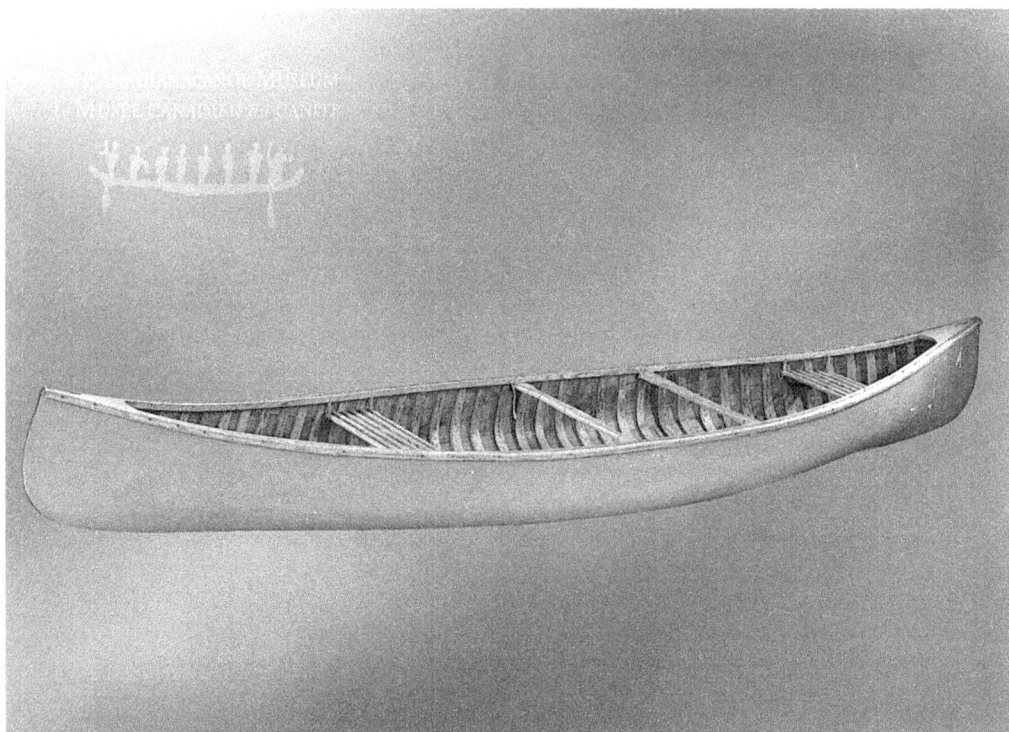

Postcard image of Bill Mason's canoe.
Courtesy of the Canadian Canoe Museum.

study suggested that the theme of the museum displays should be the history of watercraft, this direction was rejected for a number of reasons. When Executive Director Jack Matthews undertook serious fund-raising in 1990 he urged the board to change the name from 'Kanawa International Museum' to Canadian Canoe Museum, a move which he argued gave the museum a national title that was 'essential from a fund-raising point of view.'[7] An early planning document written by then-Chair Jamie Benidickson pointed out that the choice of display themes would be crucial to attracting audiences and to fund-raising. 'I have yet to meet anyone whose primary interest is kanawas,' he wrote.[8] Planning documents and the Millennium Grant application demonstrate that by 1998 the permanent displays were organized to show the history of Canada through the canoe, emphasizing the important collection of indigenous canoes but also showcasing leisure canoeing and canoe-camping, with the goal of appealing to federal funding agencies, leisure canoeists (who were also potential donors), and school groups studying the history of Canada.

The decision to make the history of Canada the focus of the display means that chronology as well as taxonomy determines the order of the canoes in the Canadian Canoe Museum. Chronological arrangement is common in museum displays because the experience of a museum is almost always linear and progressive, the linear sequence being created by the experience of a walking subject who meets a series of static objects. The order or sequence of objects can be random, or it may be controlled by their physical placement using scrims, walls or other temporary divisions of the space, numbered text panels, or narrated tours. As Michael Brawne points out in *The Museum Interior* (1982), 'the way in which any sequence is controlled or free is … likely to alter our awareness of objects and especially their initial impact.'[9] 'Very often sequence is controlled because it can ... suggest the dimension of time, as in a natural history display of evolutionary development, or in a museum showing the history of a town, or in a gallery devoted to a school of painting.'[10] The museum-goer's movement through the Canoe Museum's permanent display, titled 'The Canoe: A Canadian Cultural Icon,' is controlled by various architectural features (including stairways, railings, walls, and dividers) in order to guide the museum-goer chronologically through Canadian history from 'Origins' to the present.

The display starts in the lobby of the museum with an architectural feature consisting of a waterfall with trees beside a staircase. This is a representation of 'Grand Portage,' which invites the museum-goer to enter a vision of Canada that is dominated by waterways and the geographical features that determine them and creates a transition from the Canada outside the museum to the Canada governed by the canoe. At the top of the stairs is the 'Origins' gallery, devoted to indigenous canoes and canoe-making and representing the pre-contact period. The entrance to the gallery is dominated by the museum's Nu Chaa Nulth whaling canoe, which introduces a set of text panels and artefacts related to west coast dugout canoes; the remainder of the Origins gallery consists of bark canoes, many from the Heye Collection, and a separate section of kayaks. This gallery concludes with a selection of east coast canoes and a replica of a Mi'kmaq bark tipi, which is used for educational programs (completing a movement from west to east in the Origins gallery). The 'Trade' gallery begins with contact (in the east, in the seventeenth cen-

tury) and represents the importance of the canoe in conveying Europeans westward into the interior of the continent. The displays include
text panels describing the fur trade and a fully loaded 'North Canoe,'
and the gallery ends with a voyageur camp-site that represents the rigid
social hierarchy typical of the fur trade in the nineteenth century. The
'Preserving Skills' gallery is located in an alcove off the Trade gallery,
and it features the charming and knowledgeable Jeremy Ward creating
original artefacts and restoring older ones using traditional techniques.
The storyline continues downstairs in 'The Land Becomes Canada,' a
gallery that addresses the role of the canoe in surveying and exploration in the period after the Hudson's Bay Company ceded its lands to
the Canadian government (approximately 1880–1920). 'It Wasn't All
Work' is a gallery dedicated to leisure canoeing in the first decades of the
twentieth century, and a canoe-camping display features a summer camp
'out-tripping shed' and a salute to Kirk Wipper. A third major gallery on
the first floor displays materials related to the canoe-building industry of
Peterborough, bringing the display up to the mid-twentieth century. The
narrative concludes in the 'Reflections' gallery, which includes display
cases and text panels on popular contemporary canoeists such as Bill
Mason, Eric Morse, and Pierre Trudeau.

A linear, chronological museum display such as one in the Canadian
Canoe Museum works to construct a certain kind of subjectivity for the
museum-goer. Such displays are constructed rather like a traditional
history: they assemble artefacts into a narrative, with a definite origin,
development through a series of events linked by cause and effect, consistent themes and conflicts, and a conclusion that provides a resolution.
Such narratives often utilize third-person narration in text panels, what
literary theorists would call a 'dominant discourse,' to organize facts
and comment on them, making their meanings and links seem 'natural' or 'obvious.' Hayden White has shown how only those narratives
of historical fact that conform to a predetermined cultural pattern are
likely to be perceived as 'real' by readers; he uses the term 'narrativizing'
for the kind of history that arranges events and documentary evidence
into a seamless, single story in such a way that it appears 'natural' and
'real.'[11] The role of the museum visitor in viewing a narrativizing display
is analogous to that of a reader of a realist fiction or a narrative history.
The dominant discourse, embodied in the text panels that explain the
objects, relies on assumptions about reality, about cause and effect, and
about social value, which it assumes are also held by the reader. Thus
the display constructs a 'subject position,' a point of view from which

it makes sense, and invites the reader to identify with it. Examining the assumptions that make up the subject positions created by the display can reveal the structure of rationality that organizes it, just as an analysis of the taxonomic categories into which the collection is organized reveals the structure of rationality that animated its collector, and just as surely displays its ideological contradictions.

'The Canoe: A Canadian Cultural Icon' begins by asking the visitor to take up the position of a paddler, or more accurately, a voyageur, travelling through the Grand Portage towards the North-west of the fur trade. The metaphor initiates the idea of a journey: the traveller is headed against the water flow, as it were, back in time to the 'Origins' of the canoe and of Canada. This message is reinforced by the first text panel, titled 'The canoe: connecting us with our history and land.' The text constructs an 'us' (presumably all Canadians, paddlers, and portagers) who are in a position of ownership with respect to the history and the land represented. The text implicitly claims the 'land' for Canada, despite the fact that the display as a whole, by beginning in an Aboriginal 'Origins' gallery, represents the canoe as arising from pre-contact indigenous cultures.

The Origins gallery at the top of the stairs represents First Nations cultures in the absence of obvious European contact. Maps indicate the locations of traditional territories before contact, and panels describe traditional uses of the canoe (to hunt whales, for example) and traditional canoe-building methods, without commenting on how these changed with the coming of Europeans. The gallery implicitly invites the museum-goer to relive the moment of contact in encountering unfamiliar cultures and historical artefacts and moving through them towards the present.

The Trade gallery emphasizes the contributions of the French, British, and First Nations to fur trade society, extending back into the eighteenth and nineteenth centuries concepts of multiculturalism that typify contemporary Canadian museum representations. The commentary and text boxes offer the museum visitor the position of the liberal Canadian citizen/subject, for whom valuing the unique ethnicities and gendered perspectives of 'other' Canadians is a part of the national identity and appreciated as adding 'colour' to the 'mosaic' of the nation. However, as Deborah Doxtator puts it, this view of a partnership among races and ethnicities distorts the historic position of First Nations: 'multicultural Canadian nationalism … considers itself non-ethnic and "culture-free," with the state presenting itself as the impartial coordinator and arbitrator among … ethnic groups.'[12] Indigenous peoples become just another cultural group defined in opposition to the mainstream, 'ordinary' or 'non-hyphenated' Canadians, a category that is reified and reinforced in the process.

The museum visitor leaves the Trade gallery and descends to the main floor to encounter a large-scale wall-mounted map that illustrates the growth of European occupation. This map introduces a display that focuses on the post-Confederation activities of trade and mapping, activities that the display asserts became the basis of modern-day Canada. However, the title of the gallery, 'The Land Becomes Canada,' disguises some contradictions. While it acknowledges that land claimed by Canada was not always Canada, it stops short of saying what it was. It does this by evoking the romantic notion of a union between people and landscape, figuring 'the land' as a physical fact uninscribed by human politics and Canada as the society, people, and history that were created by the interaction between human beings and that land. However, the land was not uninscribed by human activity before Canada was created; the struggles of First Nations to resist Canadian sovereignty are elided in this statement, as are those of Euro-Canadian and mixed-race communities to oppose the centralized administration that Canada represented. More practically, the statement 'The Land Becomes Canada' seems to contradict the construction of the previous galleries as representing stages in a seamless 'Canadian' history.

The next gallery, titled 'It Wasn't All Work,' focuses on leisure canoeing in or near urban areas in Canada. The canoes are framed by enlarged photographs from popular canoe clubs in Toronto and vacation areas north of Toronto, as well as some photographs representing other parts of Canada. This section concludes with a reproduction of a summer camp 'out-tripping' shed equipped with life-jackets, tents, cooking equipment, and maps for planning summer canoe-camping trips. This display appeals strongly to nostalgia in the Toronto-based visitor: my mother recognizes the photos of the Balmy Beach Canoe Club, where my father's jazz band played in the forties and fifties; I had forgotten the word 'out-trip,' once an important part of my summer-camp vocabulary, until I was reminded on my visit to the museum. But the display's primary purpose, as well as that of the 'out-tripping' shed and the tribute to Kirk Wipper that follow, is to connect the museum-goer with a personal history of canoeing and canoeing landscapes.

The next gallery features the history of Peterborough-based canoe companies and includes descriptions of the different ways that companies tried to mass-produce canoes for sale and export, focusing on the struggle to create a watertight model that would not need the attention of skilled craftsmen but could be created by trained labourers. The text panels assume the visitor's interest in the ways that canoes are built, but do not problematize the de-skilling of jobs and their transfer to non-indigenous workmen, or the assumption that industrialization is a good thing. Instead, the gallery celebrates technological innovation and business acumen, as well as the community of Peterborough itself. This seems appropriate, given that many of the off-season visitors to the museum are likely to be Peterborough-area residents and, especially, students and school children eager to connect the gallery to their own personal histories.

The final gallery is in some ways the most interesting. 'Reflections' consists of a series of display cases featuring famous canoeists: Eric Morse, Bill Mason, Pierre Trudeau, Victoria Jason, Tony and Robin Fraser. I call it the Hall of the Saints. Each case contains objects featured in films or books about these figures – their life-jackets, map cases, paddles, caps, packs – and extensive interpretive text panels of quotations and enlarged photographs. A text box features the famous quotation from Pierre Trudeau's essay 'Exhaustion and Fulfillment': 'Travel a thousand miles by train and you are a brute; pedal five hundred miles on a bicycle and you remain basically bourgeois; paddle a hundred in a canoe and you are already a child of nature.' Bill Mason's statement of canoeing faith is similarly highlighted: 'It is as if God made the canoe, and then set about making a country in which it could flourish. That country was Canada.' This gallery promulgates a specific ideology of the canoe that links the experience of paddling with moral education, environmentalism, and patriotism. The museum visitor is invited both to 'worship' – to admire and learn from – the paddlers featured, and to identify with them, agree with them, by comparing their own experiences and views with those of the 'saints.' This impression of religious sanctity is not merely my invention: museum staff tell me that people actually do come to the museum specifically to see, or touch, Bill Mason's canoe, as though it were a sacred relic.

This reading of the Canoe Museum's permanent display demonstrates the elements of the subjectivity constructed for its viewer – an 'ordinary,' 'non-hyphenated' Canadian whose nationality has a specific content of multiculturalism and racial tolerance, respect for First Nations, and interest in a particular kind of history; that content includes belief that the experience of paddling is a means to identify with other paddlers, contemporary and historical, and with the land itself – indigenization. And, consistent with the way that the materiality of the canoes in the collection serves to demonstrate the stability of the categories they represent, this display serves as a proof of the existence of Canada, and of a particular kind of Canadian.

When the display was first mounted, the museum's academic advisory committee invited four accomplished scholars from different parts of Canada (Sylvia van Kirk, Arthur 'Skip' Ray, Doug McCalla, and Ken Cruikshank), specializing in the fields of fur trade, indigenous, and environmental history, to 'peer review' the conceptual plan and the display itself. The resulting written reports (which also summarized several hours of discussion among the reviewers, museum employees, volunteers, and committee members) succinctly pointed out the problems with choosing to display chronology while preserving the taxonomic distinctions between categories of canoes. While the Origins gallery was intended to highlight the origins of the canoe in pre-contact indigenous societies and specifically indigenous traditions of canoe construction, none of the actual canoes in the display pre-date contact. Instead, they are contemporaneous with the canoes in the galleries that represented leisure canoeing and canoe-camping in the twentieth century, even though they are separated from those galleries by the Trade display that represents the passage of more than a hundred years. They are placed at the beginning of the display in order to create a chronological distinction between indigenous and non-indigenous canoes that did not exist. Videos of contemporary indigenous canoe-builders appear in the Origins gallery, separated chronologically from discussion of contemporary non-indigenous canoe-builders. And the 'Bluebird' racing canoe, which represents the healthy and ongoing tradition of dugout canoe racing in western reserve communities, is separated from canoes that illustrate other traditions of canoe racing.

Dale Standen, the history professor at Trent who, as chair of the academic advisory committee, arranged for the external review, was optimistic that the results of the review could be incorporated into the museum display. He was critical of the chronological orientation of 'The Canoe: A Canadian Cultural Icon' because it seemed to imply a metanarrative of progress that was inherently disrespectful to indigenous canoe-builders, and he had hoped the name of the Origins gallery could be changed to 'The Inventors' to suggest the way that First Nations canoe-builders continued to innovate and adapt traditional techniques throughout the twentieth century even as the non-indigenous community shifted to

new materials and assembly-line manufacturing. 'Origins makes a powerful suggestion that the gallery is frozen in time in the past and now
everything that follows is an improvement. It's the old idea of progress
that I just want to destroy in those exhibits.' He found that despite the
reviewers' strong feeling that indigenous cultures had been represented
as anachronistic and 'frozen in time,' museum staff were committed to
the chronological format: Standen remarks, 'what I'm really struck by in
my studying of museums is how powerful ideas are once they're embedded. Once you make certain choices it's very easy for those to become
foundation assumptions whether they should be or not. You may want
to pull that out by the roots and say, hey, that doesn't work. But it's very
hard to do that, and once it's institutionalized it takes on a life of its
own.' Standen and the other academics associated with the project feel
strongly that museums 'have opportunities to bring the public in and
engage them in alternatives, ambiguities, debates, [but] that takes an
awful lot of time and thinking and care and working out and we just
didn't have it.' The opening date for the museum had been set for 1 July
2000 to take advantage of the symbolism of both Canada Day and the
new millennium, and as Standen says, 'you've got to get these things up
and running. It's worse than a publishing deadline – there's going to be
an opening, the press is going to be there.'[13] Time constraints as well as
philosophical differences among all the parties involved in the creation
of the displays meant that many of the contradictions remain.

While the Aboriginal canoes stayed in the Origins gallery, John Jennings's article 'The Canadian Canoe Museum and Canada's National
Symbol' suggests the way that the museum decided to address issues of
indigenous representation. For Jennings (a history professor at Trent
specializing in the idea of the frontier in Canada and the US, and a
former vice chair and founding member of the Canoe Museum's board
of directors), the fur trade history of Canada represents a model of multiculturalism, relying as it did on the cooperation, knowledge, and skills
of indigenous peoples, French Canadians, Metis, and Anglo-Canadians.
The canoe can thus function as a reminder that Canadian multiculturalism is not merely a recent government policy, but a founding idea: 'this
vast fur empire was held together by the canoe and by the co-operation
that existed among the main participants … Here, in the fur trade, is the
most notable example of collaboration between Native people and the
two founding peoples of Europe.'[14] Text panels in the fur trade section
of the museum emphasize the diversity of ethnic heritage among fur
trade participants and feature indigenous peoples as active and knowl-

edgeable 'partners' in the trade: one panel features 'the importance of aboriginal knowledge and skills,' while others represent 'the peoples of the fur trade' and quote a visitor to Fort William in 1817 on the 'strange medley' of ethnic diversity he encountered there. However, the choice to physically locate all the indigenous canoes together means that, despite the message on the text panels, by the time the museum visitor reaches the twentieth-century displays (back down the stairs on the first floor, separated from the lobby by dividers) the indigenous presence has disappeared; similarly, the arrival of immigrating groups from Asia and eastern Europe does not appear at all. Dale Standen points out, 'if you're going to have a museum that is using the canoe as a window into Canadian history, until you get up to dragon boats, they don't fit into the story very well.'[15]

The relegation of indigenous canoes to the Origins gallery is typical of the way that traditional museum displays in North America incorporate indigenous peoples into national histories. As Deborah Doxtator put it in her article 'Implications of Canadian Nationalism for Aboriginal Cultural Autonomy,' 'To nationalistic Euro-Canadians, the only hope for the survival of aboriginal culture … was that the culture should somehow be valued within the Canadian society … What better way was there for Canada to value aboriginal cultures than to incorporate them into Canadian cultural institutions such as museums as relics of the supplanted past?'[16] However, the emphasis on the multicultural and multiracial aspects of fur trade society in the 'dominant discourse' of text boxes and theme labels begs the question of why First Nations do not appear in a significant way on the first floor, in the twentieth-century section of the museum. The museum laments the fact that no original canots du mâitre or canots du nord have survived; it seeks to mitigate that loss with the Preserving Skills workshop, which allows techniques to be demonstrated and passed on to others by resident craftspeople. But there is no gallery to explain why canoe-making skills were lost: there is no gallery of cultural genocide.

What would such a gallery look like? And would it attract visitors? The ethnography gallery at the Royal British Columbia Museum in Victoria takes a different approach to representing the cultural effects of the invasion of First Nations territories by Euro-Canadians. The period around contact is represented by a small, round, enclosed space with a lowered ceiling, where the museum-goer is surrounded by much-larger-than-life photographs of the serious, laughing, and highly individualized faces of BC First Nations peoples. The recorded voice of Bill Reid (the well-known Haida sculptor was also a CBC announcer) describes the devastating effects of the smallpox epidemic on First Nations communities – the painful loss not only of thousands of people, but also of family memory and cultural tradition. The voice fills the small space, which is artificially screened from the rest of the display and soundproofed in order to focus attention on the voice. This gallery sets the stage for the display representing the missionization of BC Native communities and the introduction of the infamous residential school system. The use of the photographs in this Hall of Cultural Genocide (as I call it) is controversial: the photographs were taken by Edward Curtis, who is well-known to have 'faked' their look by carefully eliminating signs of white society from the framing of the pictures and by dressing his subjects in traditional clothing that he supplied himself. No names are included with the photos, and the descendants of those photographed rightly object to the way their relatives have been made into nameless 'Indians.' However, the beautiful way that Curtis caught the expression and individuality of each subject creates the effect desired by the display designers: these photographs personalize the feeling of loss and make real the historical effects of political and cultural oppression on British Columbia's First Nations. Given the age of this display (it was conceived and built over thirty years ago), its political message is remarkably contemporary.

Could the Canoe Museum have told (or yet tell) a story like this? Certainly many of the canoes in the collection, especially those acquired from the Heye Foundation in New York, might easily serve to illustrate the way that, in the early decades of the twentieth century, museums and private collectors raided First Nations families so devastated by epidemic illnesses and cultural oppression that in some cases they could not even determine the correct lines of inheritance for treasured family heirlooms and privileges.[17] The redistribution of the indigenous canoes throughout the chronology of the display could show how canoe-building and canoe use persists in indigenous communities up to the present. The emphasis on 'preserving skills' and on the revival of traditional canoe-building techniques in First Nations communities might be contextualized by a statement of *why* the skills need to be revived, and *from what* they need to be preserved. However, it seems unlikely that such a gallery would constitute a 'feel-good' heritage outing for the museum's target visitors or attract donations from wealthy individuals and corporations.

So despite the best intentions of its curators and supporters, the Canadian Canoe Museum exhibits nothing so much as the ideological contradictions that are inherent in the nationalist historiography they depict.

The vision of the multicultural but unified nation is undercut by the linear, chronological organization of the displays and the difficulty of making changes to expensive material installations, as well as by the absence of a historical link to Asian and more recent immigrant communities. While the museum remains committed to honouring First Nations as the originators of the canoe and as contributors to the building of the Canada, the liberal ideology of multiculturalism means that it is unwilling to confront the history of colonialism that the canoe also signifies. The conflicted history of how the collection and the museum itself came to be, as well as how its assemblers and preservers perceive its significance, remains inscribed in both the physical limitations of the displays and the categories that organize the collection. None of these limitations is particularly new or even unexpected: all museums confront the difficulties inherent in the interpretation of material history for the diverse requirements of the 'general public': a nostalgic reminder of childhood for one is a culpable lie to another, and even interesting and challenging text panels may be ignored by a parent supervising an outing on a wet summer day.

The Canadian Canoe Museum reiterates the way that the ideal canoe trip is supposed to create an identity between the human world and the wilderness, the nation and the landscape, and yet also inevitably demonstrates the absolute incommensurability of these opposites and the way that the desire for a nation that is material and experiential, felt in the bones as Pierre Trudeau put it, will always be frustrated. That ideal world of glaciated lakes and loons remains, and will remain, beyond my reach, in a conceptual and spiritual way, because of the contradictions that it involves. And yet despite these contradictions, like the rest of the objects and activities in this book, the Canadian Canoe Museum is a place I love, a place I find myself and my family history of complicity, complacency, patriotism, and love.

Chapter Eight

Decolonizing the Canoe

Canoe nationalism founders when it hits the Rockies: this is one 'height of land' that offered serious obstacles to canoeists. Mackenzie and Thompson found their way over the passes, carrying canoes; but the passes are few and dangerous. In the early days, fur trade posts in the BC interior were supplied by canoes that came up the Columbia from Fort Vancouver (now in Washington state) or from the east by way of the Grande Traverse portage that came over the mountains to the farthest northern curve of the Columbia. In his article 'Splendor Sine Occasu: Salvaging Boat Encampment,' Ian MacLaren recounts the lost history of Boat Encampment, the location on the Columbia that ended the six-day portage over the mountains for canoe brigades from the east: 'It was an isolated transhipment point on the transcontinental route, separated from any post by the dangerous rapids of the malevolent Columbia downstream and the punishing Grande Traverse over Athabasca Pass; the gloom of the surrounding mountains exerted itself psychologically on the men camped there, waiting.'[1] Yet the feeling of relief was palpable when the canoe brigades reached this gloomy spot, MacLaren notes, as paddlers and travellers erupted in impromptu celebration of the end of their snowy trek. While the existence of this route does legitimate the idea of 'sea to sea' canoe travel, it can't have been a section of the route that the paddlers relished, though it was in use, according to MacLaren, for four decades, from 1814 to 1855. In any case, as MacLaren points out, that east-west route by canoe is now a memory, as Boat Encampment and the canoeable portion of the Columbia have disappeared under Kinbasket Lake.

In general, British Columbia does not contain those networks of canoeable freshwater lakes and rivers that characterize the rest of the country. The long rivers are either dammed, like the Columbia, or too dangerous to canoe, like the Fraser. There are exceptions, of course: the Bowron lakes, for example, is a popular recreational canoe route, and parts of the Peace River are canoeable. But the Centennial Canoe Pageant started its trek eastward on the other side of the mountains, in Alberta. In general, BC paddlers can be found in kayaks, and we head for the ocean.

I can almost hear you say, but what about all those First Nations canoes out there on the west coast and the revival of the practice of ocean-going canoe journeys? Don't they prove that canoeing extends the whole breadth of the country and that the western Canadians participate in the 'ideology of the canoe'? It's true that there is a revival of canoe carving, and of canoe journeys among coastal First Nations in BC, and perhaps among Canadian First Nations in general, but this practice is not easily subsumed under the rubric of canoe nationalism. And the reason why is Aboriginal title.

What is Aboriginal title? I find when I talk to my friends back east there is a lot of confusion about this. In Canada, Aboriginal title (as distinct from Aboriginal rights) is the interest that First Nations had in their land when Britain extended its sovereignty over what is now Canada. This title derives from British law (by way of the Royal Proclamation of 1763) and was confirmed in Canadian law by the Supreme Court of Canada when it ruled in the Delgamuuk'w decision of 1997. Essentially, it means that indigenous people had (have, have always had) a kind of ownership of their lands, and they can only give up this ownership legally through a treaty (*some* kind of treaty: an argument can be made for almost any kind of treaty). This interest consists of something more than the right to hunt, fish, and harvest in traditional territories, according to the courts; it consists of a material interest in the land itself. This means that indige-nous people in Canada retain (at least) an interest in (at least) any lands not covered by a treaty. And that is most of British Columbia.

This is why lumber companies have to consult the Haida before they log on Haida traditional lands; this is why mining projects can be stopped when BC First Nations go to court; this is why the BC government is negotiating treaties: not because First Nations block logging roads or cause negative publicity, and certainly not because British Columbians are nice or want to be fair, but because indigenous peoples are recog-nized by the Canadian courts as part-owners of the land the province sits on. Nothing can be done on BC Crown lands without consulting all the owners, or at least buying out their interest, and BC is 94 per cent

Crown land. And remember, this is by authority of *Canadian* law, not First Nations laws or traditions. What their rights are (or should be) by their law is another matter entirely.

To introduce Aboriginal title here might seem like a non-sequitur. But it's not. Like my canoe paddle, west coast canoe journeys, as material practices, and west coast canoes, as objects, are capable of multiple and contradictory interpretations – they tell many stories, as museum people would say. They have stories, as individual objects, of manufacture and use; they have stories of provenance, that is, how they ended up in museum collections; they have stories based in tradition, signified by their decorations or their names. But the dominant story that west coast canoes tell to me these days, to me as an individual and as a Canadian, is the story of Aboriginal title and sovereignty, which includes the way my love of canoeing implicates me in theft and cultural genocide.

In order to research this chapter, I visited the U'Mista Cultural Centre, an important Native-run museum in the tiny community of Alert Bay, located a short ferry ride from Port McNeill, itself a seven-hour drive from Victoria, BC. The objects in this museum are the remains of the regalia confiscated from the Cranmer family potlatch held on Village Island in 1921. The potlatch was 'raided' by the local Indian Agent and the local police, and most of the regalia was confiscated; the Kwakwaka'wakw people lobbied for decades to have their regalia returned, and they eventually received funding from the federal government for a museum to house the collection. The artefacts, which the Kwakwaka'wakw people had been told were practically worthless, had been dispersed into the collections of, among others, the Canadian Museum of Civilization, the Royal Ontario Museum, the Museum of the American Indian, and the private collections of the government officials who participated in their confiscation; only those still owned by the government could be returned.

The U'Mista Centre displays the repatriated regalia in a room that resembles a Kwakwaka'wakw big house, with the masks and carvings grouped by the figure they represent and arranged approximately in the order they would appear at a potlatch (according to the museum video). Some artefacts are labelled with the name of the historical or supernatural figure they represent; some are labelled with the name of their owner (for each object is owned by a family, just as they were when confiscated). But there is little in the way of interpretation of who these figures were, what cultural significance they had, or why they appeared in this order at the potlatch. The traditional stories of the Kwakwaka'wakw people are not explained or even presented. Instead, the labels and text panels in the U'Mista Centre contain direct quotations from the people's correspondence with government officials about the potlatch law and the confiscation. The letters to and from D.C. Scott of the federal department of Indian Affairs; W.M. Halliday, the Indian Agent at Alert Bay; and W.E. Ditchburn, 'Chief Inspector of Indian Agencies' in Victoria – shameful letters, if you're a Canadian – demonstrate how our government officials, on our behalf, obfuscated, patronized, and lied. The only story represented here is the story of the suppression of the potlatch, and of the Kwakwaka'wakw people's battle against colonialism and cultural genocide. I went to the museum expecting a kind of anthropological display that would answer questions I had about the objects. But what I found was the story that the U'Mista Cultural Society wanted to tell me – the story about my implication in colonialism – the very story that many museum professionals had told me could not be told by museums without doing violence to museum objects as objects.

Stories and meanings are not naturally inherent in museum objects; at best, such objects are mnemonics, reminders of stories that a person or a culture tells to itself. Objects can legitimately represent many different stories, some of them contradictory; and just as my paddle can simultaneously function as a metonymic reminder of my family history and a symbolic reminder of my complicity in a history of colonialism, the potlatch collection can simultaneously represent multiple and contradictory meanings. I'm sure that for people who already know the names and histories of the supernatural beings represented by the masks, who have attended one of the potlatches or dances held by Kwakwaka'waka families since the 1950s, the mere sight of these masks is a sufficient reminder of that cultural knowledge; but for an outsider, like myself, who looks to the museum to create a context for me, those objects function as a reminder of a different kind of cultural knowledge and tell a different story.

In Alert Bay I met Bill Wasden, who is a graduate of the indigenous governance program at the University of Victoria and a respected spokesman and treaty negotiator. I also met some carvers and paddlers. These conversations started strangely, at least from my perspective. I thought I was there to find out about canoes. I had read about canoe history and design, about the different groups that were famed for canoe-making (Haida, Nuu Chaa Nulth, and Heiltsuk) and the different sizes and shapes of canoes – how they were made, how they were painted with an eye under the black overpaint so they could see where they were going, how they were living beings with names. But every conversation I started seemed to begin with a discussion about land claims and treaty. I wondered why it was taking me so long to get to canoes; my experience at the museum answered that question for me – the carvers, like the canoes, were telling the story of colonialism, colonialism not in the past, but in the present.

The coastline between Alert Bay and Victoria is an object lesson in colonialism. I took a boat tour around Village, Cormorant, and Hanson Islands, locations I know from Martin Allerdale Grainger's semi-autobiographical book, *Woodsmen of the West* (1908). I teach this book in my class on British Columbia literature, and I wanted to see where the story had taken place. By the time Grainger was writing, he considered the area along the shoreline to be nearly logged-out; he writes about the forest being 'sacked' by logging vandals taking the best trees and leaving slash behind. From the tour boat I could see how the second-growth forest rises up from the shoreline of Hanson Island in tangled green, and I tried to imagine what it was like when the huge firs could drop directly from their stumps down the slope and into the water. But I was the only British Columbian on the boat who knew any of the history of this landscape. The Europeans, in particular, kept talking about 'untouched wilderness.' But this has all been logged over at least once, I insisted; the whole province is divided up into tree-farm licenses and designated logging areas; there is no untouched landscape; it is all part of a long-term government plan for resource management, and has been for generations.

It was on my return trip to Victoria by car that I really started to understand what I had been learning about the land and its relationship to me as a Canadian. The highway between Port McNeill and Campbell River runs for miles with few houses or businesses, only a patchwork of various shades of green on either side, each rectangle showing by its colour how long ago it was logged. Helicopters, whap whap whap, shaped like red damsel-flies, crossed from hillsides over the highway with logs suspended underneath. I stopped and got out of the car to watch, mainly because I was unreasonably afraid they would fall and crush my tin-can rental. Environmental activists in British Columbia are fond of declaring that they want to stop the whole province from becoming a fibre farm. Well, too late. I sat back into the driver's seat, pulled out my notebook, and wrote, 'This whole chapter has to be the merest ruse for discussing Aboriginal title.' Because that's the real story that the big canoes tell.

The artist Bill Reid, in his statement to the provincial government's

Wilderness Advisory Committee in 1986, pointed out that the Haida
struggle against logging on South Moresby Island was not about something that had happened a hundred years ago, or two hundred years
ago; it was not about colonialism in the past, but about what we are doing
now. 'If these remnants of [the Haida's] former riches are not returned,
it will make the act of theft a conscious one, perpetuated by the people
of today, instead of just an accident of history ... And in killing the forests
... You murder once more their symbolic ancestors. That is what I think
the land claims are about.'² And this is also what the new tradition of
coastal canoe journeys is all about: not about Canada, not about Canadian unity or Canadian sovereignty, and not about preserving something
that happened in the past: 'This ... is a very powerful political message to
the world that our people are unifying and that we're using our canoes
as a symbol of our sovereignty. That's why they're so precious to me,
because of what they symbolize; they symbolize our life, or sovereign
right, our strength and power,' according to Tom Abel, a Haida from
Kuna, Alaska.³

Much has been made of the contemporary renaissance of canoe carving. But in accounts of the celebratory performances and the canoe journeys that have followed, there has been little about how and why canoe
skills were lost. I suspect this is the story that the U'Mista Centre would tell
about the canoe – the story of its suppression and loss. And of course this
is the story non-indigenous Canadians need to remember – the context
of colonialism that is everywhere present for the First Nations paddlers
and carvers but which is elided in the way that non-Natives participate in
canoe celebrations. James Raffan suggests that 'the great canoes of the
Pacific Northwest were eventually overtaken by mechanized travel,'⁴ but
this leaves out the cultural and economic forces that all but determined
their loss. The economic role of the big canoes was lost: First Nations
were encouraged to settle in one place and join the wage economy, working in canning factories or living on reserves where government agencies
could conveniently deliver services. Individual reserves rarely included
all of the several different locations and townsites that the people would
traditionally travel to at different times of the year, to harvest salmon,
or clams, or berries, or oolichans, so First Nations people did not necessarily travel for economic reasons any more. Surviving communities
adopted big boats with engines for fishing: the mechanized family fishing
boat became the norm, for after all, who would embrace the hardship
of traditional fishing for its own sake? The great whaling nations of the
Nuu Chaa Nulth and the Tlinglit joined commercial whaling and sealing

crews. The social reasons for the big canoes were also lost: the potlatch was outlawed, so there was little need for ceremonial travel (and when potlatches were held, participants did not necessarily want to draw the attention of the local police). 'Then the erosion of the societies between the fearsome grinding stones of efficient weapons, alcohol and disease, culminating in the horror of 1862, when the Haidas lost eighty-five per cent of their numbers between spring and winter, and the rest of the coast suffered almost as tragically.'[5] The evidence of the loss of generations of boat builders is there to see: Guujaaw recounts how the Haida have found over twenty unfinished canoes in the woods, 'abandoned at different stages' by canoe builders who died, were called away to other responsibilities in the midst of disease and death, or were unable to muster the considerable help needed to transport the roughed-out canoe to the water.[6]

Yet despite this, a canoe culture of a kind survived. Many First Nations carvers in British Columbia continued to create small canoes for family use and the long, narrow, low canoes used in the active First Nations canoe-racing scene. One of these canoes, Bluebird (made by respected Cowichan master carver Simon Charlie), is on display in the Canadian Canoe Museum; other examples can be seen in photographs of the regattas that were held throughout the early decades of the twentieth century on the Gorge in Victoria. Small canoes continued to be used on coastal rivers even after most boat builders shifted their efforts to making big boats able to fit engines. Simon Dick of the Nakwaxda'xw First Nation remembers, 'We used to borrow my grandfather's canoe all the time to go trout fishing, or to go hunting, or to go check the net. We always played in canoes ... In some areas, like in Kingcome [Inlet] canoes were used as recently as twenty years ago.'[7] The Royal British Columbia Museum commissioned carvers to work on-site in Victoria, creating poles, masks, and other works, including canoes; the museum website shows Nu Chaa Nulth carvers David Frank and Paul Sam working on a canoe in the museum carving shed in 1964. The memory of the big canoes and the skills to create them were passed on by elders, even though the social function of these canoes had been lost.

Kirk Wipper commissioned well-known Haida carver Victor Adams of Masset to create a canoe for his collection, housed at that time in the Kanawa museum building on the grounds of Camp Kandalore near Minden, Ontario. James Raffan recounts that Wipper took delivery of the canoe in the spring of 1971 in front of a hushed and expectant crowd; according to Raffan, Wipper's Haida hosts were expecting the canoe to

'Indian Canoe' race on Cowichan Bay, near Victoria, 1911.
Courtesy of BC Archives, b-05670.

overturn, as it had when it was tested the evening before. Despite some
confusion over which end was the bow, the crew who had accompanied
Wipper successfully tested the canoe in Masset Sound and paddled off
into Hecate Strait, expecting to be able to make Prince Rupert that after-
noon. (They were rescued off Graham Island at midnight, and the canoe
was shipped to the mainland by ferry. It's not called Hecate Strait for
nothing.) After crossing the country by road, the 'Victor Adams' canoe,
as it is known at the museum, was paddled by way of the Trent-Severn
waterway from Toronto to the Gull River near Minden by a crew including Raffan himself.[8]

  The current resurgence of west coast canoe carving is commonly dated
from the construction of LooTaas, or Wave Eater, the fifty-foot Haida

canoe built by Bill Reid and a team of Haida carvers for the celebration of the 1986 World's Fair in Vancouver. Reid had studied canoes in the Museum of Anthropology at UBC and other museums; from these, he built a model and then a twenty-seven-foot 'half-size' canoe to test the process. According to another member of the team, Guujaaw, the carvers also researched the half-finished canoes they found in the woods near historic villages on Haida Gwaii: 'Over the years we've been locating old canoes in the bush that were abandoned at different stages due to the pestilence that struck our people ... the different stages for getting to the final form soon became apparent.'[9] A small canoe was borrowed from the UBC Museum of Anthropology as a model, and advice from two elders 'who had seen canoes built in their youth'[10] was also key to their success. The final canoe, fifty feet long and nicknamed 'Murphy' to acknowledge all the things that had gone wrong, was taken to Vancouver and 'proudly paddled before an appreciative international audience on the Vancouver waterfront.'[11] Its first long sea journey was the trip back from Vancouver, paddled by Haida and welcomed to the village of Skidegate, where it is now on display in a museum. Despite its status as a work of art, LooTaas has had a storied career. In 1989 it was paddled up the Seine in France to join other works by Reid in a display at the Museum of Man. Also in 1989, it made a historic journey from Haida Gwaii to Hydaberg in Alaska, a symbolic challenge to the international border that artificially divides the Haida Nation. Fibreglass replicas of LooTaas (named Looplex, the plex traditionally signifying a copy) have served as models for other canoe-carvers and been used in numerous cultural celebrations.

However, Raffan and others who have written about the appearance of LooTaas at Expo '86 often fail to note that there was another canoe on the water that day: Glwa, from the Heiltsuk Nation. Like the Haida, the Heiltsuk are an ocean-going people, famed for their skill in carving canoes; as Reg Moody of the Heiltsuk Nation remarks in the film *Qatuwas*, in the old days the Heiltsuk did not have totem poles because they made canoes.[12] The Heiltsuk, under the leadership of Frank Brown, had not only carved their own canoe, but paddled the three hundred miles from their traditional territory in Bella Bella to Vancouver to be part of the exhibit on traditional transportation.

Brown's accomplishment caught the attention of the Suquamish Tribe of Washington, who issued an invitation to other west coast First Nations to paddle to meet them in 1989 as part of the celebration of the Washington Centennial. The 'Paddle to Seattle' included canoes from the

Hoh and LaPush Quileute communities, as well as Suquamish, Tulalip, and Lummi canoes that met with the Heiltsuk at the Golden Gardens Park outside Seattle. There Frank Brown challenged those present to do as his people had done: carve their own canoes and paddle the hundreds of miles to Heiltsuk territory for a gathering of 'Canoe Nations' in the summer of 1993. David Forlines of LaPush accepted the invitation and presented Brown with the paddle of a Quileute elder, promising to retrieve it in four years. Eventually twenty-three canoes made the trip to Bella Bella for the Qatuwas (People Gathering Together) festival in 1993, which marked the turning point in the revival of the big canoes among the west coast First Nations.

The achievement of the communities who participated in the Qatuwas festival should not be underestimated. Communities need a considerable basic infrastructure to carve a canoe and paddle it hundreds of miles. They need enough administrative structure to identify and solicit the donation of a suitable tree – usually from a logging company – and enough cash to have it transported. Communities with their own carvers need to have them commit to the project, or they need to attract and pay an accomplished carver to lead and train their own young men. People have to commit to feeding the carvers, to showing up and helping when strong backs are needed to move the canoe, or to participate in steaming it. The community needs fund-raisers – someone to coordinate salmon barbecues, t-shirt sales, and appeals to forestry companies and local businesses. David Neel estimated the cost of creating a twenty-five-foot canoe to be $30,000–$35,000 dollars in 1995. In order to participate in canoe journeys, communities must provide support boats, as well as people willing to sacrifice their time (and presumably potential income) to work in the support boats and to paddle. They need to create a functional 'canoe family,' with administrative, problem-solving, paddling, and cultural expertise spread over several generations, elders and adults and young people, and with resources to spare. In small indigenous communities in British Columbia, whose populations often number only a few hundred, including elders and children, these resources and abilities are not always a given; the legacy of residential schools, the prevalence of diabetes and other illnesses, all the effects of colonialism militate against them. For educated and successful community leaders, the demands of business, education, self-government, and treaty negotiation also conflict with the time and resources needed. The task of commissioning or building a canoe can be a great achievement in the health of a small community, signalling the growth of organizational ability, the ability to inspire young people and impose discipline, and the growth of hope and pride. As David Neel puts it in his introduction to *The Great Canoes*, 'All facets of the contemporary canoe experience – planning, building, fund-raising, practising, travelling – combine to make our communities strong and vital in the old ways.'[13]

Most of the communities who took part in the Qatuwas festival faced a substantial challenge merely in carving a canoe. Not every community had the advantage of a world-famous carver like Bill Reid, with his privileged access to museum artefacts and ability to command resources, among their members. Instead, individuals researched in museums; examined, measured, and plotted out existing canoes (including LooTaas and Looplexes); and sought advice from elders and from elderly carvers to answer questions. Which end of the log, the butt or the crown, should become the bow? (Depends on the size of the canoe.) Which side of the log should become the bottom of the canoe? (The north side, according to some, where the rings are closer together; or drop the log in the water and see which side floats downward.) How thick should the sides and the base be? And so forth. In addition, considerable experience is needed to anticipate the shape of the final canoe at the beginning of carving. The bottom of the canoe is carved straight, or even slightly convex, to allow for the way the shape changes during the final stage of steaming. The canoe is tented with tarps and filled with water, which is then heated with stones. The sides are spread open (the canoe gaining some two feet in width) and the ends rise, creating a slight rocker at the keel. A wrong judgment at any stage could mean disaster. Oral and written histories tell of big canoes that split along the grain from end to end in the dangerous seas of Hecate Strait, with all hands lost.

Securing a canoe, crew, and support boats was only the beginning of the commitment to participate in the Qatuwas festival. As the canoes travelled up (or down) the coast, elaborate protocol welcomed them ashore at neighbouring communities, where they often participated in feasts, ceremonials, and dances. The crews and the hosts had to learn the songs and dances appropriate to the protocol ceremonies, and suitable regalia for community members as well as chiefs to wear had to be created. Host communities billeted and fed the visitors. Families donated their fish, their labour, and their time. Children were taught to mind their manners according to community custom, honouring their elders by serving them first. A strict ban on alcohol and drugs was maintained.

When the twenty-three canoes reached Bella Bella in the summer of 1993, they were joined by elders and family members who had arrived

Arrival of the Tribal Journeys canoes at the North American Indigenous Games in Duncan, BC, 2008. Courtesy of the *Cowichan News Leader-Pictorial*.

by ferry; Bella Bella, an isolated community of 1,200 people accessible only by water, hosted two thousand visitors for the week-long festival. The Heiltsuk are proud of their tradition as hosts; located on Campbell Island on the central coast, about halfway between Vancouver and Haida Gwaii, they have a tradition of welcoming seafaring travellers. The success of the Qatuwas festival spawned other canoe journeys, now known under the collective title of Tribal Journeys: Victoria in 1994 for the Commonwealth Games, LaPush, Washington, in 1997, and since then Tribal Journeys have occurred yearly.[14] Ten thousand people were expected for the Paddle to Cowichan (outside Victoria, BC) to mark the opening of the World Indigenous Games in 2008, including canoes from Saskatchewan as well as from coastal communities from Alaska to Washington.

In the National Film Board video *Qatuwas* and David Neel's book *The Great Canoes*, paddlers, community members, and organizers talk about their motivations for participating in canoe journeys and what they mean to their communities. Chief among these motivations is to draw attention to their presence on the land and in the water, and to its political significance. Participants repeatedly talk of 'showing the world.' The elaborate protocol at each community, which includes asking permission from the chief to come ashore, demonstrates the borders of traditional territories and the appropriate behaviour of 'guests' (which the BC First Nations consider non-Aboriginal Canadians). The scale of the event, and its organization, demonstrates the competence and power of First Nations on the west coast. The songs and regalia demonstrate the richness of the culture and its historic roots in the land and in 'time immemorial.' The participation of communities from the US and Canada offers a challenge to the artificial separation of families and communities by the border and demonstrates unity among peoples who have traditionally been divided by rivalry or even hostility. As is the tradition in many BC First Nations, the canoe journeys perform their sovereignty.[15]

In addition to asserting sovereignty and indigenous presence, canoe journeys are processes of healing for those individuals and communities who continue to struggle with the legacy of colonialism. As Ian Campbell of the Squamish Nation puts it in *Qatuwas*, 'our communities have a lot of healing that needs to take place, because there is so much drugs and alcohol, so much abuse ... Being on a journey will help us to overcome some of those social issues, by practicing the traditions, and by being drug and alcohol free during our training, and having that moment to be ourselves.'[16] Bill Wasden, in *The Great Canoes*, says the canoe 'seems to be a healing tool, especially for the youth. When they come into the canoe, their attitudes change and their respect for their culture, and they conduct themselves with dignity when they're in the canoe.'[17] Learning community values, such as respect for the natural world, for the canoe and the water, for elders, and for yourself, is part of this healing process. According to Ann Atleo of Ahousaht, a paddler, 'you learn really quickly about how to respect the water ... you realize in that canoe that one wrong move by one of the paddlers could capsize the entire canoe, and how important life is, and how quickly it can be taken away.'[18] Respect for the canoe derives from the belief that the canoe is a living creature, created from the living tree, and the carving process includes a blessing ceremony as well as a naming. 'The canoe is a lot more than a boat. It's what the tree gave ... Everything in the world has a soul.'[19] The tree itself determines how it is carved: 'Sometimes we would let it sit for days and just look at it, and eventually it would come to you as to what to do with that log.'[20]

Discipline is also an important lesson for carvers and paddlers; in addition to paddling practice and physical training, many coastal First Nations have traditions of ritual bathing and cleansing that must be followed exactly. The goals of discipline and cooperation are emphasized in the 'Ten Rules of the Canoe,' which were formulated by the Quileute canoe contingent in 1990 at an experiential education conference that considered the canoe journey as a learning experience for young people. The rules emphasize teamwork, flexibility, self-and-other care, and the value of process: these principles have been adopted by the Tribal Journeys organization. They also inculcate the skills needed to succeed in a small community, drawing attention to the analogy made by many participants between the canoeing crew and 'your tribe.' Gerald Stewart of the Tsimshan says in *The Great Canoes*: 'For our people the canoe was basically an analogy for what a tribe was, and the water was life. How it paddled during rough waters and such was relevant ...When someone makes gestures or movements they are noticed by all, and affect the whole group ... I believe in that metaphor and what it says.'[21]

Another motivation commonly cited by participants is the desire to reconnect with ancestors and to please elders. This reconnection is often expressed in the same language used by Anglo-Canadians who retrace the routes of explorers and adventurers; many say they now appreciate the physical demands and skills required by their ancestors; they feel connected with the spirits of their forebears; they know the ancestors would be pleased because the tradition is carried on. But in retracing the routes of their ancestors, BC First Nations are making explicit what is only implicit in the journeys of Anglo-Canadian recreational canoeists: the history of canoe culture constitutes a continuing assertion of sovereignty. Bill Wasden emphasizes that these journeys are not re-enactments or entertainments; they constitute another forum for affirming the presence of First Nations on their traditional territories, as well as a mechanism for teaching young people about their culture, instilling community values, and celebrating community strength.[22]

Historian David McNab, in his account of the role of the canoe in Ojibwa history,[23] suggests that the canoe has always been a means for the defence of First Nations sovereignty in North America, not only on the west coast. The canoe was a technology of battle, transporting men and women noiselessly and in numbers to repel invaders; it was also a technology of diplomacy, providing a dignified platform for ambassadorial conferences: 'The canoe, in war and diplomacy, was the principal means by which Aboriginal autonomy and sovereignty were long secured' (237). Because its use created and facilitated the growth of the fur trade, it 'considerably slowed the process of European expansion into northeastern North America for the seventeenth to the mid-nineteenth centuries … effectively prevent[ing] the conquest of the Amerindian Nations and eventually provid[ing] one of the ways in which Aboriginal peoples have continued to survive and finally flourish once again in the late twentieth century' (243). McNab states that 'While and wherever the canoe reigned supreme, Aboriginal people were not marginalized and certainly not conquered' (249). The two rows of purple beads on a white wampum belt (the 'two-row wampum') that commemorated the treaty between the Six Nations of the Haudenosaunee and the European invaders (in 1613) are widely interpreted as signifying the journey of the two peoples, one in a canoe and the other in a European ship, each travelling separately, with their own laws and cultures, linked by respect and peace. Rather than seeing the canoe as a means to further integration into Canadian nationality, like BC First Nations many central Canadian indigenous peoples see the canoe as a technology of resisting the Canadian state, and of resisting colonialism.

The canoe also continues to have anti-colonial symbolism, both traditional and contemporary, for indigenous writers. McNab recounts how the canoe functions within the traditional spiritual beliefs of central Canadian First Nations as a symbol of balance, linking the four elements of earth, water, air, and fire with the four directions: 'Resting horizontally across a plane of water and with a paddle held vertically, the canoe represents the four sacred directions. As such, it is a holistic representation or symbol of life and the human journey through the moral world to the world of the spirits' (238). He notes that the canoe appears in some indigenous creation stories as the log upon which the first man climbed after the flood covered the earth (239); it also appears in flood stories of the west coast First Nations as the means whereby the people were enabled to survive a flood that covered all but the highest mountain tops. Contemporary anti-colonial symbolism draws on these traditional meanings by emphasizing the role of the canoe in ensuring balance, health, and survival.

Peter Cole uses the canoe journey as a rhetorical device to structure his book, *Coyote and Raven Go Canoeing*. Cole rejects traditional academic discourse, especially the convention of reference to academic sources, and looks to indigenous culture and the experience of indigenous peoples for methodologies to decolonize the representation of First Nations in the realm of academe. He structures his investigation as a canoe journey, a narrative journey upon which he and his readers have embarked

together and collaboratively: 'the means of transportation I have chosen
for this journey of journeys / besides language and spirit is a canoe /
constructed not from the forest nations but from words / and the ges-
turing of those words and the spaces around those words.'[24] The canoe
journey is a particularly appropriate metaphor for Cole's book, which
links discourses as diverse as conversations between Raven and Coyote,
poems, analysis, interviews, and reports from various locations in North
America, New Zealand, and Australia to consider and critique the representation of First Nations in academic discourse and in education.

The book begins with a poem to honour a dugout canoe that has been
removed from its useful life and put on display in a museum to signify, in
Cole's interpretation, the meaning that First Nations peoples are 'memorabilia from ages times spaces past memory' (14). The speaker wants
to see the canoe restored to use and calls on 'powers and spirits and
beings of the four directions' to 'give this canoe life again ... let it fly
through the canyons of hell's gate / through the rage and the clamour
/ let it crash onto the rocks in the land of its birth.' Rather than let it
die in the museum, 'crucified,' he would prefer to have an axe to 'end
its misery / and my own' (14). Cole's use of the canoe as a discursive
methodology restores it to life as 'a place of cultural understanding / it
transports it connects me to the forest and the water and to my spirit /
it conveys it acts as a place of gestation of birthing / in transit and final
worldly threshold for generations milleniations of my relations / if ever
there was home for our migrations / it is this form this vessel this tree
relation / this part of my word forest' (23). Coyote acts as a mock tour
guide, asking passengers in the canoe to leave behind their cell phones,
televisions, and other electronic devices ('blackberries no blueberries
yes') and to behave according to protocol, respecting both sovereignty
and traditions of good manners (20).

Cole's rejection of the conventions of academic discourse recalls similar gestures by feminists of a generation ago, and for similar reasons: its
language devalues the experiences of marginalized peoples and is in itself
tainted with colonialist assumptions. For indigenous peoples, English is
a foreign language whose concepts have been enlisted in order to rob
them of their lands: Cole points out that the idea of ownership implied by
the genitive case does not exist in his traditional language (55). English
is also the language of the torture and abuse of children in residential
schools, and Cole recalls the stories of children with pins stuck through
their tongues, with mouths washed out with soap, or beaten for speaking
their own languages. Cole argues that because it devalues the evidence of

experience and excludes indigenous voices, academic discourse is a self-referential and self-confirming system that continues to colonize indigenous peoples in the present. With his discursive canoe, Cole proposes to replace academic references with 'sound vision texture scent taste' (20), and he punctuates the beginnings and endings of sections in his book with a reminder of these sensations: '*paddle stroke paddle swooooooosh*' (28).

Cole paddles his canoe in opposition to the protocols of non-indigenous discourse: his canoe represents his resistance to the figures of incorporation and appropriation in settler/invader discourse. McNab and other indigenous commentators see the canoe as a means of historical resistance to invasion and as a reminder of traditional spirituality. West coast First Nations engage in canoe journeys to promote healing, preserve culture, and affirm Aboriginal sovereignty. Despite the way that canoe nationalism tries to incorporate indigenous peoples into the narrative of nationality by reference to the canoe, First Nations peoples reject this characterization of their own activities and their own tradition, referencing the canoe as a rhetorical figure of resistance to that very discourse and as a material practice that enacts that resistance. When indigenous people canoe, whether for recreation, cultural revival, or work, they do not imagine themselves to be voyageurs, or even the guides of the explorers: they imagine themselves in the present, fighting the ongoing consequences of colonialism as enacted in the present.

What impact does, or should, this rejection have on the nationalist justifications for canoeing practices carried out by non-indigenous Canadians? Is it possible to decolonize the Canadian canoe? In the context of current historical research, the claim that underlies the mythology of the canoe – that First Nations participated actively and self-consciously in the creation of Canada as it now exists – seems self-justifying; cultural historians like Ted Chamberlain and John Borrows have made it clear enough that in negotiating treaties with Canada, many First Nations were attempting to preserve what was left of their own cultures, not to join Canada (whatever their subsequent goals have become). The practice of retracing voyageur and explorer canoe routes seems of a piece with the practices of colonialism: by re-enacting the moment of conquest in the 'wilderness' spaces of Canada, canoeists attempt to legitimize the appropriation of Aboriginal resources and the assertion of sovereignty of the Canadian state by historicizing the land and territorializing their own history, and so take both land and history away from First Nations. Even those canoeists who profess respect for the environmental practices of First Nations peoples and use their canoeing activism to fight for the preservation of wilderness are often reluctant to acknowledge the way the idea of wilderness is implicated in colonialist practices and unwilling to grant actual First Nations sovereignty over their traditional lands, especially if the local band council does not agree to guarantee the preservation of 'untouched wilderness.' Canadian literary works, be they poems, stories, or wilderness adventures, embody the cathected emotional moment of the uncanny canoe while refusing to acknowledge its source in shame, guilt, and injustice.

The Canadian Canoe Museum recently made an attempt to address the possibility of a decolonized canoe by exhibiting 'Treaty Canoe,' a sculptural work by Alex McKay, a Windsor artist of British heritage and a dual Canadian/US citizen. The sculpture consists of a twelve-foot canoe wrapped in the texts of treaties between North Americans and First Nations, which were transcribed by hand by volunteers who, in the process, actually read the text of the treaties and so learned of their own responsibilities. The sculpture is described on McKay's website: 'Treaty Canoe speaks of mutual, sacred bonds of honour. When exhibited it hangs by a thread balanced on a central pivot point above its one thwart. It responds to the slightest breeze of a passer-by, rocking and turning. Lit from above the craft becomes translucent; in casting a shadow it becomes two canoes, floating in the same current on separate but parallel courses.'[25] The suspension of McKay's sculpture recalls the 'floating canoe' motif familiar from Canadian literature, and the creation of a shadow canoe through lighting evokes the two parallel courses of the two-row wampum; in addition, his use of transcribed treaties actively educates both the transcribers and the viewers as to the content of the 'sacred bonds of honour' that the treaties represent. The canoe's shape evokes the contradictory way that Euro-Canadian nationalism appropriates the canoe as a link to the land and to First Nations heritages even as it fails to live up to the commitments that connection implies. 'Treaty Canoe' makes visible the colonial history of the canoe, and of the relationships between invader-settler cultures and First Nations that are the themes of McKay's work, and as such, 'This exhibit represents a significant step forward for the Canoe Museum,' as Executive Director James Raffan states in the accompanying press release. 'McKay's work raises important questions about Canada's relationship with our First Nations. To have these questions posed in the form of a canoe only increases their relevance, for the canoe has been a medium of exchange and understanding between peoples just as treaties have been.'[26]

A decolonized canoe could only be paddled by an anti-colonial paddler, someone who is aware of the way they have benefited from the structural inequalites of Canadian history and who takes action to restore justice. This does not mean that non-indigenous Canadians should become what Peter Cole calls 'wies' – white Indian experts – by trying to understand and/or appropriate indigenous meanings and uses of the canoe, but rather that we should be turning our political analysis upon our own practices and our 'own role in the perpetuation of colonialism colonialist discourse genocide and coverup' (65). Find out about the specific piece of land you stand on: how it became part of Canada and what became of the people who owned/own it. Try to determine whether you can live with that process, whether it represents your idea of justice; learn appropriate protocols to acknowledge that process, and use that knowledge to guide your behaviour (and your vote). Above all, be aware that colonialism continues to exist in the present, in the practices of everyday life for white and non-indigenous Canadians, and that it should be resisted. This resistance needs to take both active and passive forms: active in the sense that we must do our research and reading and try to understand the issues, as Chippewa author Lenore Keeshig-Tobias says;[27] passive in the sense that we must resist trying to take authoritative positions in respect to First Nations internal governance structures and land use. It is not up to indigenous peoples to educate us on our colonialist practices, any more than it is up to feminists to teach men how to be acceptable members of society. Instead, we need to confront our own histories and our current practices and beliefs as euro-Canadians – to take action towards decolonizing the canoe, not by reappropriating it as part of a myth of 'three founding peoples' or as a sentimental motif of guilty 'imperialist nostalgia,' but by using it as a reminder and a spur to action.

John Ralston Saul draws attention to one way Canadians can work to decolonize our attitudes: in *A Fair Country* he emphasizes the way that the initial communities formed by the French in Quebec included many First Nations people and looked to alliances with First Nations communities for both physical survival and family bonds. Saul suggests that Canadians have forgotten the extent to which family ties between settlers and First Nations influenced the way Canadian values developed. Rather than studying the official discourse of nationality introduced through the European intellectual tradition, he suggests that individual Canadians consult their own family histories to recognize the extent to which we are a 'metis nation.' In a broad sense, this seems to be a good idea; though I suspect that many Canadians would be likely to find evidence of complicity in colonialism in their families, as well. As Saul suggests, many Europeans who came to Canada were impoverished and barely able to feed themselves in Europe; for them, joining an indigenous community would be 'marrying up.' One might argue that such people were unlikely (and literally unable) to colonize or oppress anyone, and a similar argument might be made for subsequent immigrants. However, I would argue that neither poverty nor unacknowledged indigenous ancestry provide an exemption from implication in colonialism in Canada. At the very least, non-indigenous Canadians are the beneficiaries of privileges derived solely from not being restricted by the Indian Act. No matter what class they belonged to, male Canadians of European ancestry were not barred by legislation from raising a mortgage on their own homes; from filing for ownership of homestead lands; from hiring a lawyer, voting, or raising and educating their own children; from receiving veterans benefits; or from making a will and being assured it would be executed. For most of the existence of the Canadian state, First Nations people have not been able to do any of these things. This means to me that despite whatever difficulties my ancestors laboured under, or which I labour under, we also derived benefits simply from *not* being 'an Indian' as defined by the Indian Act. These benefits were not insignificant in making it possible for my family to accumulate capital, or for my great-grandfather's great-grandchildren to earn graduate degrees and professional qualifications, own homes, and provide material benefits to children over generations. This privilege derives solely and only from the way that both legal and social norms characterize me as 'non-Indian.' To this extent, the Indian Act makes class distinctions irrelevant; the legal definition of 'status' is what counts here, however one might identify in terms of class or race.

As I said in the introduction, I do not think that the recognition that I have already benefited from genocide and theft is merely 'white guilt.' Whiteness is a social construct, not a biological category or a required identification, and so it is peripheral to the issue; the idea of guilt, it seems to me, seeks to substitute emotion for action. All nations, as Ernst Renan has pointed out, are creatures of what they seek to forget, of the originary violence that created their unity. 'Later generations … cannot be blamed for their parents' and grandparents' failure to act,' says Habermas, but is 'there still a problem of joint liability for them?' I would say, in our case, yes; we are still liable, at least by our own law, to pay compensation through the treaty process and its attendant negotiations; what happens after that is for a future of equality to determine.

This position assumes a distinction between existing First Nations and 'Canada,' rather than an identification of First Nations with a multicul-

tural nationality. This is a distinction that many First Nations communities and individuals make when they choose to travel using band- or
community-issued 'passports' rather than Canadian ones; when they sit
at the treaty table opposite representatives of a position called 'Canada';
or when they demand to be treated with the protocol granted to equal
nations by the federal government. Mohawk scholar Taiaiake Alfred has
argued that the people of the First Nations should not consider themselves citizens of Canada because Canadian citizenship has only led to
the dilution of Aboriginal land claims, languages, and traditions. Alfred
is a bit of a provocateur, but his point is well-taken, I think. When asked,
many politically active members of First Nations communities might
question the advantages conferred by Canadian citizenship and consider their 'inclusion' in a multicultural Canada to be involuntary. Kristina Fagan notes that Alfred's position angers many Canadian readers
because it challenges their 'ideas of Canadian identity'; she recounts that
when she teaches Alfred's article, many of her students demand that he
'should learn to fit' into 'the Canadian cultural mosaic' or, more radically, accept his position as a member of a conquered people.[28] I expect
that my argument that both the practice of (recreational) canoeing and
its representation in historical and literary texts in Canada attempts to
substitute a conflict-free history of inclusion for the reality of genocide
and theft will similarly anger those whose knowledge of First Nations
politics within contemporary Canada is limited. But this is exactly my
point – the emotional investments of many recreational canoeists in a
particular version of the past and present of Canada have resulted in a
defensive certainty about identity that is not inclusive at all.

How can a Canadian be alien within Canada? The answer is simple:
because non-indigenous Canadians stole the land and resources and
continue in the present day to steal and to deny justice to indigenous
Canadians. When can I claim an untroubled relationship to the land I
love? The passage of time is not the issue; my personal investment in the
land, my sense of connection or stewardship or love is not the issue; my
defence of Canadian independence or Canadian cultural uniqueness is
not the issue. I need to be able to say to myself that, *at least* by my own
standards as a member of the Canadian community, I have been just.
Until then, my canoe paddle can only be a reminder to me of what I still
need to fight for in order to be able to remain a nationalist, a lover of
that rocky Shield landscape of my childhood, and to honour the family
connections that tie me to it.

As I said, this book is about loss. It is the loss that my paddle represents to me, a loss of childhood, family, stability, but also a loss of fixed political identity that I think is common to many other Canadians of my generation. For if my paddle represents to me the attempt to bridge the gap between myself as Canadian and the landscape of Canada, this book is about the absolute incommensurability of these two, and about the way that the desire for a nation that is material and experiential will always be frustrated. And if my paddle represents my desire, as a non-indigenous Canadian, to be vitally and historically and spiritually connected to place, to be indigenous to Canada, then this book represents the loss of that dream for me, and it is my attempt to disrupt, trouble, and denaturalize that dream for other non-indigenous Canadians. It represents my attempt to do what Deborah Root suggests: 'Rather than seeking authenticity elsewhere, we need to transform how we look at our histories and traditions and find ways to unravel these from all the racist versions to which we have been subjected.'[29] Thinking about my canoe paddle has been a good way to rediscover the continuity between the personal and the cultural, to tease out my personal investments in the cultural discourses of colonialism, and also a way for me to oppose the paralysis that a burgeoning post-colonial awareness can provoke and to investigate what I might have inherited from within Western culture that can help to address the inequities that have resulted from those discourses. In this way, my canoe paddle can still represent the familial and cultural continuity I want to preserve. I still can use my inheritance of self-reliance and stillness, good memories, and commitment to place and my skills of analysis, storytelling, and research to change the way I think of Canada and my place in it.

Notes

Introduction

1 Peter Schwenger, 'Words and the Murder of the Thing,' *Critical Inquiry* 28 (autumn 2001): 100.
2 Karl Marx, 'Commodities,' in *The Marx-Engels Reader*, ed. Robert Tucker (New York: Norton, 1978): 321.
3 Schwenger, 'Words and the Murder of the Thing,' 101.
4 Schwenger, 'Words and the Murder of the Thing,' 101.
5 Pierre Trudeau, 'Exhaustion and Fulfilment: Ascetic in a Canoe' (1944), *Che-mun* 102 (2000), http://www.canoe.ca/che-mun/102trudeau.html.
6 Daniel Francis, *National Dreams* (Vancouver: Arsenal Pulp, 1997), 10. Further reference will be indicated by page number in the text.
7 Roland Barthes, *Mythologies*, trans. Annette Lavers (London: Granada Publishing, 1972), *passim*.
8 My use of the word 'metonymic' will have several resonances for readers. One of these will be Roman Jakobsen's use of the word in contradistinction to metaphoric in 'Two Aspects of Language and Two Types of Aphasic Disturbances.' Jakobsen distinguishes between metaphoric language, which relates words on the basis of similarity and substitutability, and metonymic language, which relates words by continuity and contextuality. My paddle (like Jakobsen's word) is metonymically related to a group of objects defined by their status as constituting the material context of my childhood. For Jakobsen, synecdoche is a kind of metonymy because in both cases part is related to whole by continuity. Pearce discusses Jakobsen's terms metonymy and metaphor, Barthes's first and second order signification, and her own terms intrinsic sign and metaphoric symbol as slightly different but parallel concepts. Roman Jakobsen, 'Two Aspects of Language and Two

Types of Aphasic Disturbances,' in *On Language*, ed. Linda R. Waugh and Monique Monville-Bursten (Cambridge, MA: Harvard UP, 1990): 115–33; Susan Pearce, *Museums, Objects and Collections* (Washington: Smithsonian Institution Press, 1992), 38.

9 Daniel Miller, *Material Culture and Mass Consumption* (Oxford: Basil Blackwell, 1987), 106.

10 Pearce, *Museums, Objects and Collections*, 27.

11 Renato Rosaldo, *Culture and Truth: The Remaking of Social Analysis* (Boston: Beacon), 69.

12 See Yi-Fu Tuan, *Topophilia* (Englewood Cliffs, NJ: Prentice-Hall, 1974).

13 Minnie Bruce Pratt, 'Identity: Skin Blood Heart,' in *Yours in Struggle: Three Feminist Perspectives on Anti-Semitism and Racism*, ed. Elly Bulkin, Barbara Smith, and Minnie Bruce Pratt (Ithaca: Firebrand), 35.

14 Biddy Martin and Chandra Mohanty, 'Feminist Politics: What's Home Got to Do with It,' in *Feminist Studies/Critical Studies*, ed. Teresa de Lauretis (Bloomington: Indiana UP, 1986), 196.

15 See Anna Bramwell, *Ecology in the Twentieth Century: A History* (New Haven: Yale UP, 1989), *passim*.

16 Margery Fee, 'Romantic Nationalism and the Image of Native People in Contemporary English-Canadian Literature' in *The Native in Literature*, ed. Thomas King, Cheryl Dawnan Calver, and Helen Hoy (Montreal: ECW, 1987), 17–18. Further reference will be indicated in the text by page number.

17 George Grant, 'In Defence of North America,' in *Technology and Empire* (Toronto: House of Anansi, 1969), 17.

18 Northrop Frye, 'Conclusion to *The Literary History of Canada*,' in *The Bush Garden* (Toronto: House of Anansi, 1971), 225. Further reference will be indicated in the text by page number.

19 Margaret Atwood, *Survival* (Toronto: House of Anansi, 1972), 49. Further reference will be indicated in the text by page number.

20 Dennis Lee, 'Three,' in *Civil Elegies and Other Poems* (Toronto: House of Anansi, 1972), 42.

21 Robin Mathews, 'The Social Political Novel' in *Canadian Literature: Surrender or Revolution* (Toronto: Steel Rail, 1978).

22 Earle Birney, 'Can. Lit.' in *An Anthology of Canadian Literature in English*, ed. Russell Brown, Donna Bennett, and Nathalie Cooke (Toronto: Oxford UP, 1990), 385–6.

23 Terry Goldie, *Fear and Temptation: The Image of the Indigene in Canadian, Australian, and New Zealand Literatures* (Montreal: McGill-Queen's UP, 1989), 12. Further reference will be indicated in the text by page number.

24 Deborah Root, '"White Indians": Appropriation and the Politics of Display,' in *Borrowed Power: Essays on Cultural Appropriation*, ed. Bruce Ziff and Pratima V. Rao (New Brunswick, NJ: Rutgers UP), *passim*.

25 Eva Mackey, 'Becoming Indigenous: Land, Belonging and the Appropriation of Aboriginality in Canadian Nationalist Narratives,' *Social Analysis* 42, no. 2 (July 1997): 160. Further reference will be indicated in the text by page number.

26 William Cronon, 'The Trouble with Wilderness; or, Getting Back to the Wrong Nature,' in *Uncommon Ground: Rethinking the Human Place in Nature*, ed. William Cronon (New York: W.W. Norton and Co., 1995), 71–84.

27 Trudeau, 'Exhaustion and Fulfilment'

28 Jurgen Habermas, 'On the Public Uses of History,' in *The New Conservatism*, ed. and trans. Sherry Weber Nicholson (Cambridge, MA: MIT, 1989), 232–3.

29 Root, '"White Indians,"' 232.

Chapter One

1 Duncan Campbell Scott, 'Night Hymns on Lake Nipigon,' in *A Northern Romanticism: Poets of the Confederation*, ed. Tracy Ware (Ottawa: Tecumseh), 225–7.

2 For a metrical analysis of this poem, see Carolyn Roberts, 'Words After Music: A Musical Reading of Scott's "Night Hymns on Lake Nipigon",' *Canadian Poetry*, no. 8 (1981): 56–63.

3 Of course, the students look at me as if I'm mad.

4 David Bentley, in 'Shadows in the Soul,' interprets the singing as the 'harmonious union of alterities' in contrast to the more destructive 'racial haunting' of mixed race people in Scott's poems. He also notes the way the poem evokes the four stages theory of human development, and perpetuates 'racial and linguistic stereotypes.' D.M.R. Bentley, 'Shadows in the Soul: Racial Haunting in the Poetry of Duncan Campbell Scott,' *University of Toronto Quarterly* 75, no. 2 (spring 2006): 753.

5 D.M.R. Bentley, 'Uncannyda,' *Canadian Poetry* 37 (fall/winter 1995): 1.

6 Bentley, 'Uncannyda,' 2.

7 Terry Goldie, *Fear and Temptation: The Image of the Indigene in Canadian, Australian, and New Zealand Literatures* (Montreal: McGill-Queen's UP, 1989), 12.

8 This was Professor John Milloy.

9 Homi Bhabha, 'Introduction,' in *Narrating the Nation*, ed. Homi Bhabha (London: Routledge, 1990), 2. Further reference will be indicated by page number in the text.

10 For a discussion of the mechanism of compulsive repetition, see Sigmund Freud, *Beyond the Pleasure Principle*, trans. Alix Strachey (New York: Liveright, 1970).

11 Bentley, 'Uncannyda,' 9.

12 Archibald Lampman, 'Morning on the Lièvres,' in *A Northern Romanticism: Poets of the Confederation*, ed. Tracy Ware (Ottawa: Tecumseh, 2000), 131.

13 Isabella Valancy Crawford, *Malcolm's Katie* (London, ON: Canadian Poetry, 1987).

14 James Reaney writes about this lyric in 'Isabella Valancy Crawford,' in *Our Living Tradition*, 2d and 3d ser., ed. R.L. McDougall (Toronto: U Toronto P, 1959), 277–84.

15 Robin Mathews, '*Malcolm's Katie*: Love, Wealth, and Nation Building,' *Studies in Canadian Literature* 2.1 (1997): http://www.lib.unb.ca/Texts/SCL/vol2_1/Contents.htm.

16 Robert Alan Burns, 'Crawford and Gounod: Ambiguity and Irony in *Malcolm's Katie*,' *Canadian Poetry* 15 (fall/winter 1984): 30–53, http://uwo.ca/english/canadianpoetry/cpjrn/vol15/burns.htm

17 Moore 126n; cited in Bentley, 'Uncannyda,' 9.

18 Cited in Bentley, 'Uncannyda,' 9.

19 Isabella Valancy Crawford, 'The Lily Bed,' in *A Northern Romanticism: Poets of the Confederation*, ed. Tracy Ware (Ottawa: Tecumseh, 2000), 19–21; Ian Lancashire, 'Isabella Valancy Crawford, Notes on Life and Works,' in *Representative Poetry On-line*, http://rpo.library.utoronto.ca/poet/85.html.

20 Pauline Johnson, 'The Idlers,' in *E. Pauline Johnson Tekahionwake: Collected Poems and Selected Prose*, eds. Carole Gerson and Veronica Strong-Boag (Toronto: U Toronto P, 2002), 60.

21 Nikki Strong-Boag and Carole Gerson also read 'The Song My Paddle Sings' as an allegory of sexual encounter, based on the language of 'wooing,' the subsequent 'trembling' running of the rapids, and a possibly post-coital languor in the last stanza. Maybe – I am not convinced. See Veronica Strong-Boag and Carole Gerson, *Paddling Her Own Canoe: The Times and Texts of E. Pauline Johnson* (Toronto: U Toronto P, 2000), 144.

22 See Johnson, *E. Pauline Johnson Tekahionwake*, 43. Strong-Boag and Gerson also note the recurrence of this image in Lampman's 'Morning on the Lievres' in *Paddling Her Own Canoe*, 152.

23 Glenn Willmott, 'Paddled by Pauline,' *Canadian Poetry* 46 (spring/summer 2000): http://uwo.ca/english/canadianpoetry/cpjrn/vol46/willmott.htm.

24 Marjorie Pickthall, 'The Third Generation,' in *Angel's Shoes and Other Stories* (London: Hodder and Stoughton, 1923). Further reference will be indicated by page numbers in the text.

25 Pickthall might use the name 'Montagnais' because this name for the Labrador Innu was used by Leonidas Hubbard, Mina Hubbard, and Dillon Wallace in the works about Labrador that may have provided inspiration for this story. There is no relationship to be assumed between the man in this story and any actual First Nations people; there is no evidence that Pickthall visited the Canadian North or ever met any Labrador Innu.

26 This quotation is from Exodus 20:5, King James version, but this statement is repeated at Exodus 34:7, Numbers 14:18, and Deuteronomy 5:9. It has remained controversial in Christian belief, as it seems to contradict the representation of God in the New Testament as just and merciful.

27 Goldie, *Fear and Temptation*, 13.

28 Margaret Atwood, *Surfacing* (Toronto: General Publishing, 1972), 67.

29 Margaret Atwood, *Surfacing*, 11.

30 Bentley, 'Uncannyda,' 12.

31 Margaret Atwood, 'Death by Landscape,' in *Wilderness Tips* (Toronto: McClelland and Stewart, 1992), 119. Further reference will be indicated by page number in the text.

32 Bentley, 'Uncannyda,' 14.

33 A term used by Nick Mount in *When Canadian Literature Moved to New York* (Toronto: U Toronto P, 2005).

34 William Closson James, 'The Quest Pattern and the Canoe Trip,' in *Nastawgan: The Canadian North by Canoe and Snowshoe*, ed. Bruce W. Hodgins and Margaret Hobbs (Toronto: Betelgeuse Books, 1985), 9.

35 James, 'The Quest Pattern and the Canoe Trip,' 15.

36 James, 'The Quest Pattern and the Canoe Trip,' 18.

37 James, 'The Quest Pattern and the Canoe Trip,' 18.

38 Duncan Campbell Scott, 'The Height of Land,' in *A Northern Romanticism: Poets of the Confederation*, ed. Tracy Ware (Ottawa: Tecumseh, 2000), 242–6.

39 Douglas LePan, 'Canoe-trip,' 'A Country without a Mythology,' and 'Coureur de Bois,' in *The Wounded Prince and Other Poems* (London: Chatto and Windus, 1948). Further references in the text refer to this edition.

40 James, 'The Quest Pattern and the Canoe Trip,' 16.

41 Atwood, *Survival* (Toronto: House of Anansi, 1972), 52–3.

42 Atwood, *Survival*, 53.

43 James, 'The Quest Pattern and the Canoe Trip,' 18.

44 James, 'The Quest Pattern and the Canoe Trip,' 19.

45 Hugh MacLennan, *The Watch that Ends the Night* (1958; reprint Toronto: MacMillan, 1975), 289.

Chapter Two

1 Grey Owl [pseud.], *Men of the Last Frontier* (London: Lovat Dickson, 1931), 1.
2 Grey Owl [pseud.], *Men of the Last Frontier*, 1.
3 Grey Owl [pseud.], *Men of the Last Frontier*, 2.
4 Hayden White, *The Content of the Form* (Baltimore: Johns Hopkins UP), 65.
5 Stuart Hall, cited in Eva Mackey, *The House of Difference: Cultural Politics and National Identity in Canada* (London: Routledge, 1998), 151.
6 Robin Winks, introduction to *The Fur Trade in Canada: An Introduction to Canadian Economic History*, by Harold A. Innis (Toronto: U Toronto P, 1956), xiv.
7 D.G. Creighton, *The Commercial Empire of the St. Lawrence 1760–1850* (Toronto: Ryerson P, 1937), v. Further reference will be indicated in the text by page number.
8 See A.B. McKillop, 'Historiography in English,' in *The Canadian Encyclopedia* (Historica Foundation, 2012), www.thecanadianencyclopedia.com.
9 John Jennings, ed., *The Canoe: A Living Tradition* (Toronto: Firefly, 2002), 26.
10 A.R.M. Lower, *Canadians in the Making: A Social History of Canada* (Toronto: Longmans, 1958), 47.
11 Lower, cited in Carl Berger, *The Writing of Canadian History*, Toronto: Oxford UP, 1976), 115.
12 Bruce Hodgins, 'Refiguring Wilderness: A Personal Odyssey,' *Journal of Canadian Studies* 33, no. 2 (summer 1998): 12–26.
13 Hugh MacLennan, *Seven Rivers of Canada* (Toronto: Macmillan, 1961), 11. Further reference is indicated in the text by page number.
14 W.J. Eccles, 'A Belated Review of Harold Adams Innis, *The Fur Trade in Canada*,' *Canadian Historical Review* 40, no. 4 (1979): 420. Further reference is indicated in the text by page number.
15 Bruce Hodgins, 'Canoe Irony: Symbol and Harbinger,' in *Canexus: The Canoe in Canadian Culture*, ed. James Raffan and Bert Horwood (Toronto: Betelgeuse Books, 1998), 55.
16 Daniel Francis, *National Dreams* (Vancouver: Arsenal Pulp, 1997), 129.
17 Bruce Willems-Braun, 'Buried Epistemologies: The Politics of Nature in (Post)colonial British Columbia,' *Annals of the Association of American Geographers* 87, no. 1 (1997): 21.
18 Mackey, *House of Difference*, 152.
19 Robert E. Pinkerton, 'The Canoe – Half Stolen,' *Outing* 62 (May 1913): 159.
20 Pinkerton, 'The Canoe – Half Stolen,' 160.

21 C.E.S.Franks, *The Canoe and White Water: From Essential to Sport* (Toronto: U Toronto P, 1977), 41.

22 Terry Goldie, *Fear and Temptation: The Image of the Indigene in Canadian, Australian, and New Zealand Literatures* (Montreal: McGill-Queen's UP, 1989), 20.

23 Goldie, *Fear and Temptation*, 36.

24 Mackey, *House of Difference*, 158.

25 Kirk Wipper, foreword to Raffan and Horwood, *Canexus*, ix.

26 James Raffan, *Bark, Skin and Cedar: Exploring the Canoe in Canadian Experience* (Toronto: Harper Perennial, 1999), 89.

27 Raffan, *Bark, Skin and Cedar*, 2.

28 Peter Labor, 'The Canot du Maitre: Master of the Inland Seas,' in *The Canoe in Canadian Cultures*, ed. John Jennings, Bruce Hodgins, and Doreen Small (Toronto: Natural History/National Heritage Inc., 1999), 93.

29 Peter Labor, 'The Canot du Maitre: Master of the Inland Seas,' 95.

30 Bill Mason, *Canoescapes* 10.

31 Samuel de Champlain, *Des sauvages, ou Voyage de Sieur de Champlain fait en l'an 1603*, trans. H.H. Langton (Toronto: Champlain Society), 152; cited in John Murray Gibbon, *The Romance of the Canadian Canoe* (Toronto: Ryerson P, 1951), 17. Also cited in Raffan, *Bark, Skin and Cedar*, 24; Ralph Frese 'Canadians and the Canadian Canoe in the Opening of the American Midwest,' in Jennings, et al., *The Canoe in Canadian Cultures*, 161; and David McNab et al., 'Black with Canoes: Aboriginal Resistance and the Canoe: Diplomacy, Trade and Warfare in the Meeting Grounds of Northeastern North America,' in *Technology, Disease and Colonial Conquests, Sixteenth to Eighteenth Centuries*, ed. George Raudzens (Leiden: Brill, 2002), 252.

32 Raffan, *Bark, Skin and Cedar*, 3.

33 John Wadland, 'Wilderness and Culture,' in *Nastawgan*, ed. Bruce Hodgins and Margaret Hobbs (Toronto: Betelgeuse Books, 1985), 223.

34 Peter Labor, 'The Canot du Maitre: Master of the Inland Seas,' 95.

35 Eric Morse, 'Notes on the Fond du Lac River,' Eric Morse Fonds, R8288, vol. 1-23, Library and Archives Canada.

36 James N. Gladden, *The Boundary Waters Canoe Area* (Ames: Iowa State UP, 1990), 10.

37 Raffan, *Bark, Skin and Cedar*, 24. Grace Lee Nute has pointed out that the sled and snowshoes were at least as important. See Nute, 'Knights of the Waterways,' *The Beaver* 298 (summer 1967): 11–17.

38 Peter Labor, 'Alexander Mackenzie Voyageur Route: Community Survey Discussion: A Cultural Context I,' [1996] http://www.amvr.org/page50.htm.

39 Susanna Moodie, *Roughing It in the Bush*, vol. 2 (London: Bentley, 1852),
    26; also cited in Beverly Haun-Moss, 'Layered Hegemonies: The Origins of
    Recreational Canoeing Desire in the Province of Ontario,' *Topia: Canadian
    Journal of Cultural Studies* 7 (spring 2002): 43; Jamie Benidickson, *Idleness,
    Water, and a Canoe: Reflections on Paddling for Pleasure* (Toronto: U Toronto P,
    1997), 78; William Closson James, 'The Quest Pattern and the Canoe Trip,'
    in Hodgins and Hobbs, *Nastawgan*, 12; Marsh 'The Heritage of Peterbor-
    ough Canoes,' in Hodgins and Hobbs, *Nastawgan*, 211; James Raffan, 'Being
    There: Bill Mason and the Canadian Canoeing Tradition,' in Jennings et
    al., *Canoe in Canadian Cultures*, 18; and Johnston, 'Canoe Sport in Canada:
    Anglo-American Hybrid?' in Raffin and Horwood, *Canexus*, 64.
40 Anna Jameson, *Winter Studies and Summer Rambles in Canada*, vol. 3 (London:
    Saunders and Otley, 1838), 198–9; also cited in James 'The Quest Pattern
    and the Canoe Trip,' 12; Benidickson, *Idleness, Water, and a Canoe: Reflections
    on Paddling for Pleasure*, 96; and Haun-Moss, 'Layered Hegemonies,' 44.
41 Frances Simpson, 'Journal of a Voyage from Montreal, thro' the Interior of
    Canada to York Factory on the Shores of Hudson Bay,' in *Canadian Explora-
    tion Literature*, ed. Germaine Warkentin (Toronto: Oxford UP, 1993), 388.
42 Haun-Moss, 'Layered Hegemonies,' 44. Further reference will be indicated
    in the text by page number.
43 Denis Coolican, 'Canoe Trip Diary,' *Fishing*, 77, clipping in Eric Morse
    Fonds, R8288, Churchill River 2 file, Library and Archives Canada.
44 Raffan, *Bark, Skin and Cedar*, 112.
45 Hodgins, 'Canoe Irony,' 46–7. Hodgins recognizes in his later work that
    this may be an oversimplification. See Bruce Hodgins and Gwyneth Hoyle,
    Canoeing North into the Unknown: A Record of River Travel: 1874–1974 (Toron-
    to: Natural Heritage, 1994), 23.
46 John Jennings, 'The Canadian Canoe Museum and Canada's National Sym-
    bol,' in Jennings et al., *The Canoe in Canadian Cultures*, 6.
47 Eric Morse, *Freshwater Saga: Memoirs of a Lifetime of Wilderness Canoeing in
    Canada* (Toronto: U Toronto P, 1968), 9.
48 Eric Morse, 'Canoe Routes of the Voyageurs: The Geography and Logistics
    of the Canadian Fur Trade' (Ottawa: Royal Canadian Geographical Society
    [1962]), 41.
49 Harold A. Innis, *The Fur Trade in Canada: An Introduction to Canadian Eco-
    nomic History* (Toronto: U Toronto P, 1956), 118.
50 Canadian Canoe Museum, 'Our Canoeing Heritage,' http://www.canoemu-
    seum.net/heritage/.
51 Eric Morse, *Fur Trade Canoe Routes of Canada, Then and Now* (Toronto: U
    Toronto P, 1968), 75.

52 John J. Bigsby, *The Shoe and the Canoe, or Pictures of Travel in the Canadas* (1850; reprint New York: Paladin, 1969), 240–1.

53 Grace Lee Nute, 'Knights of the Waterways,' 12.

54 Hugh MacLennan, *Seven Rivers of Canada*, 17.

55 Morse, *Fur Trade Canoe Routes*, 77. Further reference will be indicated in the text by page number.

56 Grace Lee Nute, 'Knights of the Waterways,' 9, 11.

57 Timothy Kent, 'Manufacture of Birchbark Canoes for the Fur Trade in the St. Lawrence,' in Jennings et al., *Canoe in Canadian Cultures*, 113.

58 Timothy Kent, 'Manufacture of Birchbark Canoes,' 113.

59 Franks, *Canoe and White Water*, 53–4. Further reference will be indicated in the text by page number.

60 McNab et al., 'Black with Canoes,' 237.

61 Raffan, 'Being There,' 19.

62 Craig MacDonald, 'The Nastawgan: Traditional Routes of Travel in the Temagami District,' in Hodgins and Hobbs, *Nastawgan*, 187.

63 Jennings, 'Canadian Canoe Museum,' 1.

64 Furniss, Elizabeth, *The Burden of History: Colonialism and the Frontier Myth in a Rural Canadian Community*, 65. Further reference will be indicated in the text by page number.

65 For example, Treaty 9 (which was signed in 1906) was negotiated specifically to allow development of mineral and other resources on what was acknowledged to be First Nations land in the northern part of Ontario and Quebec. See D.C. Scott, 'The Last of the Indian Treaties,' in *The Circle of Affection* (Toronto: McClelland and Stewart, 1947), 109–22.

66 Saul, on his website www.johnralstonsaul.com; see also John Ralston Saul, *A Fair Country: Telling Truths about Canada* (Toronto: Viking, 2008).

Chapter Three

1 Beverly Haun-Moss, 'Layered Hegemonies: The Origins of Recreational Canoeing Desire in the Province of Ontario,' *Topia: Canadian Journal of Cultural Studies* 7 (spring 2002): 50.

2 Eric Morse, *Freshwater Saga: Memoirs of a Lifetime of Wilderness Canoeing in Canada* (Toronto: U Toronto P, 1968), 5. Further reference will be indicated in the text by page number.

3 The Canadian Club website, www.canadianclub.org.

4 This information is condensed from the selection of papers of the Ottawa Canadian Club, 1949–1950, available on their website, www.canadianclubottawa.org.

5 Morse's thesis was titled 'Immigration and the Status of British East Indians in Canada: A Problem in Imperial Relations' (M.A. thesis, Queen's University, 1936). His supervisor was R.G. Trotter, an early member of what J.M.S. Careless has called the 'Political Nationhood' school of Canadian history, which focused on the 'paper-strewn path' that traced the formation of Canada's independent political institutions. J.M.S. Careless, 'Frontierism, Metropolitanism, and Canadian History,' *Canadian Historical Review* 35, no. 1 (March 1954): 3.

6 Identified as such in a list of 'EM's main summer canoe trips from 1951 onwards' (perhaps prepared by Pamela Morse?) in Morse's papers. Eric Morse Fonds, R8288, file 1-1, Library and Archives Canada.

7 Bruce Hodgins and Gwyneth Hoyle, *Canoeing North into the Unknown: A Record of River Travel: 1874–1974* (Toronto: Natural Heritage, 1994), 17–18.

8 'List of Guests,' Eric Morse Fonds, R8288, vol. 3, file 3-49, 'Clippings and Memorabilia,' Library and Archives Canada.

9 Eric Morse, 'On the Trail of La Verendrye,' clipping in Eric Morse Fonds, R8288, file 1-4, Library and Archives Canada.

10 Blair Fraser, 'We Went La Verendrye's Way,' *Maclean's* (1 October 1954): 19, clipping in Eric Morse Fonds, R8288, file 1-5, Library and Archives Canada.

11 Eric Morse, 'Voyageurs 1958: Ile a la crosse to Waterways,' typescript in Eric Morse Fonds, R8288, file 1-26, Library and Archives Canada.

12 Sigurd Olsen, *The Lonely Land*, 11–12.

13 Fraser, 'We Went La Verendrye's Way,' 19.

14 See Morse, *Freshwater Saga*, 11; also Sigurd Olsen, 'Memo to Voyageurs,' 19 June 1954, in Eric Morse Fonds, R8288, file 1-1, Library and Archives Canada.

15 Stuart Hall, 'Cultural Identity and Diaspora,' in *Identity: Community, Culture, Difference*, ed. Jonathan Rutherford (London: Lawrence and Wishart, 1990), 225.

16 Some of the posts were in 'dry' areas (where the sale of liquor was not allowed), so they had to order ahead and immediately take the alcohol out of town.

17 Morse does not provide any information about his marriage in *Freshwater Saga* other than the fact of its having taken place – an interesting example of gender and genre decorum.

18 When Trudeau later won his first election as prime minister, the group sent a telegram: 'The Coppermine Voyageurs warmly and proudly salute their most intrepid member on a rapid neatly run without dumping and bow first, an approved change in style.' Eric Morse Fonds, R8288, Coppermine River 1 file, Library and Archives Canada.

19 Angus Scott, foreword to Morse, *Freshwater Saga*, xi.

20 Of course, this was in the days before modern satellite telephones and GPS made wilderness tripping much safer.

21 Morse to Rodger, 11 February 1957, in Eric Morse Fonds, R8288, file 1-23, Library and Archives Canada. The quotation from Grant can be found in George Grant, *Ocean to Ocean* (London: Sampson Low, Marston, Low and Searle, 1873), 32.

22 Haun-Moss, 'Layered Hegemonies,' 40.

23 Christy Collis, 'The Edge Men: Narrating Late Twentieth-Century Exploration on Australia's Desert and Antarctic Frontiers' (PhD diss., LaTrobe University, 2000), 11. Further reference will be indicated in the text by page number.

24 This is not to say that land claims were not an issue in this period, just that in public discourse the 'Canadian identity' debate was much more visible. Anxiety about land became much more marked in Canada in the 1990s after the Delgamuuk'w decision.

25 Tony Bennett, *The Birth of the Museum: History, Theory, Politics* (London: Routledge, 1995), 141.

26 Carol Duncan, *Civilizing Rituals* (London: Routledge, 1995), 24.

27 Duncan, *Civilizing Rituals*, 12.

28 Olsen, 'Memo to the Voyageurs,' 19 June 1954.

29 David F. Pelly, *Arctic Cairn Notes* (Toronto: Betelgeuse Books, [1997]), 98.

30 See Collis, 'The Edge Men,' *passim.*

31 Morse, 'On the Trail of La Verendrye.'

32 Morse, 'Voyageurs 1958 Ile a la Crosse to Waterways,' 7.33. Olsen, *The Lonely Land*, 125. Further reference will be indicated in the text by page number.

34 See Hodgins, 'Canoe Irony: Symbol and Harbinger,' in *Canexus: The Canoe in Canadian Culture*, ed. James Raffan and Bert Horwood (Toronto: Betelgeuse Books, 1998).

35 Cited by Morse in the *Ottawa Journal*, 26 September 1959.

36 Hodgins and Hoyle, *Canoeing North into the Unknown*, 23.

Chapter Four

1 Prince Edward Island and Newfoundland did not participate; the Nova Scotia team did not receive support from their provincial government, but participated anyway using a combination of commercial support and personal funds.

2 'Front Page–Coverage–Summary,' Centennial Commission Records, RG 69, vol. 545, 'Canoe Pageant 1967 Publicity' file, Library and Archives Canada.

3 Daniel Francis, *National Dreams* (Vancouver: Arsenal Pulp, 1997), 12. Further reference will be indicated in the text by page number.

4 Undated press release, Centennial Commission Records, RG 69, vol. 545, 'Press Releases' file, Library and Archives Canada.

5 Pierre Berton, *1967: The Last Good Year* (Toronto: Doubleday, 1997), 48–57.

6 According to Judy Lamarsh in her autobiography, *Memoirs of a Bird in a Gilded Cage*, the idea originated with Gene Rheaume, then MP for the Northwest Territories (192). Charbonneau's memo of 27 August 1964 identifies the idea as originating with Gene Rheaume, and the authors of the plan as Tyson and John Nikel (Centennial Commission Records, RG 69, vol. 505, 'Minutes and Reports Volume 1' file, Library and Archives Canada). Rheaume's brother Jim Rheaume became Chief Voyageur (coach) of the Manitoba team.

7 A.J. Charbonneau, 'Memo,' 17 August 1964 , Centennial Commisson Records, RG 69, vol. 505, Library and Archives Canada. Further reference will be indicated in the text.

8 Morse's thesis supervisor was R.G. Trotter, an early member of what J.M.S. Careless has called the 'Political Nationhood' school of Canadian history, which focused on the 'paper-strewn path' that traced the formation of Canada's independent political institutions. J.M.S. Careless, 'Frontierism, Metropolitanism, and Canadian History,' *Canadian Historical Review* 45, no. 1 (March 1954).

9 Alan Filewod 'The Face of Re-enactment,' *Canadian Theatre Review* 121 (winter 2005), 14.

10 Michael Dawson, *The Mountie: From Dime Novel to Disney* (Toronto: Between the Lines), 111.

11 See also H.V. Nelles, *The Art of Nation-Building: Pageantry and Spectacle at Quebec's Tercentenary* (Toronto: U Toronto P, 1999) for an example of the way that contemporary aims influence the representation of the past in historical re-enactments.

12 Anne McClintock, *Imperial Leather: Race, Gender and Sexuality in the Colonial Contest* (New York: Routledge, 1995), 374. Further reference will be indicated in the text by page number.

13 This shift is a result of a process that Marx called the fetishism of commodities, whereby the social relations that produce value in objects are obscured and value is taken to inhere in objects themselves rather than in the social relations that produced them. Thus 'productions of the human brain appear as independent beings endowed with life, and entering into relation both with one another and the human race.' Karl Marx, 'Commodities,' in *The Marx-Engels Reader*, ed. Robert Tucker (New York: Norton, 1978), 321.

14 James Raffan, *Fire in the Bones: Bill Mason and the Canadian Canoeing Tradition* (Toronto: Harper Collins, 2002), 125. Raffan notes that Mason was one of the crew that originally was contracted to film the portion of the race that ran through Quetico Park, but he was prevented from participating by the onset of his first heart attack.

15 A journal of this trip written by G.H.U. Bayley, 'Canoe Trip from Fort MacPherson to Fort Yukon 1965,' is available in the Trent University Archives (93-016/3/87).

16 See G.H.U. Bayley, 'To Whom It May Concern,' Centennial Commission Records, RG 69, vol. 505, Library and Archives Canada.

17 Olsen also provided a sixty-page typescript that compiled the comments of explorers and historical travellers along the Grand Portage and border lakes route, with his own annotations and instructions designed for present-day travellers. This manuscript was duplicated and passed on to provincial commodores. Matthews to Olsen, 23 December 1966, Centennial Commission Records, RG 69, vol. 506, 'Centennial Voyageur Canoe Pageant General Correspondence (1966) vol 1b' file, Library and Archives Canada.

18 This corresponds with the conclusions reached by Haun-Moss and by Hodgins and Hoyle that recreational canoeists in general are male and belong to privileged classes in Canada, with high levels of income and education. I would add that David F. Pelly's book *Arctic Cairn Notes* (Toronto: Betelgeuse Books, [1997]), which documents dozens of handwritten notes left by recreational canoeists in stone cairns on the Hanbury-Thelon and Kazan Rivers, shows that recreational canoeists are startlingly good spellers, even on vacation – additional evidence of their high socio-economic and education level.

19 For example, the inaugural meeting of the 'Professional Canoe Racers Association' organized by John Nikel at the annual regatta in Shawinigan in 1965 was attended by five established two-man teams who would all eventually be part of the Voyageur Canoe Pageant: Crerar and McEachern, Michelle and Carrier (Manitoba), Maxwell and Nikel (Alberta), Bellemare and Chevalier (Quebec), and Hart and Fraser (BC). Minutes, 2 September 1965, courtesy of Jim Rheaume. See also the interview with Don Starkell, originally published in *Che-Mun* 86 (autumn 1996), at http://cgi.canoe.ca/che-mun/interview.html.

20 J.A. Mitchell, 'Commodore's Report,' 11 September 1965, Centennial Commission Records, RG 69, vol. 505, Library and Archives Canada.

21 John Nikel, 'Commodore's Report on the 1965 Trial,' Centennial Commission Records, RG 69, vol. 505, Library and Archives Canada.

22 Mitchell, 'Commodore's Report,' 11 September 1965.

23 Nikel to Matthews, 11 December 1966, Centennial Commission Records, RG 69, vol. 505, Library and Archives Canada. Nikel was evidently so upset at the way he had been shuffled out of a central role that he distributed this letter, in which he also declined employment with the Centennial Commission, to all the provincial commodores (Jim Rheaume, private communication).

24 According to Norm Crerar, there had been a mix-up about the time (private communication).

25 'Centennial Report Number 9,' [1966?], Provincial Centennial Commission Records, GR 1449, box 45, file P-V-2 'Voyageur Canoe Pageant Vol 3,' British Columbia Public Archives, Victoria.

26 'The Boat that Built Canada,' *Hunting and Fishing in Canada* (March 1966), clipping in Centennial Commission Records, RG 69, vol. 547, Library and Archives Canada.

27 Norm Crerar, private communication.

28 The canoes were typically governed by a hierarchical management team that included a 'bourgeois' (the white trader); a 'gouvernnail,' (overseer or crew chief who made decisions about routes and personnel); a steersman for each canoe and his assistant, a bowman, both of whom needed experience in personnel management and white water; and the paddlers, at the bottom of the hierarchy.

29 'Centennial Report Number 9,' [1966?].

30 Undated press release, Centennial Commission Records.

31 Undated press release, Centennial Commission Records.

32 'Centennial Report Number 9,' [1966?].

33 Jack Struthers, 'Easy Life of Early Voyageurs Envy of Centennial Paddlers,' *Cariboo Observer* (Quesnel, BC). Clipping dated 20 July 1967, Provincial Centennial Commission Records, GR 1449, box 45, file P-V-2 vol 4, British Columbia Public Archives, Victoria.

34 'Scientific Aid Helps Voyageurs Float down Saskatchewan River,' *Globe and Mail*, 12 June 1967.

35 According to Pierre Berton, the Voyageur Canoe Pageant was listed in the *Guinness Book of World Records* as the longest ever canoe race on the initiative of Don Starkell (Berton, *The Last Good Year*, 56).

36 The seats might not have broken accidentally. Norm Crerar points out that racing paddlers each need a separate thwart to facilitate changing sides in mid-stroke; Crerar remembers pageant paddlers greeting the Governor General in pants with holes worn in the seats from sliding back on forth over the thwarts so frequently. Canoes built with two seats and two thwarts, like the ones ordered from Chestnut, would have been useless to teams of

six paddlers, and Crerar suggests the racers may have taken steps to make this point clear to more nostalgic race organizers.

37 I thank Norm Crerar for allowing me to consult the written record of the points awarded to various candidates under his selection system.

38 For example, the Peter Ballantyne Cree Nation team description declared that the race will be 'following ancient routes that have been used by PBCN First Nations from time immemorial and later used by the fur traders' on the canoequest website (www.saskatchewancentennialcanoequest.info, 2005, no longer available).

38 See for example, Barb Cranmer, *Qatuwas: People Gathering Together* (National Film Board of Canada, 1997), a film about the first west coast Aboriginal canoe festival held at Bella Bella.

39 Neil Loutit, 'La Verendrye Legend Re-enacted,' *Winnipeg Free Press*, 6 July 1967.

40 Brown, 'Commodore's Report on the NWT Team's Participation in the Eastern Trials of the Centennial Canoe Pageant during August 1965,' Centennial Commission Records, RG 69, vol. 505, Library and Archives Canada.

41 Brown, 'Commodore's Report on the NWT Team's Participation.'

42 'An Incident of Discrimination against Indians and Eskimos on the Canadian National Toronto-North Bay: August 7 1965,' 15 October 1965, p. 2, Centennial Commission Records, RG 65, vol. 505, file 'NWT National Project.' Library and Archives Canada.

43 Jim Rheaume, private communication.

44 Both the *Daily News* (New York) (30 August 1966) and the *New York Times* (30 August 1966) ran the same photograph of the NWT team eating ice cream.

45 Ken Ouellette to Matthews, 4 April 1967, Centennial Commssion Records, RG 69, vol. 505, Library and Archives Canada.

46 Skwah First Nation website, http://www.skwahnation.net/activities.html (2005).

47 This vote, moved by New Brunswick commodore John Murrant and seconded by Vic Chapman, then Alberta commodore (later the project officer for the pageant for the Centennial Commission), is recorded in the minutes of a meeting of the Provincial Commodores on 21 August 1966, p. 1. Centennial Commisson Records, RG 69, vol. 505, file 'Centennial Voyageur Canoe Pageant Minutes and Reports Vol II,' Library and Archives Canada. Subsequent newspaper ads for these positions specified that one of the qualifications was gender. Incidentally, I have not met anyone yet who would admit to having attended this meeting.

48 An exception was Adeline Rheaume, wife of Manitoba commodore Jim Rheaume, who reported on the pageant from day-to-day for the *Flin Flon Daily Reminder*.

49 I thank reader C of my article for *Journal of Canadian Studies* for suggesting a little context was in order here.
50 These initiatives eventually led to the founding of Collège militaire royal de Saint-Jean.
51 Matthews to Simon-Pierre Rainville, 1 mai 1967; Matthews to Simon-Pierre Rainville, 26 April 1967; Chapman to Simon-Pierre Rainville, Centennial Commission Records, RG 69, vol. 505, Library and Archives Canada.
52 Margery Fee, 'Romantic Nationalism and the Image of Native People in Contemporary English-Canadian Literature,' in *The Native in Literature*, ed. Thomas King, Cheryl Dawnan Calver, and Helen Hoy (Montreal: ECW, 1987), 16. Further reference will be indicated in the text by page number.
53 McClintock, *Imperial Leather*, 375.

Chapter Five

1 John Moss, *Enduring Dreams* (Toronto: House of Anansi, 1996), 55. Further reference will be indicated in the text.
2 There are, of course, other accounts of canoe trips that followed Hornby's route, or part of it, that I have excluded because the references to Hornby are minor or because the paddlers are primarily British or American citizens. These include: Christopher Norment, *In the North of Our Lives* (Camden, ME: Down East Books, 1989); Helge Instad, *The Land of Feast and Famine*, trans. Eugene Gay-Tifft (New York: A.A. Knopf, 1933); and George Grinnell, *A Death on the Barrens* (Toronto: Northern Books, 1996). Norment's book is particularly well-written. John Moss also mentions Hornby in *Enduring Dreams*. There are numerous accounts of recent retracings of Hornby's trip on the Internet: Shipp and Mo's 'Thelon River Expedition' is fun: www.shippw.homestead.com/Thelon1.html; see also Craig Walker's site at http://www.aoc.nrao.edu/~cwalker/photos/Thelon04/index.html.
3 Hayden White, 'The Value of Narrativity in the Representation of Reality,' *Critical Inquiry* 7, no. 1 (autumn 1980): 15.
4 Malcolm Waldron, *Snowman: John Hornby in the Barren Lands* (1931; reprint Montreal: McGill-Queen's UP, 1997), 287. Further reference will be indicated in the text by page number.
5 Sherrill Grace, *Canada and the Idea of North* (Montreal: McGill-Queen's UP, 2001), 145. Further reference will be indicated in the text by page number.
6 Renee Hulan, *Northern Experience and the Myths of Canadian Culture* (Montreal: McGill-Queen's UP, 2002), 4–5. Further reference will be indicated in the text by page number.
7 See William Closson James, 'The Quest Pattern and the Canoe Trip,' in *Nas-*

tawgan, ed. Bruce W. Hodgins and Margaret Hobbs (Toronto: Betelgeuse Books, 1985). See also Chapter One.

 8 George Whalley, *The Legend of John Hornby* (Toronto: Macmillan, 1962), 1. Further reference will be indicated in the text by page number.

 9 George Whalley, 'Notes on a Legend,' *Queen's Quarterly* 76 (1969): 614.

10 Whalley, 'Notes on a Legend,' 616–17.

11 Northrop Frye, *Anatomy of Criticism* (Princeton, NJ: Princeton UP, 1957), 237.

12 Whalley, 'Notes on a Legend,' 617.

13 George Whalley, *Poetic Process* (London: Routledge and Kegan Paul, 1953), 170. Further reference will be indicated in the text by page number.

14 Whalley, 'Notes on a Legend,' 618.

15 Randall Jarrell, 'Death of the Ball Turret Gunner'; Timothy Findlay, *The Wars* (Toronto: Clarke Irwin, 1977).

16 Thomas York, *Snowman: A Novel* (Toronto: Doubleday, 1976), 39. Further reference will be indicated in the text by page number.

17 The fictionalizing of the historical Arimo is particularly offensive, since the novel represents her as married against her will and abused by her husband, D'Arcy Arden. The real Arimo and Arden were interviewed by Whalley, and they seemed to him to have a happy and successful marriage.

18 James, 'The Quest Pattern and the Canoe Trip,' 18.

19 Laurence Jeffrey, *Who Look in Stove and The Edgar Christian Diary* (Toronto: Exile Editions, 1993), 24. Further reference will be indicated in the text by page number.

20 Clive Powell-Williams, *Cold Burial: A True Story of Endurance and Disaster* (New York: St. Martin's Griffin, 2002), 19. Further reference will be indicated in the text by page number.

21 Elizabeth Hay, *Late Nights On Air* (Toronto: McClelland and Stewart, 2007), 43. Further reference will be indicated in the text by page number.

22 Elizabeth Hay, 'Three for Thought: Everything You Need to Know about … Cold,' *Globe and Mail*, 24 January 2004.

23 The story of Leonidas Hubbard is told in Mina Hubbard, *A Woman's Way through Unknown Labrador* (New York: McClure, 1908) and Dillon Wallace, *The Lure of the Labrador Wild* (New York: F. Revell, 1905); the St. John's school disaster is the focus of James Raffan's *Deep Waters: Courage, Character and the Lake Timiskaming Canoeing Tragedy* (Toronto: Harper Collins, 2002).

24 From Matthew Arnold, 'Stanzas from the Grand Chartreuse.'

Chapter Six

 1 Bill Mason, *Waterwalker* (National Film Board of Canada, 1984). Further reference will be indicated in the text.

2 Bill Mason, *Path of the Paddle Solo Basic* (National Film Board of Canada, 1976). Further reference will be indicated in the text.

3 Beverly Haun-Moss, 'Layered Hegemonies: The Origins of Recreational Canoeing Desire in the Province of Ontario,' *Topia: Canadian Journal of Cultural Studies* 7 (spring 2002), 51.

4 According to Ken Buck, 'His films were consistently among the ten most frequently rented films from the NFB. For several years, he had four films in the top ten – an amazing feat.' Ken Buck, *Bill Mason, Wilderness Artist* (Surrey, BC: Rocky Mountain Books, 2005), 12. Two of his films were nominated for Academy Awards, and all won numerous national and international awards.

5 Ken Buck, *Bill Mason, Wilderness Artist*, 28; 11.

6 Kevin Callan, cited in Don Stanfield and Liz Lundell, *Stories from the Bow Seat: The Wisdom and Waggery of Canoe Tripping* (Erin, ON: Boston Mills, 1999), 140.

7 James Raffan, *Fire in the Bones: Bill Mason and the Canadian Canoeing Tradition* (Toronto: Harper Collins, 1996), xviii.

8 James Raffan, introduction to *Voyages: Canada's Heritage Rivers* (St. John's, NF: Breakwater), viii.

9 Haun-Moss, 'Layered Hegemonies,' 52.

10 Eva Mackey, 'Becoming Indigenous: Land, Belonging and the Appropriation of Aboriginality in Canadian Nationalist Narratives,' *Social Analysis* 42, no. 2 (July 1997),160.

11 Eva Mackey, 'Becoming Indigenous: Land, Belonging and the Appropriation of Aboriginality in Canadian Nationalist Narratives,' 161.

12 William Cronon, 'The Trouble with Wilderness; or, Getting Back to the Wrong Nature,' in *Uncommon Ground: Rethinking the Human Place in Nature*, ed. William Cronon (New York: W.W. Norton and Co., 1995), 79.

13 James Raffan, *Fire in the Bones*, 141.

14 Bill Mason, *Death of a Legend* (National Film Board of Canada, 1968). Further reference will be indicated in the text.

15 Tina Loo, *States of Nature: Conserving Canada's Wildlife in the Twentieth Century* (Vancouver: UBC P, 2005), 177.

16 Bill Mason, *Path of the Paddle* (Toronto: Key Porter Books, 1995) 191.

17 But not so far, anyway. Bill Mason, *Waterwalker*. Further reference will be indicated in the text.

18 Bill Mason, *Song of the Paddle* (National Film Board of Canada, 1976).

19 Bill Mason, cited in Raffan, *Fire in the Bones*, 228.

20 Bill Mason, *Path of the Paddle* (book), 3.

21 Bill Mason, *Path of the Paddle* (book), 168.

22 See Bruce Hodgins, 'Canoe Irony: Symbol and Harbinger,' in *Canexus: The*

Canoe in Canadian Culture, ed. James Raffan and Bert Horwood (Toronto: Betelgeuse Books, 1988).

23 Bill Mason, *Song of the Paddle* (Toronto: Key Porter Books, 1988), 14. Further reference in this paragraph by page number.

24 Renato Rosaldo *Culture and Truth: The Remaking of Social Analysis* (Boston: Beacon Press, 1989), 69.

25 Raffan, *Fire in the Bones*, 78.

26 Mason, *Path of the Paddle* (book), 194.

27 Mason, *Path of the Paddle* (book), 192.

28 Loo, *States of Nature*, 180.

29 Bill Mason, cited in Raffan, *Fire in the Bones*, 188. Raffan describes this document as an 'Undated, unpublished, mimeographed manuscript, probably written about 1978.' It is held by the family.

30 Carolyn Merchant, *ReInventing Eden: The Fate of Nature in Western Culture* (New York: Routledge, 2004), 24; Cronon, *Uncommon Ground*, 134–6. Tina Loo discusses various interpretation of 'dominion' among conservationists in Canada in *States of Nature*.

31 Buck, *Bill Mason, Wilderness Artist*, 22.

32 Cronon, 'The Trouble with Wilderness,' 73.

33 Cronon, 'The Trouble with Wilderness,' 73.

34 Haun-Moss, 'Layered Hegemonies,' 42.

35 Cronon, 'The Trouble with Wilderness,' 73.

36 Haun-Moss, 'Layered Hegemonies,' 42–3.

37 Mason's paintings are published in Bill Mason, *Canoescapes* (1995) and *Bill Mason, Wilderness Artist* by Ken Buck (2005).

38 Jonathan Bordo, 'Picture and Witness at the Site of Wilderness,' *Critical Inquiry* 26, no. 2 (winter 2000): 227.

39 Cronon, 'The Trouble with Wilderness,' 79.

40 Cronon, 'The Trouble with Wilderness,' 79–80.

41 Cronon, 'The Trouble with Wilderness,' 80.

42 Cronon, 'The Trouble with Wilderness,' 79.

43 Cronon, 'The Trouble with Wilderness,' 83.

44 Cronon, 'The Trouble with Wilderness,' 83–4.

45 Cited in Raffan, *Fire in the Bones*, 237.

46 Mason ignores the rest of the book, which consists of quotations that stress the rights of First Nations and the failure of governments to live up to their treaty obligations.

47 Raffan, *Fire in the Bones*, 239.

48 Raffan, *Fire in the Bones*, 269.

49 Anachronistic space is a term coined by Anne McClintock in *Imperial Leather:*

Race, Gender and Sexuality (New York: Routledge, 1995) to indicate the trope in colonialist discourse that locates indigenous peoples in a 'space' that is somehow co-existent with modernity yet 'primitive,' pre-modern.

50 Mason quoted in Raffan, *Fire in the Bones*, 37.

51 Mason, *Song of the Paddle* (book), 1; Mason, *Death of a Legend*; Bill Mason, *Cry of the Wild* (National Film Board of Canada, 1971).

52 Mason, *Path of the Paddle* (book), 3.

53 Buck, *Bill Mason, Wilderness Artist*, 11, 28.

54 Buck, *Bill Mason, Wilderness Artist*, 215.

55 Brind quoted in Raffan, *Fire in the Bones*, 191.

56 James Raffan, 'Being There: Bill Mason and the Canadian Canoeing Tradition,' in *The Canoe in Canadian Cultures*, ed. John Jennings et al. (Toronto: Natural Heritage, 1999), 17.

57 Mason, *Path of the Paddle* (book), 2.

58 Raffan, 'Being There,' 25. Mason famously advocated in his books and his films a four-sided canvas 'Baker' or 'Campfire' tent with one side open and facing the campfire. The open side featured flaps that could be adjusted to shelter the opening from wind and rain. Mason offers a pattern for making such a tent in *Song of the Paddle* (book); many commercial companies now make this tent and specifically reference Mason's recommendation.

59 Bert Horwood, 'Canoe Trips: Doors to the Primitive,' in Raffan and Horwood, *Canexus*, 133.

60 Alister Thomas, 'Paddling Voices: There's a Poet, Voyageur Adventurer and Explorer in All of Us,' in Jennings et al., *Canoe in Canadian Cultures*, 176.

61 Alister Thomas, 'Paddling Voices,' 178.

62 Bob Henderson, 'The Canoe as a Way to Another Story,' in Jennings et al., *Canoe in Canadian Cultures*, 184.

63 Daniel Francis, *National Dreams* (Vancouver: Arsenal Pulp, 1997), 10, 129.

Chapter Seven

1 See Shanna Balazs, 'Aboriginal Involvement in Selected Canadian Museums' (MA thesis, Trent University, 1999), 99–127, for a history of the development of the museum. Additional information is available in documents held in the archives of the Canoe Museum at Trent University. I am grateful to Bruce Hodgins, John Jennings, and Dale Standen for sharing their knowledge of the museum with me and for confirming (or sometimes correcting) my interpretation of the documentary evidence.

2 See Brian Young, *The Making and Unmaking of a University Museum: The McCord* (Montreal: McGill-Queen's UP, 2000), for the history of the McCord

Museum; for information on the struggle for control over the McMichael Gallery, see Margaret Cannon, 'Plaintiff: Robert McMichael's Legal Battle against the Kleinburg Gallery that Bears His Name Is Sending Shock Waves through the World,' *Toronto Life* 33, no. 5 (April 1999): 100–4, 106.

3 Jamie Benidickson, Memo to the Board, 17 September 1992, Canadian Canoe Museum Fonds, 93-016/12/25, Trent University Archives.

4 The museum conservation staff and volunteers led by Collections Manager Dawn McQuade did an important job with few resources and with wonderful imagination and initiative. One story that commands particular admiration concerns the initial treatment of the canoes to remove insects and fungus. Most historical museums have a freezer, which kills the insects and other agents of deterioration that often live in organic artefacts and could spread to other objects in the collection storage areas. The Canoe Museum needed a large and expensive freezer facility to accommodate their canoes, a facility they could not afford to build. Museum staff contacted Baskin-Robbins, the ice cream company, and borrowed one of their freezer trucks to treat artefacts before they were brought into the climate-controlled main building (now called the Weston National Heritage Centre). Like the staff of many of Canada's museums, they are experts at doing a lot with a little.

5 Susan Pearce, *Museums, Objects and Collections* (Washington: Smithsonian Institution, 1992), 38.

6 See Pearce, *Museums, Objects and Collections*, 40–3, for the extended account upon which this description of fetishization of objects is based.

7 Memo, Jennings and Matthews to Board, 11 July 1990, Canadian Canoe Museum Fonds, 93-016/12/22, Trent University Archives.

8 Jamie Benidickson, Planning Document, , 17 September 1992, Canadian Canoe Museum Fonds, 93-016/1225, Trent University Archives.

9 Michael Brawne, *The Museum Interior* (London: Thames and Hudson, 1982), 10.

10 Michael Brawne, *The Museum Interior*, 11.

11 See Hayden White, 'The Value of Narrativity in the Representation of Reality,' *Critical Inquiry* 7, no. 1 (autumn 1980): 5–27.

12 Deborah Doxtator, 'Implications of Canadian Nationalism for Aboriginal Cultural Autonomy,' in *Curatorship: Indigenous Perspectives in Post-Colonial Societies* (Hull, QC: Canadian Museum of Civilization, 1994), 61.

13 Dale Standen, private communication.

14 John Jennings, 'The Canadian Canoe Museum and Canada's National Symbol,' in *The Canoe in Canadian Culture*, ed. John Jennings, Bruce Hodgins, and Doreen Small (Toronto: Natural History/Natural Heritage Inc., 1999), 6.

15 Dale Standen, private communication.

16 Doxtator, 'Implications of Canadian Nationalism for Aboriginal Cultural Autonomy,' 61

17 See Douglas Cole, *Captured Heritage: The Scramble for Northwest Coast Artifacts* (Vancouver: UBC P, 1985), *passim*.

Chapter Eight

1 I.S. MacLaren, 'Splendor Sine Occasu: Salvaging Boat Encampment,' *Canadian Literature* 170–1 (summer 2001): 166.

2 Bill Reid, *Solitary Raven: The Selected Writings of Bill Reid* (Vancouver: Douglas and McIntyre, 2000), 217.

3 Tom Abel, quoted in David Neel, *The Great Canoes: Reviving a Northwest Coast Tradition* (Vancouver: Douglas and McIntyre, 1995), 44.

4 James Raffan, *Bark, Skin and Cedar: Exploring the Canoe in Canadian Experience* (Toronto: Harper Perennial, 1999), 216.

5 Reid, *Solitary Raven*, 223.

6 Guujaaw, quoted in Neel, *The Great Canoes*, 26.

7 Simon Dick, quoted in Neel, *The Great Canoes*, 36.

8 James Raffan recounts this story in *Bark, Skin and Cedar*.

9 Guujaaw, quoted in Neel, *The Great Canoes*, 26.

10 Guujaaw, quoted in Neel, *The Great Canoes*, 26.

11 Raffan, *Bark, Skin and Cedar*, 213.

12 Barb Cranmer, *Qatuwas* (National Film Board of Canada, 1997).

13 Neel, *The Great Canoes*, 2.

14 Puyallup, WA, in 1998; Ahousaht, BC, in 1999, Songees, BC, in 2000; Squamish, BC, in 2001; the Quinault in Taholah, WA, in 2002; Tulalip, WA, in 2003; Chemainus, BC, in 2004; Lower Elwha Klallam in Port Angeles, WA, in 2005; Muckleshoot in Auburn, WA, in 2006; Lummi, WA, in 2007; and Cowichan, BC, in 2008. This account of the story of the Qatuwas Festival is taken from 'American Indian Film Festival: Frank Brown,' in *Wavelength* (December/January 2005), accessed at http://bellevuecollege.edu/diversitycaucus/AIFF2006/FrankBrown.htm.

15 Neil Sterritt et al., *Tribal Boundaries in the Nass Watershed* (Vancouver: UBC P, 1998), explains how the performance of dances and songs operates as a kind of land title system for the Giksaan and Wetsue'ten people of northern BC.

16 Ian Campbell, in Cranmer, *Qatuwas* (film).

17 Bill Wasden, quoted in Neel, *The Great Canoes*, 98.

18 Ann Atleo, in Cranmer, *Qatuwas* (film).

19 Quoted in Neel, *The Great Canoes*, 92.

20 Quoted in Neel, *The Great Canoes*, 92.

21 Quoted in Neel, *The Great Canoes*, 68.

22 Bill Wasden, private communication.

23 David McNab et al., 'Black with Canoes: Aboriginal Resistance and the Canoe: Diplomacy, Trade and Warfare in the Meeting Grounds of Northeastern North America,' in *Technology, Disease and Colonial Conquests, Sixteenth to Eighteenth Centuries*, ed. George Raudzens (Leiden: Brill, 2002). Further reference will be indicated in the text by page number.

24 Peter Cole, *Coyote and Raven Go Canoeing* (Montreal: McGill-Queen's UP, 2006), 21. Further reference will be indicated in the text by page number.

25 Alex McKay, 'A. McKay, Portfolio,' http://web.mac.com/aamckay/Claudemirror.com/McKay_Portfolio,_1988-1999.html

26 Canadian Canoe Museum, 'Press Release,' 26 February 2009, http://www.canoemuseum.ca/index.php/Treaty-Canoe-Exhibit/treaty-canoe.html.

27 Lenore Keeshig-Tobias, 'Stop Stealing Native Stories,' in *Borrowed Power: Essays on Cultural Appropriation*, ed. Bruce Ziff and Pratima V. Rao (New Brunswick, NJ: Rutgers UP, 1997), 73.

28 Taiaiake Alfred, 'Who Are You Calling Canadian?' *Windspeaker* (1 September 2000): 4–5; Kristina Fagan, 'Tewatatha:wi: Aboriginal Nationalism in Taiaiake Alfred's *Peace, Power, Righteousness: An Indigenous Manifesto*,' *American Indian Quarterly* 28, no. 1–2 (winter-spring 2004): 13.

29 Deborah Root, '"White Indians": Appropriation and the Politics of Display,' in Ziff and Rao, *Borrowed Power*, 232.

Works Cited

Alfred, Taiaiake. 'Who Are You Calling Canadian?' *Wavelength*, September 2000.

'American Indian Film Festival: Frank Brown.' *Wavelength*, December/January 2005. http://bellevuecollege.edu/diversitycaucus/AIFF2006/FrankBrown.htm.

Atwood, Margaret. *Surfacing*. Toronto: General Publishing, 1972.

– *Survival*. Toronto: House of Anansi, 1972.

– 'Death of a Young Son by Drowning.' In *Selected Poems, 1966–1984*. Toronto: Oxford UP, 1990.

– 'Death by Landscape.' In *Wilderness Tips*. Toronto: McClelland and Stewart, 1992.

Balazs, Shanna. 'Aboriginal Involvement in Selected Canadian Museums.' MA thesis, Trent University, 1999.

Barthes, Roland. *Mythologies*. Translated by Annette Lavers. London: Granada Publishing, 1972.

Bayley, G.H.U. 'Canoe Trip from Fort MacPherson to Fort Yukon 1965.' Trent University Archives, 93-016/3/87.

Benidickson, Jamie. 'Idleness, Water and a Canoe: Canadian Recreational Paddling Between the Wars.' In *Nastawgan*, edited by Bruce Hodgins and Margaret Hobbs. Toronto: Betelgeuse Books, 1985.

– *Idleness, Water, and a Canoe: Reflections on Paddling for Pleasure*. Toronto: U Toronto P, 1997.

Bennett, Tony. *The Birth of the Museum: History, Theory, Politics*. London: Routledge, 1995.

Bentley, D.M.R. 'Uncannyda.' *Canadian Poetry* 37 (fall/winter 1995). www.uwo.ca/english/Canadianpoetry/cpin/vol37/bentley.htm.

– 'Shadows in the Soul: Racial Haunting in the Poetry of Duncan Campbell Scott.' *University of Toronto Quarterly* 75, no. 2 (spring 2006): 752–70.

Berger, Carl. 'The True North Strong and Free.' 1966. Rpt. in *Canadian Culture*, edited by Elspeth Cameron. Toronto: Canadian Scholars Press, 1997.

– *The Writing of Canadian History*. Toronto: Oxford UP, 1976.

Berton, Pierre. *1967: The Last Good Year*. Toronto: Doubleday, 1997.

Bhabha, Homi. Introduction to *Narrating the Nation*, edited by Homi Bhabha. London: Routledge, 1990.

– *The Location of Culture*. London: Routledge, 1994.

Bigsby, John J. *The Shoe and the Canoe, or Pictures of Travel in the Canadas*. 1850. Reprint, New York: Paladin Press, 1969.

Birney, Earle. 'Can. Lit.' In *An Anthology of Canadian Literature in English*, edited by Russell Brown, Donna Bennett, and Nathalie Cooke. Toronto: Oxford UP, 1990.

Blanchet, M. Wylie. *The Curve of Time*. 1968. Reprint, Vancouver: Whitecap Books Ltd., 1985.

Bordo, Jonathan. 'Jack Pine – Wilderness Sublime or the Erasure of the Aboriginal Presence from the Landscape.' *Journal of Canadian Studies* 27, no. 4 (winter 1992): 98–129.

– 'Picture and Witness at the Site of Wilderness.' *Critical Inquiry* 26, no. 2 (winter 2000): 224–47.

Borrows John 'Wampum at Niagara: Canadian Legal History, Self-Government, and the Royal Proclamation.' In *Aboriginal and Treaty Rights in Canada* edited by Michael Asch. Vancouver: UBC P, 1998.

Bowering, George. 'Hero Without Motive.' *Canadian Literature* 17 (1963): 72–3.

Bramwell, Anna. *Ecology in the Twentieth Century: A History*. New Haven: Yale UP, 1989.

Brawne Michael. *The Museum Interior*. London: Thames and Hudson, 1982.

Buck, Ken. *Bill Mason, Wilderness Artist*. Surrey, BC: Rocky Mountain Books, 2005.

Burke Edmund. *A Philosophical Enquiry into the Origin of Our Ideas of the Sublime and Beautiful*. London: Dodsley, 1759. www.gender.amdigital.co.uk.

Burns, Robert Alan. 'Crawford and Ground: Ambiguity and Irony in *Malcolm's Katie*.' *Canadian Poetry* 15 (fall/winter 1984): 30–53. www.uwo.ca/english/Canadianpoetry/cpjn/vol15/burns.htm.

Canadian Canoe Museum Fonds. Trent University Archives.

Cannon, Margaret. 'Plaintiff: Robert McMichael's Legal Battle against the Kleinburg Gallery that Bears His Name Is Sending Shock Waves through the World.' *Toronto Life* 33, no. 5 (April 1999): 100–4, 106.

Careless, J.M.S. 'Frontierism, Metropolitanism, and Canadian History.' *Canadian Historical Review* 45, no. 1 (March 1954): 1–21.

– *Frontier and Metropolis*. Toronto: U Toronto P, 1989.

Centennial Commission Records. RG 65. Vol. 505. Library and Archives Canada.

– RG 69. Vol. 505–507, 545, 547. Library and Archives Canada.

Chamberlin, J. Edward. 'Culture and Anarchy in Indian Country.' In *Aboriginal and Treaty Rights in Canada*, edited by Michael Asch. Vancouver: UBC P, 1998.

Champlain, Samuel de. *Des sauvages, ou Voyage de Sieur de Champlain fait en l'an 1603*. Translated by H.H. Langton. Toronto: Champlain Society.

Christian, Edgar. *Unflinching: A Diary of Tragic Adventure*. London: John Murray, 1937.

– *Death in the Barren Ground*. Edited by George Whalley. Ottawa: Oberon, 1980.

Cole, Douglas. *Captured Heritage: The Scramble for Northwest Coast Artifacts*. Vancouver: UBC P, 1985.

Cole, Peter. *Coyote and Raven Go Canoeing*. Montreal: McGill-Queen's UP, 2006.

Collis, Christy. 'The Edge Men: Narrating Late Twentieth-Century Exploration on Australia's Desert and Antarctic Frontiers.' PhD diss., LaTrobe University, 2000.

Cranmer, Barb (dir.). *Qatuwas: People Gathering Together*. National Film Board of Canada, 1997.

Crawford, Isabella Valancy. *Malcolm's Katie*. London, ON: Canadian Poetry, 1987.

– 'The Lily Bed' In *A Northern Romanticism: Poets of the Confederation*, edited by Tracy Ware. Ottawa, Tecumseh, 2000.

Creighton, D.G. *The Commercial Empire of the St. Lawrence 1760–1850*. Toronto: Ryerson P, 1937.

Crerar, Norm. Private communication. 2–3 August 2005.

Cronon ,William. 'The Trouble with Wilderness; or, Getting Back to the Wrong Nature.' In *Uncommon Ground: Rethinking the Human Place in Nature*, edited by William Cronon. New York: W.W. Norton and Co., 1995.

Dawson, Michael. *The Mountie: From Dime Novel to Disney*. Toronto: Between the Lines, 1998.

DeLaute, Frank. 'The Voyageurs Canoe Trip Diary, Hayes River 1956.' Ottawa: Reprinted by arrangement with the *Ottawa Journal*, 1957.

Doxtator, Deborah. 'Implications of Canadian Nationalism for Aboriginal Cultural Autonomy.' In *Curatorship: Indigenous Perspectives in Post-Colonial Societies*. Hull, QC: Canadian Museum of Civilization, 1994.

Duncan, Carol. *Civilizing Rituals*. London: Routledge, 1995.

Eccles, W.J. 'A Belated Review of Harold Adams Innis, *The Fur Trade in Canada*.' *Canadian Historical Review* 40, no. 4 (1979): 419–41.

Eric Morse Fonds. R 8288. Library and Archives Canada.

Fee, Margery. 'Romantic Nationalism and the Image of Native People in Con-

temporary English-Canadian Literature.' In *The Native in Literature*, edited by
  Thomas King, Cheryl Dawnan Calver, and Helen Hoy. Montreal: ECW, 1987.

Filewod, Alan. 'The Face of Re-enactment.' *Canadian Theatre Review* 121 (winter
  2005): 9–16.

Findley, Timothy. *The Wars*. Toronto: Clarke Irwin, 1977.

Francis, Daniel. *National Dreams*. Vancouver: Arsenal Pulp Press, 1997.

Franks, C.E.S. *The Canoe and White Water: From Essential to Sport*. Toronto: U
  Toronto P, 1977.

Fraser, Blair. 'We Went La Verendrye's Way.' *Maclean's*, 1 October 1954, 18–19,
  52–7.

Frese, Ralph. 'Canadians and the Canadian Canoe in the Opening of the American Midwest.' In *The Canoe in Canadian Culture*, edited by John Jennings, Bruce
  Hodgins, and Doreen Small. Toronto: Natural History/Natural Heritage Inc.,
  1999.

Freud, Sigmund. *Beyond the Pleasure Principle*. Translated by Alix Strachey. New
  York: Liveright, 1970.

Frye, Northrop. *Anatomy of Criticism*. Princeton: Princeton UP, 1957.

– 'Conclusion to *The Literary History of Canada*.' In *The Bush Garden*. Toronto:
  House of Anansi, 1971.

Furniss, Elizabeth. *The Burden of History*. Vancouver: UBC P, 2000.

Gerson, Carole, and Veronica Strong-Boag. *E. Pauline Johnson Tekahionwake: Collected Poems and Selected Prose*. Toronto: U Toronto P, 2002.

Gibbon, John Murray. *The Romance of the Canadian Canoe*. Toronto: Ryerson P,
  1951.

Gladden, James N. *The Boundary Waters Canoe Area*. Ames: Iowa State UP, 1990.

Glickman. Susan. *The Picturesque and the Sublime: A Poetics of the Canadian Landscape*. Montreal: McGill-Queen's UP, 2005.

Goldie, Terry. *Fear and Temptation: The Image of the Indigene in Canadian, Australian, and New Zealand Literatures*. Montreal: McGill-Queen's UP, 1989.

Grace, Sherrill. *Canada and the Idea of North*. Montreal: McGill-Queen's UP, 2001.

Grant, George. *Lament for a Nation* Toronto: McClelland and Stewart, 1965.

– 'In Defence of North America.' In *Technology and Empire*. Toronto: House of
  Anansi, 1969.

Grey Owl [pseud.]. *Men of the Last Frontier*. London: Lovat Dickson, 1931.

– *Tales of an Empty Cabin*. London: Lovat Dickson, 1936.

Grinnell, George. *A Death on the Barrens*. Toronto: Northern Books, 1996.

Grove, F.P. *Fruits of the Earth*. Toronto: McClelland and Stewart, 1989.

Habermas, Jurgen. 'On the Public Uses of History.' In *The New Conservatism*,
  edited and translated by Sherry Weber Nicolsen. Cambridge: MIT P, 1989.

Hall, Stuart. 'Cultural Identity and Diaspora.' In *Identity: Community, Culture,*

Difference, edited by Jonathan Rutherford. London: Lawrence and Wishart, 1990. Haun-Moss, Beverly. 'Layered Hegemonies: The Origins of Recreational Canoeing Desire in the Province of Ontario.' *Topia: A Journal of Cultural Studies* 7 (spring 2002): 39–46.

Hay, Elizabeth. 'Three for Thought: Everything You Need to Know about ... Cold.' *Globe and Mail*, 24 January 2004.

– *Late Nights On Air*. Toronto: McClelland and Stewart, 2007.

Hearne, Samuel. *A Journey from Prince of Wales's Fort, in Hudson's Bay, to the northern ocean: undertaken by order of the Hudson's Bay Company for the discovery of copper mines, a north west passage, &c. in the years 1769, 1770, 1771 & 1772*. London: Printed for A. Strahan and T. Cadell, 1795. Electronic file, available at www.canadiana.org.

Henderson, Bob. 'The Canoe as a Way to Another Story.' In *The Canoe in Canadian Culture*, edited by John Jennings, Bruce Hodgins, and Doreen Small. Toronto: Natural History/Natural Heritage Inc., 1999.

Hodgins, Bruce. 'Canoe Irony: Symbol and Harbinger.' In *Canexus: The Canoe in Canadian Culture*, edited by James Raffan and Bert Horwood. Toronto: Betelgeuse Books, 1998.

– 'Refiguring Wilderness: A Personal Odyssey.' *Journal of Canadian Studies* 33, no. 2 (summer 1998): 12–27.

– Personal Interview.

Hodgins, Bruce, and Margaret Hobbs, eds. *Nastawgan*. Toronto: Betelgeuse Books, 1985.

Hodgins Bruce, and Gwyneth Hoyle. *Canoeing North into the Unknown: A Record of River Travel: 1874–1974*. Toronto: Natural Heritage, 1994.

Horwood, Bert. 'Canoe Trips: Doors to the Primitive.' In *Canexus: The Canoe in Canadian Culture*, edited by James Raffan and Bert Horwood. Toronto: Betelgeuse Books, 1998.

– 'The Dao of Paddling.' In *The Canoe in Canadian Culture*, edited by John Jennings, Bruce Hodgins, and Doreen Small. Toronto: Natural History/Natural Heritage Inc., 1999.

Hubbard, Mina. *A Woman's Way through Unknown Labrador*. New York: McClure, 1908.

Hulan, Renee. *Northern Experience and the Myths of Canadian Culture*. Montreal: McGill-Queen's UP, 2002.

Innis, Harold A. *The Fur Trade in Canada: An Introduction to Canadian Economic History*. Rev. ed. Toronto: U Toronto P, 1956.

Instad, Helge. *The Land of Feast and Famine*. Translated by Eugene Gay-Tifft. New York: A.A. Knopf, 1933.

Jakobsen, Roman. 'Two Aspects of Language and Two Types of Aphasic Disturbances.' In *On Language*, edited by Linda Waugh and Monique Monville Bursten. Cambridge, MA: Harvard UP, 1990.

James, William Closson. 'The Quest Pattern and the Canoe Trip.' In *Nastawgan*, edited by Bruce Hodgins and Margaret Hobbs. Toronto: Betelgeuse Books, 1985.

Jameson, Anna. *Winter Studies and Summer Rambles in Canada*. London: Saunders and Otley, 1838. www.canadiana.org.

Jeffrey, Laurence. *Who Look in Stove and The Edgar Christian Diary*. Toronto: Exile Editions, 1993.

Jennings, John. 'The Canadian Canoe Museum and Canada's National Symbol.' In *The Canoe in Canadian Culture*, edited by John Jennings, Bruce Hodgins, and Doreen Small. Toronto: Natural History/Natural Heritage Inc., 1999.

– Personal Interview.

Jennings, John, ed. *The Canoe: A Living Tradition*. Toronto: Firefly, 2002.

Jennings, John, Bruce Hodgins, and Doreen Small, eds. *The Canoe in Canadian Cultures*. Toronto: Natural History/Natural Heritage Inc., 1999.

Johnson, Pauline. 'The Idlers.' In *E. Pauline Johnson Tekahionwake, Collected Poetry and Selected Prose*, edited by Carole Gerson and Veronica Strong-Boag. Toronto: U Toronto P, 2002.

– 'Shadow River: Muskoka' In *E. Pauline Johnson Tekahionwake, Collected Poetry and Selected Prose*, edited by Carole Gerson and Veronica Strong-Boag. Toronto: U Toronto P, 2002.

Johnston, C. Fred. 'Canoe Sport in Canada: Anglo-American Hybrid?' In *Canexus: The Canoe in Canadian Culture*, edited by James Raffan and Bert Horwood. Toronto: Betelgeuse Books, 1998.

Keeshig-Tobias, Lenore. 'Stop Stealing Native Stories.' In *Borrowed Power: Essays on Cultural Appropriation*, edited by Bruce Ziff and Pratima V. Rao. New Brunswick, NJ: Rutgers UP, 1997.

Kelly, M.T. *Out of the Whirlwind*. Toronto: Stoddart, 1995.

Kent, Timothy. 'Manufacture of Birchbark Canoes for the Fur Trade in the St. Lawrence.' In *The Canoe in Canadian Culture*, edited by John Jennings, Bruce Hodgins, and Doreen Small. Toronto: Natural History/Natural Heritage Inc., 1999.

Kincaid, Jamaica. *Lucy*. London: Jonathan Cape, 1991.

King, Thomas. 'Joe the Painter and the Deer Island Massacre.' In *One Good Story, That One*. Toronto: Harper Collins, 1993.

Labor, Peter. 'The Canot du Maitre: Master of the Inland Seas.' In *The Canoe in Canadian Culture*, edited by John Jennings, Bruce Hodgins, and Doreen Small. Toronto: Natural History/Natural Heritage Inc., 1999.

– 'Alexander Mackenzie Voyageur Route: Community Survey Discussion: A

Cultural Context I.' Website. http://www.amvr.org/page50.htm n.d. [1996]

LaMarsh, Judy. *Memoirs of a Bird in a Gilded Cage.* Toronto: McClelland and Stewart, 1968.

Lampman, Archibald. 'Morning on the Lièvres.' In *A Northern Romanticism: Poets of the Confederation,* edited by Tracy Ware. Ottawa, Tecumseh, 2000.

Lancashire, Ian. 'Isabella Valancy Crawford, Notes on Life and Works.' *Representative Poetry On-line.* http://rpo.library.utoronto.ca/poet/85.html

Landow, George P. 'The Sublime.' *The Victorian Web.* www.victorianweb.org/philosophy/sublime

Laurence, Margaret. *The Diviners.* Toronto: McClelland and Stewart, 1974.

Lee, Dennis. *Civil Elegies and Other Poems.* Toronto: House of Anansi, 1972.

LePan, Douglas. *The Wounded Prince and Other Poems.* London: Chatto and Windus, 1948.

Loo, Tina. *States of Nature: Conserving Canada's Wildlife in the Twentieth Century.'* Vancouver: UBC P, 2005.

Loutit, Neil. 'La Verendrye Legend Re-enacted.' *Winnipeg Free Press,* 6 July 1967.

Lower, A.R.M. *Unconventional Voyages.* Toronto: Ryerson P, 1953.

– *Canadians in the Making: A Social History of Canada.* Toronto: Longmans, 1958.

McClintock, Anne. *Imperial Leather: Race, Gender and Sexuality in the Colonial Contest.* New York: Routledge, 1995.

MacDonald, Craig. 'The Nastawgan: Traditional Routes of Travel in the Temagami District.' In *Nastawgan,* edited by Bruce Hodgins and Margaret Hobbs. Toronto: Betelgeuse Books, 1985.

McKay, Alex. 'A. McKay, Portfolio.' http://web.mac.com/aamckay/Claudemirror.com/McKay_Portfolio,_1988-1999.html.

McKay, Don. *Vis a Vis: Fieldnotes on Poetry and Wilderness.* Wolfville, NS: Gaspereau, 2001.

McKay, Ian. *The Quest of the Folk.* Montreal: McGill-Queen's UP, 1994.

Mackey, Eva. 'Becoming Indigenous: Land, Belonging and the Appropriation of Aboriginality in Canadian Nationalist Narratives.' *Social Analysis* 42, no. 2 (July 1997): 150–78.

– *The House of Difference: Cultural Politics and National Identity in Canada.* London: Routledge, 1998.

McKillop, A.B. 'Historiography in English.' *The Canadian Encyclopedia.* Historica Foundation, 2012. www.thecanadianencyclopedia.com.

Maclaren, I.S. 'Splendor Sine Occasu: Salvaging Boat Encampment.' *Canadian Literature* 170–1 (summer 2001): 162–87.

MacLennan Hugh. *The Watch that Ends the Night.* 1958. Reprint, Toronto: MacMillan, 1975.

– *Seven Rivers of Canada.* Toronto: MacMillan, 1961.

McNab, David, Bruce Hodgins and Dale Standen. 'Black with Canoes: Aboriginal Resistance and the Canoe: Diplomacy, Trade and Warfare in the Meeting Grounds of Northeastern North America.' In *Technology, Disease and Colonial Conquests, Sixteenth to Eighteenth Centuries,* edited by George Raudzens. Leiden: Brill, 2002.

Marsh, John. 'The Heritage of Peterborough Canoes.' In *Nastawgan,* edited by Bruce Hodgins and Margaret Hobbs. Toronto: Betelgeuse Books, 1985.

Martin, Biddy, and Chandra Mohanty. 'Feminist Politics: What's Home Got To Do with It.' *Feminist Studies/Critical Studies,* edited by Teresa de Lauretis. Bloomington: Indiana UP, 1986.

Marx, Karl. 'Commodities.' In *The Marx-Engels Reader,* edited by Robert Tucker. New York: Norton, 1978. 302–29.

Mason, Bill. *Path of the Paddle.* 1980: Toronto: Key Porter Books, 1995.

– *Song of the Paddle.* Toronto: Key Porter Books, 1988.

– *Paddle to the Sea.* National Film Board of Canada, 1964.

– *The Rise and Fall of the Great Lakes.* National Film Board of Canada, 1966.

– *Death of a Legend.* National Film Board of Canada, 1968.

– *Wolf Pack.* National Film Board of Canada, 1971.

– *Cry of the Wild.* National Film Board of Canada, 1971.

– *Path of the Paddle.* National Film Board of Canada, 1976.

– *Song of the Paddle.* National Film Board of Canada, 1976.

– *Waterwalker.* National Film Board of Canada, 1984.

Mathews, Robin. '*Malcolm's Katie:* Love, Wealth and Nation-Building.' *Studies in Canadian Literature* 2.1 (1977). www.lib.unb.ca/Texts/SCL/online_contents .htm.

– *Canadian Literature: Surrender or Revolution.* Toronto: Steel Rail, 1978.

Merchant, Carolyn. *The Death of Nature.* San Francisco: Harper Row, 1980.

– *ReInventing Eden.* New York: Routledge, 2003.

Miller, Daniel. *Material Culture and Mass Consumption.* Oxford: Basil Blackwell, 1987.

Moodie, Susanna. *Roughing It in the Bush.* London: Bentley, 1852. Electronic edition available at www.canadiana.org.

Morse, Eric. 'Voyageurs 1957: Reindeer Lake to Stoney Lake.' *Ottawa Journal,* 17–24 August 1957. Ottawa: Reprinted by arrangement with the *Ottawa Journal* [1958].

– 'Diary of Methye and Clearwater River (1958).' *Ottawa Journal,* 30 August, 3–4 September 1958.

– 'Lake Superior by Canoe.' 1960. Reprint from *Ottawa Journal.* Eric Morse Fonds, R8288 1-31, Library and Archives Canada.

- 'Canoe Routes of the Voyageurs: The Geography and Logistics of the Fur Trade.' Reprint of three articles from the *Canadian Geographical Journal* (May, July, and August 1961) by the Minnesota Historical Society and the Quetico Foundation of Canada, 1961.
- 'Canoe Routes of the Voyageurs: The Geography and Logistics of the Canadian Fur Trade.' Ottawa: Royal Canadian Geographical Society [1962].
- [Voyageurs Highway]. *Canadian Geographical Journal* (May 1962).
- Notes on a Canoe Journey from Aylmer Lake to Rae via the Lockhart and Snare Rivers, July 1964.' *Arctic Circular* 16, no. 3 (1963–64): 40–5.
- 'Freshwater Northwest Passage.' *Canadian Geographical Journal* 70, no. 6 (1965): 182–91.
- 'The Rat-Bell-McDougall Pass Canoe Trip.' *Arctic Circular* 17, no. 3–4 (1965–67): 37–46.
- *Summer Travel in the Canadian Barrens* (pamphlet). Reprint, *Canadian Geographical Journal* (May 1967). Ottawa: Northwest Territories Tourist Office. Eric Morse Fonds, R8288, 2-6, Library and Archives Canada.
- *Fur Trade Canoe Routes of Canada, Then and Now.* Toronto: U Toronto P, 1968.
- 'Was this Hearne's Thelewy-aza-yeth?' *Beaver* (winter 1971) 56–9.
- 'Modern Maps Throw New Light on Samuel Hearne's Route.' *Cartographica* 18, no. 4 (winter 1981): 23–35.
- *Freshwater Saga: Memoirs of a Lifetime of Wilderness Canoeing in Canada.* Toronto: U Toronto P, 1987.
- 'Re-Tracing Franklin's First Arctic Expedition.' Yellowknife: NWT Centennial Commission. Eric Morse Fonds, R8288, 1-31 Library and Archives Canada.
Moss, John. *Enduring Dreams.* Toronto: House of Anansi, 1996.
Mount, Nick. *When Canadian Literature Moved to New York.* Toronto: U Toronto P, 2005.
Neel, David. *The Great Canoes: Reviving a Northwest Coast Tradition.* Vancouver: Douglas and McIntyre, 1995.
Nelles, H.V. *The Art of Nation Building: Pageantry and Spectacle at Quebec's Tercentenary.* Toronto: U Toronto P, 1999.
Noel, Lynn, ed. Maps and illustrations by Hap Wilson. *Voyages: Canada's Heritage Rivers.* St. John's: Breakwater, 1995.
Norment, Christopher. *In the North of our Lives.* Camden Maine: Down East Books, 1989.
Nute, Grace Lee. 'Knights of the Waterways.' *The Beaver* 298 (summer 1967): 11–17.
Olsen, Sigurd. *The Lonely Land.* New York: Knopf, 1961.
Pearce, Susan. *Museums, Objects and Collections.* Washington: Smithsonian Institution, 1992.
Pelly, David F. *Arctic Cairn Notes.* Toronto: Betelgeuse Books, [1997].

Perrault, Gib. Interview. 3 August 2005.

Pickthall, Marjorie. *Angel's Shoes and Other Stories*. London: Hodder and Stoughton, 1923.

Pinkerton, Robert E. 'The Canoe – Half Stolen.' *Outing* 62 (May 1913): 159–63.

Powell-Williams, Clive. *Cold Burial: A True Story of Endurance and Disaster*. New York: St Martin's Griffin, 2002.

Pratt, Minnie Bruce. 'Identity: Skin Blood Heart.' In *Yours In Struggle: Three Feminist Perspectives on Anti-Semitism and Racism*, edited by Elly Bulkin, Barbara Smith, and Minnie Bruce Pratt. Ithaca: Firebrand, 1984.

Provincial Centennial Commission Records. GR 1449 Box 45 File P-V-2. British Columbia Public Archives, Victoria.

Qatuwas: People Gathering Together. Dir. Barb Cranmer. National Film Board of Canada. 1996.

Raffan, James. Introduction. *Voyages: Canada's Heritage Rivers*. St. John's: Breakwater, 1995.

– *Fire in the Bones: Bill Mason and the Canadian Canoeing Tradition*. Toronto: Harper Collins, 1996.

– 'Being There: Bill Mason and the Canadian Canoeing Tradition.' *The Canoe in Canadian Cultures*, edited by John Jennings, Bruce Hodgins, and Doreen Small. Toronto: Natural History/Natural Heritage Inc., 1999.

– *Bark, Skin and Cedar: Exploring the Canoe in Canadian Experience*. Toronto: Harper Perennial, 1999.

– *Deep Waters: Courage, Character and the Lake Timiskaming Canoeing Tragedy*. Toronto: Harper Collins, 2002.

Raffan, James, and Bert Horwood, eds. *Canexus: The Canoe in Canadian Culture*. Toronto: Betelgeuse Books, 1988.

Reaney, James. 'Isabella Valancy Crawford.' In *Our Living Tradition*, 2d and 3d ser., edited by R.L. McDougall. Toronto: U Toronto P, 1959.

Reid, Bill. *Solitary Raven: The Selected Writings of Bill Reid*. Vancouver: Douglas and McIntyre, 2000.

Renan, Ernest. 'What Is a Nation?' *Nation and Narration*, edited by Homi Bhabha. London: Routledge, 1990.

Rheaume, Jim., Interview. 4 August 2005.

Roberts, Carolyn. 'Words After Music: A Musical Reading of Scott's "Night Hymns on Lake Nipigon."' *Canadian Poetry* 8 (1981): 56–63.

Rockingham, J.M. 'Les Voyageurs 1958.' *Canadian Army Journal*. Undated clipping in Eric Morse Fonds, R8288, Library and Archives Canada.

Root, Deborah. '"White Indians": Appropriation and the Politics of Display.' In *Borrowed Power: Essays on Cultural Appropriation*, edited by Bruce Ziff and Patrima V. Rao. New Brunswick, NJ: Rutgers UP, 1997.

Rosaldo, Renato. *Culture and Truth: The Remaking of Social Analysis*. Boston: Beacon Press, 1989.

Rothbauer Kevin '10,000 Expected for Tribal Journeys.' *Cowichan Valley Citizen*, 18 July 2008. www.canada.com/cowichanvalleycitizen/news.

Rutstrum, Calvin. *Way of the Wilderness: A complete Camping Manual: A How to Do It Camping Guide*. Minneapolis: Burgess Pub. Co., 1946.

Sartre, J.P. Preface. *The Wretched of the Earth*, by Frantz Fanon. New York: Grove Press, 1963.

Saul, John Ralston. *A Fair Country*. Toronto: Viking, 2008.

Schwenger, Peter. 'Words and the Murder of the Thing.' *Critical Inquiry* 28 (autumn 2001): 99–113.

'Scientific Aid Helps Voyageurs Float down Saskatchewan River.' *Globe and Mail*, 12 June 1967.

Scott, Angus. Foreword. *Freshwater Saga: Memoirs of a Lifetime of Wilderness Canoeing in Canada*, by Eric Morse. Toronto: U Toronto P, 1987.

Scott, Duncan Campbell. 'The Last of the Indian Treaties.' In *The Circle of Affection*. Toronto: McClelland and Stewart, 1947.

– 'The Height of Land.' In *A Northern Romanticism: Poets of the Confederation*, edited by Tracy Ware. Ottawa, Tecumseh, 2000.

 – 'Night Hymns on Lake Nipigon.' In *A Northern Romanticism: Poets of the Confederation*, edited by Tracy Ware. Ottawa: Tecumseh, 2000.

Simpson, Frances. 'Journal of a Voyage from Montreal, thro' the Interior of Canada to York Factory on the Shores of Hudson Bay.' In *Canadian Exploration Literature*, edited by Germaine Warkentin. Toronto: Oxford UP, 1993.

Standen, Dale. Interview.

Stanfield, Don, and Liz Lundell. *Stories from the Bow Seat: The Wisdom and Waggery of Canoe Tripping*. Erin, ON: Boston Mills, 1999.

Sterritt, Neil J., et al. *Tribal Boundaries in the Nass Watershed*. Vancouver: UBC Press, 1998.

Strong-Boag, Veronica, and Carole Gerson. *Paddling Her Own Canoe: The Times and Texts of E. Pauline Johnson*. Toronto: U Toronto P, 2000.

Struthers, Jack. 'Easy Life of Early Voyageurs Envy of Centennial Paddlers.' *Cariboo Observer* (Quesnel, BC). Clipping dated 20 July 1967. GR 1449, box 45, file P-V-2 vol. 4. BC Archives.

Thomas, Alister. 'Paddling Voices: There's a Poet, Voyageur Adventurer and Explorer in All of Us.' In *The Canoe in Canadian Cultures*, edited by John Jennings, Bruce Hodgins, and Doreen Small. Toronto: Natural History/Natural Heritage Inc., 1999.

Traill, Catharine Parr. *Backwoods of Canada*. 1836. Reprint, Toronto: McClelland and Stewart, 1989.

Trudeau, Pierre. 'Exhaustion and Fulfilment: Ascetic in a Canoe.' 1944.
    Reprint, *Che-mun* 102 (2000). http://www.canoe.ca/che-mun/102trudeau
    .html.
Tuan, Yi-Fu. *Topophilia.* Englewood Cliffs, NJ: Prentice-Hall, 1974.
Van Kirk, Sylvia. *Many Tender Ties: Women in Fur Trade Society 1670–1870.* Mon-
    treal: McGill-Queen's UP, 1980.
Wadland, John. 'Wilderness and Culture.' In *Nastawgan*, edited by Bruce Hodg-
    ins and Margaret Hobbs. Toronto: Betelgeuse Books, 1985.
Waldron, Malcolm. *Snow Man: John Hornby in the Barren Lands.* 1931. Reprint
    with an introduction by Lawrence Millman, Montreal: McGill-Queen's UP,
    1997.
Wallace, Dillon. *The Lure of the Labrador Wild.* New York: F. Revell, 1905.
Ware, Tracy, ed. *A Northern Romanticism: Poetry of the Confederation.* Ottawa:
    Tecumseh, 2000.
Warkentin, Germaine, ed. *Canadian Exploration Literature.* Toronto: Oxford UP,
    1993.
Whalley, George. *Poetic Process.* London: Routledge and Kegan Paul, 1953.
– 'The Legend of John Hornby.' *Tamarack Review* 5 (autumn 1957): 2–26.
– *The Legend of John Hornby.* Toronto: MacMillan, 1962.
– 'Notes on a Legend.' *Queen's Quarterly* 76 (1969): 613–19.
Wipper, Kirk. Foreword. In *Canexus: The Canoe in Canadian Culture*, edited by
    James Raffan and Bert Horwood. Toronto: Betelgeuse Books, 1998.
White, Hayden. 'The Value of Narrativity in the Representation of Reality.' *Criti-
    cal Inquiry* 7, no. 1 (autumn 1980): 5–27.
White, Hayden. *The Content of the Form.* Baltimore: Johns Hopkins UP, 1987.
Willems-Braun, Bruce. 'Buried Epistemologies: The Politics of Nature in (Post)
    colonial British Columbia.' *Annals of the Association of American Geographers* 87,
    no. 1 (1997): 3–31.
Willmott, Glenn. 'Paddled by Pauline.' *Canadian Poetry* 46 (spring/summer
    2000). www.uwo.ca/english/canadianpoetry/cpjn/vol46/willmott.htm.
Wilson, Ethel. *Swamp Angel.* Toronto: Macmillan, 1954.
Winks, Robin. Introduction to *The Fur Trade in Canada: An Introduction to
    Canadian Economic History*, by Harold A. Innis. Rev. ed. Toronto: U Toronto P,
    1956.
Young, Brian. *The Making and Unmaking of a University Museum: The McCord*
    Montreal: McGill-Queen's UP, 2000.
York, Thomas. *Snowman: A Novel.* Toronto: Doubleday, 1976.

Index

Standen, Dale, 59, 154–6, 200n1; 'Black with Canoes,' 69; and Canadian Canoe Museum, 154–6

Stewart, Gerald, 172

St. Lawrence River, 27, 39, 43–44, 51, 57, 126, 133; importance in imperialism, 43, 56, 126, 133; as spiritual, 44

subjectivity: Canadian nationality, 10, 32, 75, 151, 153; defined by objects, 149–51; of the explorer/voyageur, 63, 71, 75, 87, 93, 96; of indigenous peoples, 15; and interpellation, 16, 71; and rationality, 146. See also identity; objects

sublime. See Romantic tradition

suspended canoe, the literary motif of, 25–9, 32–4; and the Canadian Canoe Museum, 146, 176. See also uncanny; 'uncannyda'

Temagami, ON, 59

Theall, Donald, 142

Thomas, Alister, 138; 'Paddling Voices,' 138

Tlinglit nation, 174. See also whaling

Toronto, ON, 65, 97, 140, 142–3, 152, 166

tourism, 49, 63, 76

Traill, Catherine P., 14,

transportation, 44, 46–8, 51, 53–4, 57, 81, 85–7, 128, 167, 174

treaty negotiations, 55, 114, 160, 163, 168, 173, 178–9, 189n65, 199n46

Trudeau, Pierre, 7, 16, 68, 72, 140, 150, 153, 158

Tuan, Yi-Fu, 11

Turner, J.M.W., 133–4

Turner, John, 78, 140

Tyson, Norm, 84–5, 90, 192n6

U'Mista Cultural Centre, 161–2, 164. See also Kwakwaka'wakw

uncanny, 18, 22–3, 25–7, 29, 31–3, 36, 39, 103, 121–2, 176. See also 'uncannyda'

'uncannyda,' 18, 23, 26, 27. See also Bentley, D.M.R.

urbanization, 8, 35, 36, 38, 48, 53, 75, 78, 87. See also cities; civilization; New Romantics

US Cold War, 11, 66

Victoria, British Columbia, 4, 7, 56, 90, 161–2, 165–6, 170

Victorian culture, 36, 52–3, 107, 112

voyageurs, 18, 46, 47, 55–7, 62–3, 70, 71, 78, 80, 82, 84–5, 88–9, 92–3, 95, 96, 99, 123, 129, 150–1, 175

Voyageurs (Morse's canoe group). See Morse, Eric

Wadland, John, 50

Waldron, Malcolm, 103, 105–8, 114–15, 118; Snow Man, 103, 105–6, 114

Ward, Jeremy, 150

Wasden, Bill, 162, 171–2

Webster Treaty of 1823, 56

whaling canoes, 149, 164. See also Nuu Chaa Nulth nation; Tlinglit nation

Whalley, George, 7, 103, 107–15, 118–21; The Legend of John Hornby, 7, 103, 107–14, 120–1; Poetic Process, 107, 110, 112

White, Hayden, 41, 105, 150

whiteness, the identification of,

CULTURAL SPACES

Cultural Spaces explores the rapidly changing temporal, spatial, and theoretical boundaries of contemporary cultural studies. Culture has long been understood as the force that defines and delimits societies in fixed spaces. The recent intensification of globalizing processes, however, has meant that it is no longer possible – if it ever was – to imagine the world as a collection of autonomous, monadic spaces, whether these are imagined as localities, nations, regions within nations, or cultures demarcated by region or nation. One of the major challenges of studying contemporary culture is to understand the new relationships of culture to space that are produced today. The aim of this series is to publish bold new analyses and theories of the spaces of culture, as well as investigations of the historical construction of those cultural spaces that have influenced the shape of the contemporary world.

Evelyn Ruppert, *The Moral Economy of Cities: Shaping Good Citizens*

Mark Coté, Richard J.F. Day, and Greg de Peuter, eds., *Utopian Pedagogy: Radical Experiments against Neoliberal Globalization*

Michael McKinnie, *City Stages: Theatre and the Urban Space in a Global City*

David Jefferess, *Postcolonial Resistance: Culture, Liberation, and Transformation*

Mary Gallagher, ed., *World Writing: Poetics, Ethics, Globalization*

Maureen Moynagh, *Political Tourism and Its Texts*

Erin Hurley, *National Performance: Representing Quebec from Expo 67 to Céline Dion*

Lily Cho, *Eating Chinese: Culture on the Menu in Small Town Canada*

Rhona Richman Kenneally and Johanne Sloan, eds, *Expo 67: Not Just a Souvenir*

Gillian Roberts, *Prizing Literature: The Celebration and Circulation of National Culture*

Lianne McTavish, *Defining the Modern Museum: A Case Study of the Challenges of Exchange*

Misao Dean, *Inheriting a Canoe Paddle: The Canoe in Discourses of English-Canadian Nationalism*